Reading
EXPLORER 3

Nancy Douglas

HEINLE
CENGAGE Learning™

Australia • Brazil • Japan • Korea • Mexico • Singapore • Spain • United Kingdom • United States

Reading Explorer 3
Nancy Douglas

VP and Director of Operations: Vincent Grosso
Publisher: Andrew Robinson
Editorial Manager: Sean Bermingham
Senior Development Editor: Derek Mackrell
Assistant Editor: Claire Tan
Technology Development Manager: Debie Mirtle
Technology Project Manager: Pam Prater
Director of Global Marketing: Ian Martin
Director of US Marketing: Jim McDonough
Content Project Manager: Tan Jin Hock
Senior Print Buyer: Mary Beth Hennebury
National Geographic Coordinator: Leila Hishmeh
Contributing Writers: Julie Deferville, Angela Dove
Cover/Text Designer: Page 2, LLC
Compositor: Page 2, LLC
Cover Images: (Top) Rich Reid/National Geographic Image Collection, (bottom) Todd Gipstein/National Geographic Image Collection

Credits appear on pages 191–192, which constitutes a continuation of the copyright page.

Acknowledgments
The Author and Publishers would like to thank the following teaching professionals for their valuable feedback during the development of this series.

Jamie Ahn, English Coach, Seoul; **Heidi Bundschoks**, ITESM, Sinaloa México; **José Olavo de Amorim**, Colégio Bandeirantes, São Paulo; **Marina Gonzalez**, Instituto Universitario de Lenguas Modernas Pte., Buenos Aires; **Tsung-Yuan Hsiao**, National Taiwan Ocean University, Keelung; **Michael Johnson**, Muroran Institute of Technology; **Thays Ladosky**, Colégio Damas, Recife; **Mohamed Motala**, University of Sharjah; **David Persey**, British Council, Bangkok; **David Schneer**, ACS International, Singapore; **Atsuko Takase**, Kinki University, Osaka; **Deborah E. Wilson**, American University of Sharjah

Additional thanks to Yulia P. Boyle, Jim McClelland, and Jim Burch at National Geographic Society; and to Paul MacIntyre for his helpful comments and suggestions.

This series is dedicated to the memory of Joe Dougherty, who was a constant inspiration throughout its development.

Student Book ISBN-13: 978-1-4240-2935-8
Student Book ISBN-10: 1-4240-2935-X
Student Book + Student CD-ROM ISBN-13: 978-1-4240-2938-9
Student Book + Student CD-ROM ISBN-10: 1-4240-2938-4
Student Book (US edition) ISBN-13: 978-1-4240-4370-5
Student Book (US edition) ISBN-10: 1-4240-4370-0

Heinle
20 Channel Center Street
Boston, Massachusetts 02210
USA

Cengage Learning is a leading provider of customized learning solutions with office locations around the globe, including Singapore, the United Kingdom, Australia, Mexico, Brazil, and Japan. Locate our local office at: **international.cengage.com/region**

Cengage Learning products are represented in Canada by Nelson Education, Ltd.

Visit Heinle online at **elt.heinle.com**
Visit our corporate website at **www.cengage.com**

Printed in Canada
3 4 5 6 7 – 13 12 11

Contents

Get ready to Explore Your World!

A soccer player from **Alabama** scored more goals for her country than any other player in the world. Who is she? **p. 12**

July 9, 2005, was an important day at the Smithsonian Zoo in **Washington, D.C.** Why? **p. 5**

A plastic surgeon from **California** has created "the perfect face." What does it look like? **p. 23**

People in the **Dominican Republic** help save rainforests by producing chocolate. How? **p. 98**

Mexico's Mt. Popocatépetl is one of the world's most dangerous volcanoes. Why is it so deadly? **p. 54**

The novel *The Lost World* was published in 1912. Which mysterious landform in **Venezuela** was it based on? **p. 46**

In 1972, a plane went missing in the **Andes** mountains. What happened to it? **p. 119**

NORTH AMERICA

SOUTH AMERICA

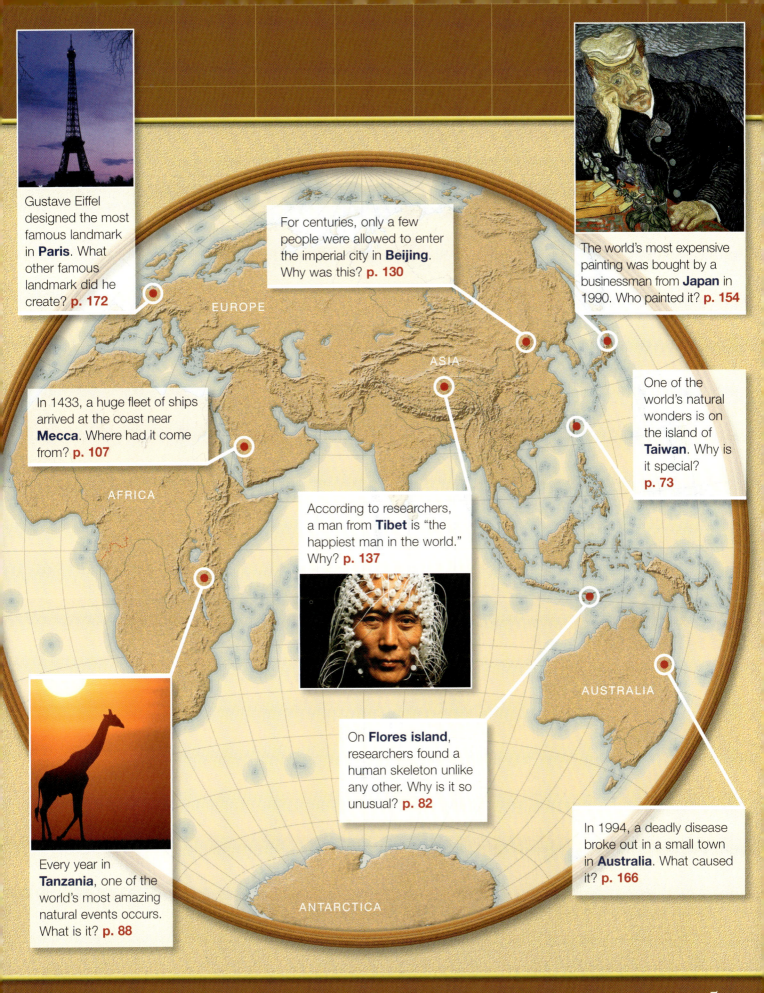

Gustave Eiffel designed the most famous landmark in **Paris**. What other famous landmark did he create? **p. 172**

For centuries, only a few people were allowed to enter the imperial city in **Beijing**. Why was this? **p. 130**

The world's most expensive painting was bought by a businessman from **Japan** in 1990. Who painted it? **p. 154**

In 1433, a huge fleet of ships arrived at the coast near **Mecca**. Where had it come from? **p. 107**

One of the world's natural wonders is on the island of **Taiwan**. Why is it special? **p. 73**

According to researchers, a man from **Tibet** is "the happiest man in the world." Why? **p. 137**

EUROPE

ASIA

AFRICA

On **Flores island**, researchers found a human skeleton unlike any other. Why is it so unusual? **p. 82**

AUSTRALIA

Every year in **Tanzania**, one of the world's most amazing natural events occurs. What is it? **p. 88**

In 1994, a deadly disease broke out in a small town in **Australia**. What caused it? **p. 166**

ANTARCTICA

Scope and Sequence

Introduction

Welcome to Reading Explorer!

In this book, you'll travel the world, explore different cultures, and discover interesting topics. You'll also become a better reader!

Reading will be easier—and you'll understand more—if you ask yourself these questions:

What do I already know?

- Before you read, look at the photos, captions, charts, and maps. Ask yourself: *What do I already know about this topic?*
- Think about the language you know—or may need to know— to understand the topic.

What do I want to learn?

- Look at the title and headings. Ask yourself: *What is this passage about? What will I learn?*
- As you read, check your predictions.

What have I learned?

- As you read, take notes. Use them to help you answer questions about the passage.
- Write down words you learn in a vocabulary notebook.

How can I learn more?

- Practice your reading skills and vocabulary in the Review Units.
- Explore the topics by watching the videos in class, or at home using the CD-ROM.

Now you're ready to explore your world!

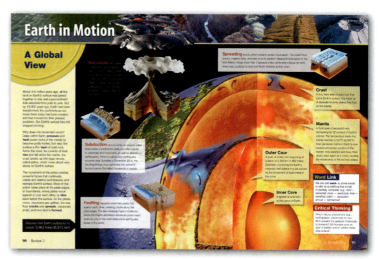

UNIT 1

Sport and Fitness

WARM UP

Discuss these questions with a partner.

1. What sports are popular in your country?

2. Are any sports from your country popular in other countries?

3. Which types of athletes do you think are the most fit?

▲ A hiker in Alaska, U.S.A. jumps with excitement.

9

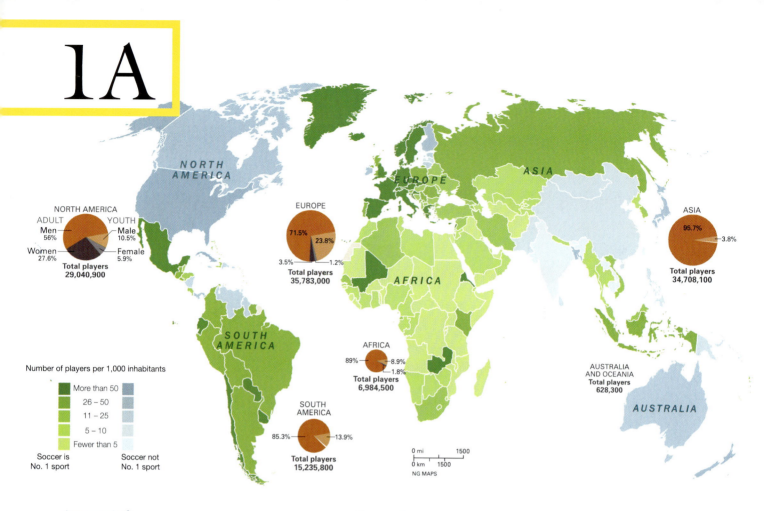

The World's Game

Before You Read

A. True or False. Look at the information about soccer above. Are these statements true (**T**) or false (**F**)?

1. More women play soccer in North America than in South America. **T** **F**

2. Soccer is the most popular sport in the majority of European countries. **T** **F**

3. Soccer is the most popular sport in most countries of the world. **T** **F**

4. The continent with the largest number of soccer players is Europe. **T** **F**

B. Predict. Look quickly at the title, headings, images, and captions on pages 11–12. Check (✔) the information you think you'll read about.

❑ where soccer started

❑ the history of the soccer World Cup

❑ areas where soccer is growing in popularity

❑ how soccer can bring people together

Planet Football

Widely considered the greatest soccer player of all time, Brazilian star Pelé is the only person to have won three World Cup tournaments as a player.

1 Throughout history, people have played some version of a kicking game. What the world now calls football, or soccer in the U.S., began as far back as 2500 B.C. with the
5 Chinese game of tsu chu. The sport we're familiar with today originated in Britain; by the 1840s, England's Football Association[1] had established a set of rules, and the modern game was born. Today, more than
10 120 million regular players from all over the globe participate in the game annually, truly making soccer the world's sport.

Europe: Home of the Rich and Famous

15 Europe has the largest number of soccer players on Earth and is also home to the world's richest and best-known professional teams. Europe's major clubs—such as Spain's Real Madrid and England's
20 Manchester United— have evolved from local teams to global brands,[2] with supporters all over the world. Some are owned by foreign businessmen, who invest large
25 amounts of money in their clubs, hoping to earn significant returns on ticket sales, television, and advertising deals.

Asia: A Growing Passion

30 Over the past two decades, an intense soccer competition among Japan, China, and South Korea has helped to increase enthusiasm for the sport across Asia. In China, for example,
35 recent data suggest that soccer is now more popular than traditional Chinese favorites, such as table tennis and basketball. This enthusiasm has also helped to bridge differences and bring people together. The 2002 World Cup,
40 co-hosted by South Korea and Japan, was a victory for cooperation and friendship, and in the Middle East, youth soccer teams have also helped to promote peace.

Australia and Oceania: Soccer Down Under

45 For decades, Australian sports have been dominated by cricket, rugby, and Australian rules football. Today, this region still has the fewest number of
50 soccer players and teams. But interest in soccer is growing, as immigrants[3] from the Balkans[4] and other countries bring the sport and their enthusiasm for it to their new country. The result: in 2006, Australia's national
55 team (nicknamed the "Socceroos") made its first appearance at the World Cup Finals in 32 years.

A skilled midfielder, England's David Beckham is also a globally recognized "brand," known for his celebrity lifestyle.

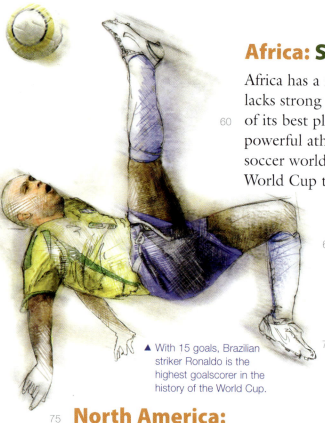

Africa: Soccer's New Frontier

60 Africa has a number of talented players; however, the continent lacks strong domestic teams and faces the prospect of losing many of its best players to the European clubs. Several national teams have powerful athletes, though, and Africa's more prominent[5] role in the soccer world was established in 2004, when FIFA[6] awarded the 2010 World Cup tournament to South Africa.

South America: Unbeatable Talent

65 South America produces some of the most exciting soccer on Earth, and many of the most admired players. Brazil has won the most World Cup Finals ever, and is the only team to have participated in every World Cup to date. Youth soccer is also an 70 enormous business in South America (third after Europe and North America), but as with Africa and Asia, many of the best players join the wealthy European teams for the chance to earn big money and international recognition.

▲ With 15 goals, Brazilian striker Ronaldo is the highest goalscorer in the history of the World Cup.

75 North America: A Sport for Everyone

In North America, almost 28 percent of the professional players are women—the largest number in the world. The women's World Cup finals are a hugely popular event; one match held in Los Angeles drew a crowd 80 of over 90,000, one of the largest ever for a women's sport. Men's soccer is also gaining in popularity throughout North America, despite tough competition from other popular team sports, such as baseball, American football, and (especially in Canada) ice hockey.

▼ U.S. star Mia Hamm scored more goals for her country than any other player in history.

85 Soccer: A Global Force

Thanks to its worldwide popularity and the reach of satellite television, soccer has experienced a major evolution in recent years. Today's major teams import both players and coaches from abroad, and clubs once supported only by their local communities now 90 have fans all over the world. In the last quarter century, soccer has succeeded in cutting across national lines to become a global, interconnected sport—one that has the power to unite us all.

---

[1] An **association** is an official group of people who have the same job, aim, or interest.

[2] A **brand** usually refers to a type of product that is made by a certain company and is known by many people.

[3] An **immigrant** is a person who has come to live in a country from another country.

[4] The **Balkans** is a region in southeastern Europe that includes Albania, Bosnia, and Croatia.

[5] Someone or something that is **prominent** is important and well-known.

[6] **FIFA** is the *Fédération Internationale de Football Association* (French for International Federation of Association Football). It is the international governing organization of soccer.

☐ Reading Comprehension

A. Multiple Choice. Choose the best answer for each question.

Gist

1. What is this reading mainly about?
   a. the history of soccer
   b. the popularity of soccer around the world
   c. the increasing popularity of women's soccer
   d. China's passion for soccer

Detail

2. Which game is NOT mentioned in the passage as a popular sport in China?
   a. table tennis
   b. basketball
   c. badminton
   d. soccer

Critical Thinking

Do you think soccer can be used to improve international relations? Why or why not?

Main Idea

3. What is the main idea of the third paragraph?
   a. In Asia, soccer is a very competitive sport.
   b. In Asia, soccer has increased in popularity in recent years.
   c. Soccer has helped to promote peace in the Middle East.
   d. The 2002 World Cup was held in Asia.

Inference

4. According to the passage, South American soccer teams don't pay as well as _____.
   a. African teams
   b. Asian teams
   c. European teams
   d. North American teams

Vocabulary

5. In line 79, the word *drew* could be replaced with _____.
   a. painted
   b. controlled
   c. arrived
   d. attracted

B. Classification. Match each sport (**a–h**) with the region in which it is most popular, according to the passage.

a. American football
b. Australian rules football
c. baseball
d. basketball
e. cricket
f. ice hockey
g. rugby
h. table tennis

Asia _____

Australia _____

North America _____

☐ Vocabulary Practice

A. Completion. Complete the information using the correct form of words from the box. One word is extra.

version   enthusiasm   evolve   award   prospect   intense

Soccer is an extremely popular sport, supported by **1.** _____ fans all over the world. There is, however, an indoor **2.** _____ of the game that **3.** _____ in Europe, particularly in the United Kingdom, where it was known as "table football," because it was played on top of a table. In addition, Germany developed a similar game, called "kicker." The games eventually crossed the Atlantic to America, where the game of "Foosball" was born.

Foosball is played on a special table where each player controls their "team" by turning sticks, to which the "players" are attached. As in real soccer, points are **4.** _____ by putting the ball in the other player's goal. Foosball, or table soccer, requires **5.** _____ focus, and excellent hand-eye coordination,[1] making it a fast and exciting game.

[1] **Coordination** means using the different parts of your body together efficiently.

▲ A table soccer game

B. Words in Context. Complete each sentence with the best answer.

1. For many things, _____ is an excellent source of data.
  a. the Internet   b. a supermarket

2. A decade is a period of _____ years.
  a. ten   b. twenty

3. An example of an enormous animal is _____.
  a. a mouse   b. a whale

4. The frontiers of science are things that are _____.
  a. known by everyone   b. near its limits

5. If we are talking about something's prospects, we are interested in its _____.
  a. future   b. past

Word Partnership

Use **prospect** with:
(*n*.) prospect **for/of peace**, prospect **for/of war**
(*v*.) prospect **of being (something)**, prospect **of having (something)**

Pushing the Limit

▲ Usain Bolt celebrates winning the final of the men's 200 meters at the 2008 Olympic Games in Beijing. He set a new world record for the race: 19.30 seconds.

☐ Before You Read

A. Completion. Look at the pictures and read the information below. Then complete sentences **1–4** using the correct form of the words in blue.

Many athletes made the news headlines during the 2008 Beijing Olympics. Some, like Michael Phelps, were already famous before the games. Phelps set an all-time world record for gold medals, receiving a total of eight in Beijing. Others, such as Usain Bolt, were less famous than Phelps before Beijing 2008. However, his years of training finally paid off, when he broke both world and Olympic records for the 100 m and 200 m races.

1. The world's biggest athletics competition—held once every four years—is the _____.
2. If you want to award someone for something they have done, you might give them a(n) _____.
3. Athletes need to _____ very hard before a competition.
4. Michael Phelps is one of the world's most famous _____.

B. Discussion. Discuss these questions. Then read the passage to learn more about Olympic athletes.

1. Do you think anyone can train to become an Olympic athlete?
2. Do you think the life of an Olympic athlete is enjoyable?

Michael Phelps ▶ receives his eighth gold medal of the 2008 Olympic Games in Beijing.

What Makes an Olympic Champion?

1 How does a person become an Olympic champion—someone capable of winning
5 the gold? In reality, a combination of biological, environmental, and psychological factors, as well as training and
10 practice, all go into making a super athlete.

▲ Weightlifters such as U.S. national champion Shane Hamman have incredibly strong leg muscles.

Perhaps the most important factor involved in becoming an elite[1] athlete is genetics. Most Olympic competitors are equipped
15 with certain physical characteristics that differentiate them from the average person. Take an elite athlete's muscles, for example. In most human skeletal muscles (the ones that make your body move),
20 there are fast-twitch fibers[2] and slow-twitch fibers. Fast-twitch fibers help us move quickly. Olympic weightlifters, for example, have a large number of fast-twitch fibers in their muscles—many more than the
25 average person. These allow them to lift hundreds of kilos from the ground and over their heads in seconds. Surprisingly, a large, muscular body is not the main requirement to do well in this sport. It is
30 more important to have a large number of fast-twitch fibers in the muscles.

The legs of an elite marathon runner, on the other hand, might contain up to 90 percent slow-twitch muscle fibers. These
35 generate energy efficiently and enable an athlete to control fatigue and keep moving for a longer period of time. When we exercise long or hard, it's common to experience tiredness, muscle pain, and difficulty breathing.
40 These feelings are caused when the muscles produce high amounts of lactate and can't remove it quickly enough. Athletes with many slow-twitch muscle fibers seem to be able to clear the lactate[3] from their muscles faster as
45 they move. Thus, the average runner might start to feel discomfort halfway into a race. A trained Olympic athlete, however, might not feel pain until much later in the competition.

[1] **Elite** refers to the most powerful, rich, or talented people within a particular group.
[2] **Fibers** are thin, thread-like pieces of flesh that make up the muscles in your body.
[3] **Lactate** is a substance produced by your muscles when you have been exercising a lot.

A crowd of 30,000 ▶ runners of all ages streams across a bridge during the New York City marathon.

For some Olympic competitors, size is important. Most male champion swimmers are 180 cm (six feet) or taller, allowing them to reach longer and swim faster. For both male and female gymnasts, though, a smaller size and body weight mean they can move with greater ease, and are less likely to suffer damage when landing on the floor from a height of up to 4.5 meters (15 feet).

Some athletes' abilities are naturally enhanced by their environment. Those raised at high altitudes in countries such as Kenya, Ethiopia, and Morocco have blood that is rich in hemoglobin. Large amounts of hemoglobin carry oxygen[4] around the body faster, enabling these athletes to run better. Cultural factors also help some athletes do well at certain sports. Tegla Loroupe, a young woman from northern Kenya, has won several marathons. She attributes some of her success to her country's altitude (she trains at about 2,400 meters or 8,000 feet) and some to her cultural background. As a child, she had to run ten kilometers to school every day. "I'd be punished if I was late," she says.

Although genetics, environment, and even culture play a part in becoming an elite athlete, training and practice are needed to succeed. Marathon runners may be able to control fatigue and keep moving for long periods of time, but they must train to reach and maintain their goals. Weightlifters and gymnasts perfect their skills by repeating the same motions again and again until they are automatic. Greg Louganis, winner of four Olympic diving gold medals, says divers must train the same way to be successful: "You have less than three seconds from takeoff until you hit the water, so it has to be reflex. You have to repeat the dives hundreds, maybe thousands of times." Training this way requires an athlete to be not only physically fit but psychologically healthy as well. "They have to be," says Sean McCann, a sport psychologist at the Olympic Training Center in the U.S. "Otherwise they couldn't handle the training loads we put on them. [Athletes] have to be good at setting goals, generating energy when they need it, and managing anxiety."

How do athletes adjust to such intense pressure? Louganis explains how he learned to control his anxiety during a competition: "Most divers think too much . . . ," he says. "They're too much in their heads. What worked for me was humor. I remember thinking about what my mother would say if she saw me do a bad dive. She'd probably just compliment[5] me on the beautiful splash."[6]

Kenyan athletes such as Irene Lemika benefit from training at high altitude, which develops the body's ability to transfer oxygen quickly.

---

[4] **Oxygen** is a colorless gas in the air that is needed by all plants and animals.
[5] If you **compliment** someone, you say something polite to them to show that you like their appearance, or approve of what they have done.
[6] A **splash** is the sound made when something hits water or falls into it.

Reading Comprehension

A. Multiple Choice. Choose the best answer for each question.

Gist **1.** What is this reading mainly about?
   a. factors that make someone a super athlete
   b. the different muscle types of a super athlete
   c. the size of a super athlete
   d. how to qualify for the Olympics

Reference **2.** The word *more* in line 24 refers to _____.
   a. Olympic weightlifters   c. muscles
   b. fast-twitch fibers   d. the average person

Detail **3.** When lactate builds up in their muscles, athletes feel _____.
   a. strong   c. dizzy
   b. energized   d. pain

Inference **4.** Having a lot of slow twitch muscle fibers is particularly important for _____.
   a. cyclists   c. weightlifters
   b. divers   d. table tennis players

Critical Thinking

One of the aims of the Olympics is to improve relationships between countries. Do you think it achieves this?

Main Idea **5.** What is the main idea of paragraph 6?
   a. Genetics is an important part of athletic success.
   b. Divers must train to be successful.
   c. Marathon runners must train hard to succeed.
   d. Success in sports comes with a lot of practice.

B. Classification. According to the passage, are the following related to marathon runners, to gymnasts, or to both? Write each answer (**a–f**) in the correct place in the chart.

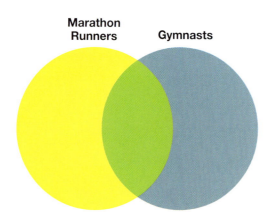

Marathon Runners   Gymnasts

a. training
b. slow twitch muscles
c. repeated motions
d. psychological health
e. ability to control fatigue and keep moving for a long time
f. small body size

Vocabulary Practice

A. Completion. Complete the information with the correct form of words from the box. Three words are extra.

champion	**genetic**	**attribute**	**enhance**	**adjust**
motion	**automatic**	**generate**	**psychological**	**differentiate**

Oscar Pistorius, the Paralympics **1.** _____ known as "The Blade Runner," has pushed forward the boundaries of what those who are physically challenged can do. Because of a **2.** _____ problem—a bone missing from both his lower legs—he had both legs amputated[1] below the knee when he was 11 months old. Now he runs on artificial versions of his lower legs, made of carbon fiber.

Pistorius's artificial legs make his running **3.** _____ the same as other runners. They enable him to run as fast as, or even faster than, a man can on human legs. In fact, some other athletes **4.** _____ his success to his artificial legs, and think that they **5.** _____ his speed compared to other runners. This has **6.** _____ intense debate about whether he should be allowed to compete in able-bodied sporting events, and has even led to some sports organizations trying to **7.** _____ their rules to exclude athletes with artificial legs.

Despite this, Pistorius's enthusiasm for success and spirit for life has won him not only medals (he was awarded three gold medals at the 2008 Paralympics in Beijing), but also international respect and admiration.

[1] To **amputate** part of the body means to cut it off in an operation.

B. Definitions. Match the definitions to words from the box in **A**.

1. working by itself   _____

2. related to the human mind   _____

3. show dissimilarities between two things   _____

4. make something better, improve it   _____

5. produce or cause something to begin   _____

6. regulate or change something to fit properly   _____

◀ Oscar Pistorius running in the men's 200-meter final at the 2008 Paralympic Games in Beijing. He won the gold medal in a time of 21.67 seconds.

Word Link

The suffix **-ic** or **-atic** can be used to form an adjective, e.g. *genet**ic***, *photograph**ic***, *problem**atic***, *autom**atic***.

High Altitude Peoples

A. Preview. You will hear these words or phrases in the video. Match each word or phrase with its definition.

1. ___ mountain sickness
2. ___ hemoglobin
3. ___ altitude
4. ___ oxygen
5. ___ lungs

a. the red substance in blood that carries oxygen around the body

b. height above sea level

c. the two organs in your chest that fill with air when you breathe in

d. a medical problem caused by low air pressure at high places

e. a colorless gas in the air that people and animals need to live

▲ The bodies of people who live at high altitude, such as these Tibetans, are adapted to life in a low-oxygen environment.

B. Summarize. Watch the video, *High Altitude Peoples*. Then complete the summary below using the correct form of words from the box. Two words are extra.

adjust	attribute	automatic	data	differentiate	enhance
evolve	generate	genetic	intense	motion	prospect

At high altitudes, simply walking can be tiring. That's because the air **1.** _____ becomes thinner the higher you climb, so that you take in less oxygen with each breath. This causes mountain sickness, or *hypoxia*.

Researchers are studying high-altitude peoples to learn how they have **2.** _____ different ways to live in such extreme environments. For example, anthropologist Dr. Aldenderfer **3.** _____ Tibetans' high-altitude survival to their fast breathing; this allows them to take in more oxygen. Other biological changes have enabled Andeans to **4.** _____ to living at high altitudes. For example, their bodies **5.** _____ more hemoglobin—the substance in red blood that carries oxygen to the rest of the body—and this **6.** _____ their ability to take in oxygen.

According to anthropologists, ancient peoples were originally attracted to mountain heights by the **7.** _____ of good hunting. Cultural developments, such as the ability to use fire and make clothes, helped them to survive the **8.** _____ cold.

Now, **9.** _____ from DNA studies may provide us with proof that it is not just cultural changes that have helped people to adapt to high-altitude environments; **10.** _____ changes inside the human body may also have played an important role.

C. Think About It.

1. What factors do you think enable people to survive in extreme environments?

2. What advice would you have for someone who wanted to be fitter?

To learn more about sport and fitness, visit elt.heinle.com/explorer

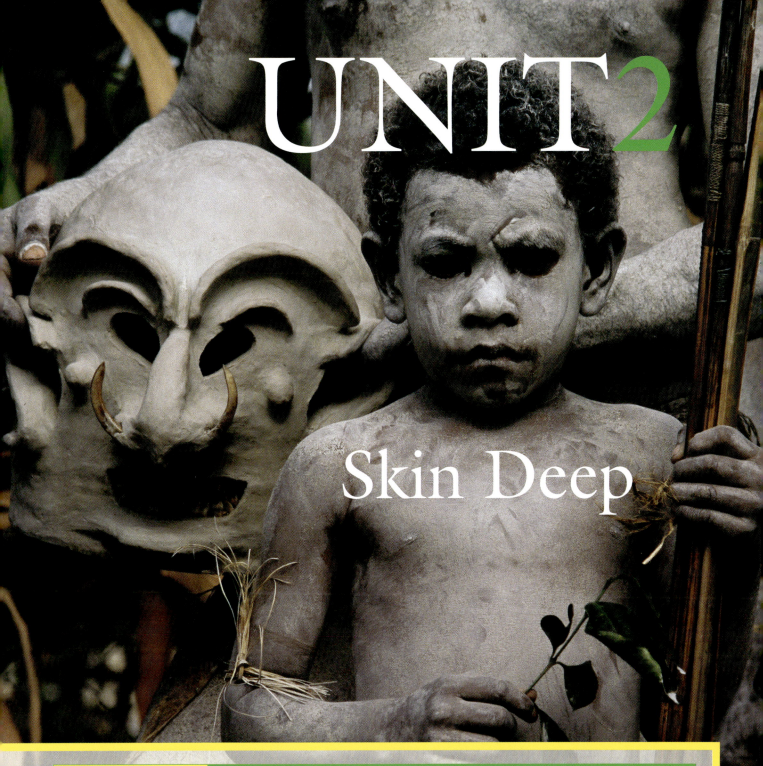

UNIT 2

Skin Deep

Discuss these questions with a partner.

1. How would you define "beauty"?

2. What do you think the expression, "beauty is only skin deep" means? Do you think it is true?

3. What do people in your country do to make themselves more beautiful?

▲ A young Asaro mudman from Papua New Guinea stands next to an adult holding a mask. "Here," says scientist Nancy Sullivan, ". . . to be masculine is to be well made-up."

21

2A   What is Beauty?

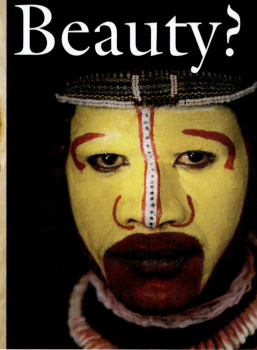

▲ A trainee geisha puts on her makeup in Kyoto, Japan.

▲ A model receives a gold facial valued at US$300, New York, U.S.A.

▲ A Huli Wigman in Garoka, Papua New Guinea is prepared for a ceremonial dance.

Before You Read

A. Survey. Complete the survey about beauty. Then explain your answers to a partner.

1. I spend a lot of time thinking about my appearance.		**Yes**	**No**
2. I think good-looking people have easier lives than other people.		**Yes**	**No**
3. I think it's fine for men to wear makeup.		**Yes**	**No**
4. Women are judged on their looks more than men are.		**Yes**	**No**
5. If I lost my hair, I might consider wearing a wig.		**Yes**	**No**
6. I notice someone's face before I notice their body.		**Yes**	**No**
7. Too many people diet to make themselves more attractive.		**Yes**	**No**

B. Scan. Quickly scan the reading. Match the people with their attitudes towards beauty.

People	Attitudes
1. ____ The ancient Maya	**a.** smaller noses and chins are attractive
2. ____ Most women	**b.** men with painted faces are attractive
3. ____ People of the Huli culture	**c.** cross-eyed people are attractive
4. ____ 18th-century French people	**d.** large shoulders and narrow waists are attractive
5. ____ Most men	**e.** large wigs are attractive

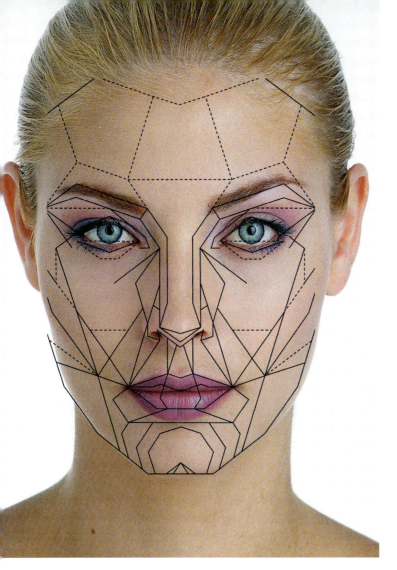

▲ **The face of beauty.** According to plastic surgeon Stephen Marquardt, this diagram shows the proportions of the ideally attractive face.

The Enigma[1] of Beauty

"one out of three consumers globally say they are spending more money today on beauty
20 and health care products . . . than ever before." Worldwide, sales of makeup, dieting, hair- and skin-care products, as well as gym memberships and cosmetic surgery,[3] generate billions of dollars every year.

25 And there is at least one good reason for the desire to be attractive: beauty is power. Studies suggest that good-looking people make more money, get called on more often in class, and are perceived as friendlier.

30 But what exactly *is* beauty? Trying to define it is difficult, and yet we know it when we see it—or so we think. "Beauty is health," says one psychologist. "It's a billboard saying 'I'm healthy. I can pass on your genes.'"
35 And our awareness of it may start at a very early age. In one set of studies, six-month-old babies were shown a series of photographs. The faces in the pictures had been rated for attractiveness by a group of college students.
40 In the studies, the babies spent more time looking at the attractive faces than the unattractive ones.

1 The search for beauty spans centuries and continents. Paintings of Egyptians dating back over 4,000 years show both men and women painting their nails and wearing makeup.
5 On the other side of the globe, the ancient Maya of Central America considered crossed eyes[2] beautiful, and hung little balls between children's eyes to develop this look. In 18th-century France, wealthy noblemen wore large
10 wigs of long, white hair to make themselves attractive. In cultures throughout the world, people have gone to extreme lengths to achieve the goal of beauty.

Today, people continue to devote a lot of time
15 and money to their appearance. According to a recent report by the Nielsen Company, a global information and marketing corporation,

[1] An **enigma** is something that is mysterious or difficult to understand.
[2] **Crossed eyes** are eyes that seem to look towards each other.
[3] **Cosmetic surgery** is surgery done to make someone look more attractive.

◄ Men of the Huli people of Papua New Guinea prepare for a *sing-sing* (an annual festival). They dress in feathers and paint to resemble the local birds of paradise. "Here men are the objects of beauty," says scientist Nancy Sullivan.

The idea that even babies judge appearance makes perfect sense to many researchers. In studies done by psychologists such as Victor Johnston at New Mexico State University and David Perrett at St. Andrews University in Scotland, men regularly showed a preference for women with certain features: larger eyes, fuller lips, and a smaller nose and chin. Another study suggests that women prefer men with large shoulders and a narrow waist. According to scientists, the mind unconsciously tells men and women that these traits—the full lips, clear skin, strong shoulders—equal health and genetic well-being. In other words, it's a fundamental part of human nature to look for these qualities in a mate.

Not everyone agrees with this notion, however. "Our hardwiredness can be altered by all sorts of expectations—predominantly cultural," says C. Loring Brace, an anthropologist at the University of Michigan. What is considered attractive in one culture might not be in another. Look in most Western fashion magazines, for example, and the women on the pages are thin. But is this the "perfect" body type for women worldwide? Douglas Yu, a biologist from Great Britain, and Glenn Shepard, an anthropologist at the University of California at Berkeley, say no; what is considered beautiful is subjective and varies around the world. Yu and Shepard found in one study, for example, that native peoples in southeast Peru preferred shapes regarded as overweight in Western cultures.

Take another example: in every culture, one's hairstyle sends a clear message. In the Huli culture of Papua New Guinea (an island nation north of Australia), men grow their hair long as a symbol of health and strength. Teenage boys in this culture learn from a young age to style and decorate their hair—a behavior more commonly associated with the opposite gender in many cultures. It is also the men (not women) in this culture who are the objects of beauty. For certain festivals and celebrations, men dress up and paint their faces. The more colorful a man is, the more masculine[4] —and attractive—he is considered.

For better or worse, beauty plays a role in our lives. But it is extremely difficult to define exactly what makes one person attractive to another. Although there do seem to be certain physical traits that are considered universally appealing, it is also true that beauty does not always conform to a single, uniform standard. A person's cultural background, for example, may influence what he or she finds attractive in others. In the end, beauty really is, as the saying goes, in the eye of the beholder.

[4] **Masculine** qualities and things are typical for men, in contrast to women.

▼ A New York model prepares for a beauty competition by having her hair cut and colored.

☐ Reading Comprehension

A. Multiple Choice. Choose the best answer for each question.

Gist

1. What is this reading mainly about?
  a. the search for the true definition of beauty
  b. the history of beauty
  c. the world's most beautiful people
  d. how beauty is power

Critical Thinking

In the last line, the author says that "beauty really is . . . in the eye of the beholder." What do you think this means? Do you agree?

Vocabulary

2. In line 29, *perceived* can be replaced with _____.
  a. known   c. treated
  b. seen   d. compared

Detail

3. In paragraph 4, the babies in the study _____.
  a. were shown photos of college students
  b. were entered in a beauty contest
  c. were rated for beauty
  d. were able to tell attractive from unattractive faces

Detail

4. What is NOT mentioned in the passage as a sign of a genetically acceptable partner?
  a. strong shoulders   c. a straight nose
  b. full lips   d. clear skin

Inference

5. Perceptions of beauty _____.
  a. change over time
  b. are the same for every person
  c. have little influence on a person's success
  d. can be easily defined

B. Summarizing. Complete the summary using words from the passage.

Beauty has been an important part of many cultures for at least **1.** _____ years, and people have gone to great lengths to achieve the perceived ideal look of beauty. Today, people spend a lot of **2.** _____ on how they look; spending on cosmetics, fitness programs, and aesthetic surgery ranges in the billions of dollars a year. The reason for this desire to be beautiful? It is proven that good-looking people get noticed more often in class, seem friendlier to others, and **3.** _____.

However, the different sexes view beauty in different ways. For example, men show **4.** _____ for women with large eyes, while women think men with wide shoulders and a narrow waist are attractive.

Differences in perception of beauty appear to be mainly **5.** _____. In the Western world, people strive to be thin, while natives of **6.** _____, for example, prefer a heavier figure. Beauty is really in the eye of the beholder.

Vocabulary Practice

A. Completion. Complete the information using the correct form of words from the box. Two words are extra.

> fundamental   alter   predominately   notion   conform   devote   gender   uniform

Anita Roddick

Anita Roddick, founder of the Body Shop, was a person who was committed to enhancing the world we live in. She was not prepared to **1.** _____ to business practices that she saw as destructive to the environment, or harmful to people's well-being. Her beliefs in social and environmental responsibility were **2.** _____ to the way in which she established her own business, and led her to **3.** _____ energy to raise awareness of the need to protect the environment. She insisted that her business was "green," and supported developing countries. When Roddick died in 2007, Adrian Bellamy, chairman of Body Shop International, said that one of Roddick's achievements was to **4.** _____ the world of business. She believed that, traditionally, the business world does things **5.** _____ for personal gain. However, she believed in the **6.** _____ that "business can and must be a force for positive social change. It must not only avoid evil . . . it must also actively do good."

▲ Anita Roddick

B. Completion. Complete the sentences using the correct form of words from the box. Three words are extra.

> mate   uniform   gender   subjective   notion   predominant   devote

1. People don't have _____ ideas on what beauty is; opinions vary greatly.

2. Nowadays, in many places, people of both _____ buy and use cosmetics; it is not a practice restricted to women.

3. When looking for a(n) _____, female peacocks are attracted by the male peacock's large, brightly-colored tail.

4. Our ideas of what is beautiful can be highly _____. What one person finds attractive may be unattractive to another.

Usage

The word **uniform** can be used as a noun or an adjective. As a noun, it refers to a special set of clothes which some people wear to work or school, e.g. *a school uniform, a police uniform*; as an adjective it means *even and regular throughout*, e.g. *cut food into uniform shapes; uniform price rises across the country*.

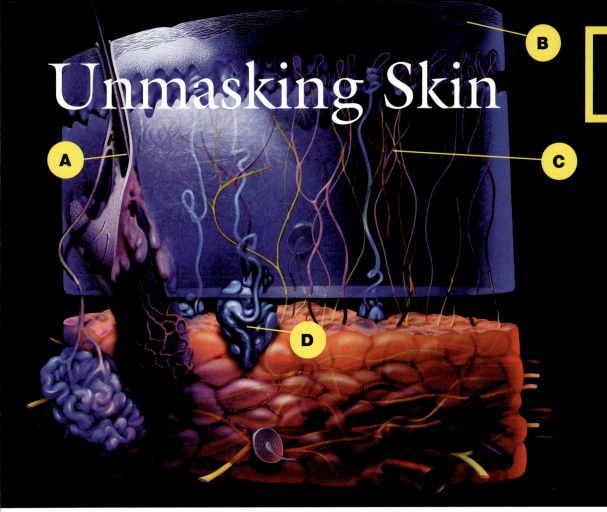

Unmasking Skin

2B

A

B

C

D

☐ Before You Read

A. Labeling. The diagram above shows a close-up of human skin. Read the descriptions (**1–4**) of each part of the skin, and write which feature (**A–D**) it refers to.

1. The epidermis is the skin's outer layer. It is replaced about once every month. ____

2. Hair follicles and surrounding nerves send messages to the brain. ____

3. Glands produce sweat to cool the body. ____

4. Thin blood vessels, just below the epidermis, help distribute nutrients and remove waste. ____

B. Scan. Quickly scan the reading. Match each practice with the place in the world where it takes place.

Place	Practice
1. ____ Modern Europe	**a.** full body tattoos
2. ____ New Zealand	**b.** sun tanning in a salon
3. ____ Japan	**c.** scarring (cutting or burning the skin)
4. ____ West Africa	**d.** full facial tattoos

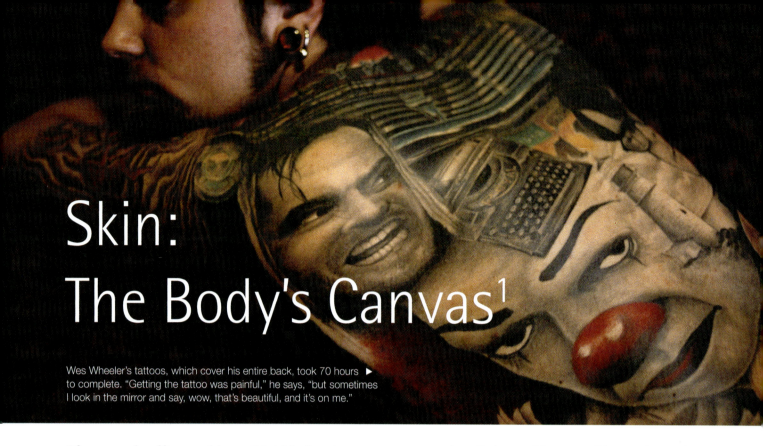

Skin:
The Body's Canvas[1]

Wes Wheeler's tattoos, which cover his entire back, took 70 hours ▶ to complete. "Getting the tattoo was painful," he says, "but sometimes I look in the mirror and say, wow, that's beautiful, and it's on me."

1 If you took off your skin and laid it flat, it would cover an area of about 1.9 square meters (21 square feet), making it by far the body's largest organ. Covering almost the entire body,
5 skin protects us from a variety of external forces, such as extremes of temperature, damaging sunlight, harmful chemicals, and dangerous infections. Skin is also packed with nerves, which keeps the brain in touch with the
10 outside world.

The health of our skin and its ability to perform its protective functions are crucial to our well-being. However, the appearance of our skin is equally—if not more—important to
15 many people on this planet.

Take skin color, for example. Your genes determine your skin's color, but for centuries, humans have tried to lighten or darken their skin in an attempt to be more attractive. In
20 the 1800s, white skin was desirable for many Europeans. Skin this color meant that its owner was a member of the upper class and did not have to work in the sun. Among darker-skinned people in some parts of the world, products
25 used to lighten skin are still popular today. In other cultures during the 20th century, as cities grew and work moved indoors, attitudes toward light skin shifted in the opposite direction. Tanned skin began to indicate leisure
30 time and health. In many places today, sun tanning on the beach or in a salon[2] remains popular, even though people are more aware of the dangers of UV rays.[3]

Just as people have altered their skin's color
35 to denote wealth and beauty, so too have cultures around the globe marked their skin to indicate cultural identity or community status. Tattooing, for example, has been carried out for thousands of years. Leaders in places
40 including ancient Egypt, Britain, and Peru wore tattoos to mark their status, or their bravery. Today, among the Maori people of New Zealand as well as in cultures in Samoa, Tahiti, and Borneo, full facial tattoos, called *moko*, are
45 still used to identify the wearer as a member of a certain family and to symbolize the person's achievements in life.

[1] **Canvas** is a strong, heavy cloth often used to do oil pants on.
[2] A **salon** is a place where people have their hair cut or colored, or have beauty treatments.
[3] **UV rays** (or **ultaviolet rays**) are what causes your skin to go darker in color after having been in sunlight.

▲ A group of children from Washington International Primary School shows a range of different skin tones.

In Japan, tattooing has been practiced since around the fifth century B.C. The government made tattooing illegal in 1870, and though there are no laws against it today, tattoos are still strongly associated with criminals—particularly the *yakuza*, or the Japanese mafia,[4] who are known for their full-body tattoos. The complex design of a yakuza member's tattoo usually includes symbols of character traits that the wearer wants to have. The process of getting a full-body tattoo is both slow and painful and can take up to two years to complete.

In some cultures, scarring—a marking caused by cutting or burning the skin—is practiced, usually among people who have darker skin on which a tattoo would be difficult to see. For many men in West Africa, for instance, scarring is a rite of passage—an act that symbolizes that a male has matured from a child into an adult. In Australia, among some native peoples, cuts are made on the skin of both men and women when they reach 16 or 17. Without these scars, members were traditionally not permitted to trade, sing ceremonial songs, or participate in other activities.

Not all skin markings are permanent, though. In countries such as Morocco and India, women decorate their skin with colorful henna designs for celebrations such as weddings and important religious holidays. The henna coloring, which comes from a plant, fades and disappears over time.

In recent years in many industrialized nations,[5] tattooing, henna body art, and, to a lesser degree, scarring have been gaining in popularity. What makes these practices appealing to those living in modern cities? According to photographer Chris Rainier, whose book *Ancient Marks* examines body markings around the globe, people are looking for a connection with the traditional world. "There is a whole sector of modern society—people in search of identity, people in search of meaning . . .," says Rainier. "Hence, [there has been] a huge explosion of tattooing and body marking . . . [I]t's . . . mankind wanting identity, wanting a sense of place . . . and a sense of culture within their community."

[4] The **mafia** is a criminal organization that makes money illegally.
[5] An **industrialized nation** is a country that has a lot of industry, such as factories, businesses, etc.

▲ The scars on the face of a Gobir woman from Niger indicate her membership in the tribe.

Reading Comprehension

A. Multiple Choice. Choose the best answer for each question.

Gist
1. What is this reading mainly about?
   a. the importance of skin to health
   b. the ways people change the appearance of their skin
   c. reasons people get tattoos
   d. cultural ceremonies

Detail
2. Why are tattoos disapproved of in Japanese society?
   a. They are often associated with crime.
   b. They are painful.
   c. They take too long to complete.
   d. They are illegal.

Detail
3. What is NOT true about henna tattoos?
   a. They are used to celebrate religious holidays.
   b. Some Indian brides decorate their skin with them.
   c. They are permanent.
   d. They are made with ink.

Vocabulary
4. In the final paragraph, the word *explosion* can be replaced with _____.
   a. bombing
   b. destruction
   c. increase
   d. decrease

Main Idea
5. What is the main idea of paragraph 8 (starting line 81)?
   a. Body marking is used today as a means of identity.
   b. Body marking is a dying art.
   c. Body marking is an old practice.
   d. Body marking is a modern phenomenon.

B. Matching. Match the ways in which people have changed the appearance of their skin (**1–5**) with their reasons for doing so (**a–e**).

Ways of changing appearance	Reasons
1. _____ henna	**a.** to show bravery or indicate achievements
2. _____ tattooing	**b.** to celebrate weddings and festivals
3. _____ scarring	**c.** to show leisure time and health
4. _____ tanning	**d.** to indicate membership of the upper class
5. _____ skin whitening	**e.** to mark the reaching of adulthood, particularly on darker-skinned people

Critical Thinking

How are tattoos viewed in your culture? Do you have one, or would you consider getting one?

Vocabulary Practice

A. Completion. Complete the information with the correct form of words from the box. Two words are extra.

fade	denote	criminal	chemical	bravery
permanent	crucial	external	mature	leisure

Tattooing was traditionally a(n) **1.** _____ part of life for members of the Iban tribe of Sarawak, Malaysia. Iban tattooing was considered a spiritual art form, and it was believed that the tattoos helped protect the Iban people from harm and disease. Common images for tattoos related to the world around them, and images of plant and animal life were predominant.

By simply looking at the tattoos, which were first done when a child grew into a(n) **2.** _____ adult, other members of the tribe could know things about the wearer, such as his or her life experiences. Specific designs like flowers and spirals **3.** _____ concepts such as a man's skill and **4.** _____ in fighting, or a woman's skill in weaving, dancing, or singing. In the past, weaving was considered the female's equivalent to fighting, and was known as "women's war." Nowadays, Iban women weave as a(n) **5.** _____ activity, or to provide souvenirs for the tourist market.

Originally, the tattooing was done using ancient recipes involving natural dyes from plants and traditional wooden tools. The dyes are **6.** _____; they cannot be removed. Newly-done, Iban tattoos look dark, but they gradually **7.** _____ somewhat from sunlight, or as the dye is absorbed into the skin. Today, for the Iban people, Western tattoos are more popular than traditional designs, and modern tattooing machines are used. Modern **8.** _____ dyes have mainly replaced the plant-based ones.

▲ An Iban man's hands show traditional Iban tattoos.

B. Definitions. Use the correct form of words in the box in **A** to complete the definitions.

1. A person who breaks the law is a(n) _____.

2. If you walk at a slow pace, you are walking _____.

3. If something is _____, it lasts forever.

4. If something is on the outside rather than the inside, it is _____.

5. You need to be _____ to handle the extreme pain of getting a traditional tattoo.

6. A person's _____ can be measured by their physical and mental development.

7. If something has become lighter in color over time, it has _____.

8. Substances that are created by a reaction between two or more other substances are _____.

Word Link

The letters **–al** at the end of a word often mean that the word is an adjective, e.g., *chemical, external, crucial,* and *criminal*. (**Note:** *criminal* is also a noun meaning a person who commits a crime.)

Skin Mask

A. Preview. You will hear these words in the video. Use the words to label the picture.

1. _____

2. _____

3. _____
made from 4. _____

silicon	lashes
mask	eyebrows

B. Summarize. Watch the video, *Skin Mask*. Then complete the summary below using the correct form of words from the box. Two words are extra.

▲ silicon mask of a model's face.

alter	chemical	conform	crucial
gender	devote	notion	permanent
predominantly	mature	subjective	uniform

The **1.** _____ of beauty is a(n) **2.** _____ one—different for everyone—but in the hands of trained special effects artists, the process of creating beauty is very precise.

To begin, they must first make a silicon mold[1] of the model's face. First, they place a cap over her hair. Then they brush Vaseline[2] on her lashes and eyebrows. The next **3.** _____ step in the process is to paint the model's face with quick-drying silicon. She has to sit motionless, as they **4.** _____ about an hour to brushing it on. When the material hardens, it forms a mold that **5.** _____ to the shape of the model's face.

At their workshop, the artists then prepare a mold. The mask itself will be made **6.** _____ of silicon. **7.** _____ are added that will **8.** _____ the mask's color to a natural shade, **9.** _____ in color, similar to human skin.

The mixture is then injected into the mold and when it's dry, a face is created. The completed mask becomes a(n) **10.** _____ record of one person's face, preserved in a moment in time.

[1] A **mold** is a hollow container that you pour liquid into. When the liquid becomes solid, it takes the same shape as the mold.

[2] **Vaseline** is a brand name for a soft clear jelly made from petroleum, which is used to protect the skin.

C. Think About It.

1. Would you like to have a mask created of your own face? Why or why not?

2. Which people do you think are the most beautiful in the world? What makes them beautiful?

To learn more about skin and beauty, visit elt.heinle.com/explorer

UNIT 3
Animals in Danger

A dogfish shark (*Squalus acanthias*) caught in a net off the coast of New Zealand.

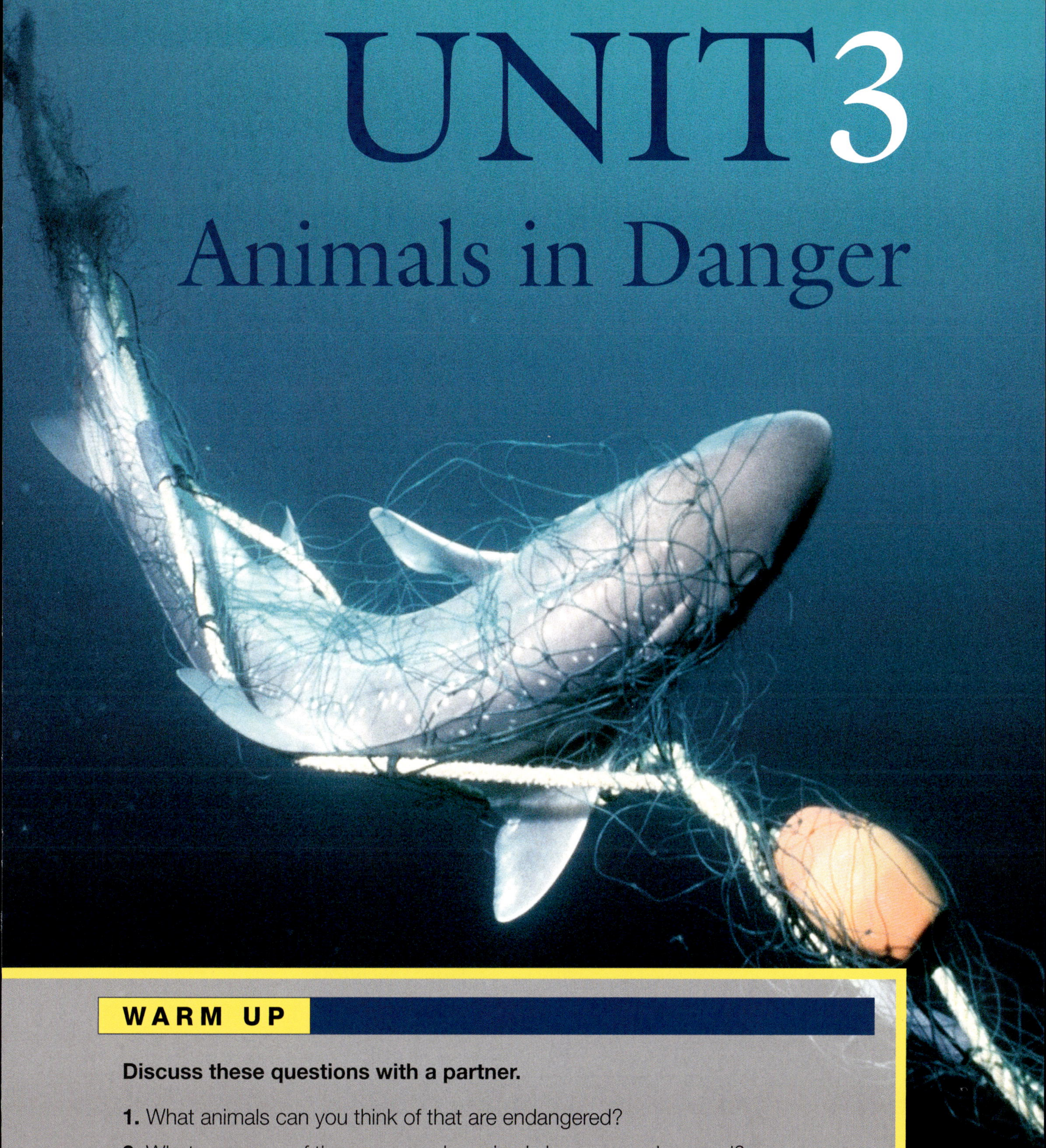

WARM UP

Discuss these questions with a partner.

1. What animals can you think of that are endangered?
2. What are some of the reasons why animals become endangered?
3. Do you think that it is important for humans to protect endangered species? Why or why not?

3A

Panda Protectors

☐ Before You Read

A. Matching. Match each description below with the picture it describes.

1. A newborn panda cub looks nothing like its mother. It's pink, hairless, and blind. Baby pandas don't open their eyes until they're six weeks old. _____

2. At three months old, baby pandas are just starting to move on their own. This cub, born in captivity in a zoo, is being weighed and measured. _____

3. Little pandas living in their natural habitat—the mountain ranges of central China—usually stay with their mothers for three years. _____

4. A fully-grown panda eats about 18 kg (40 pounds) of bamboo shoots and leaves every day. Adults stand up to 1.8 meters (6 feet) tall and weigh up to 113 kg (250 pounds). That's about 900 times the size of a newborn. _____

B. Scan. Quickly scan the reading to answer the questions below. Then read again to check your answers.

1. How much does it cost a zoo each year to look after one panda?

2. Why is it so expensive to care for pandas?

Saving the Panda

▲ Tai Shan, just before his first birthday

1 July 9, 2005, was an important day at the Smithsonian National Zoological Park in Washington, D.C. The zoo had a new arrival that morning: Tai Shan, the first baby of Tian
5 Tian and Mei Xiang, male and female giant pandas. Tai Shan's birth, like any panda's, was a cause for celebration. In the first three months that the cub was on public display following his birth, visits to the zoo increased
10 by 50 percent over prior years.

Around the world, conservation centers and zoos like the Smithsonian are working to ensure that pandas survive, whatever the cost. But what makes these animals so special?
15 Aside from their cuteness, their scarcity makes them important: giant pandas are extremely rare. Even other endangered animals—tigers, gorillas, Asian elephants—outnumber them, both in the wild and in captivity. Recently,
20 China reported that about 1,590 of the black-and-white bears survive in the hills of

Sichuan, Shaanxi, and Gansu provinces. In captivity, there are only about 200: some are in the U.S. and a few others are in Mexico,
25 Japan, Thailand, Germany, and Austria. Most captive pandas, though, are in zoos and research centers in their native China.

Their shortage makes pandas precious, but caring for them isn't easy. The cost of
30 hosting a giant panda at each zoo can exceed two and a half million U.S. dollars a year, and that's without babies. Add a couple of cubs (nearly a half of all panda births produce twins), and the bill approaches four million
35 dollars. Of course, at any zoo, the arrival of a panda or the birth of cubs brings an increase in attendance, but the crowds rarely translate into sufficient revenue. Even with tickets and gift shop sales, no zoo has collected enough
40 money to offset the costs of hosting one of these animals.

3A Panda Protectors   **35**

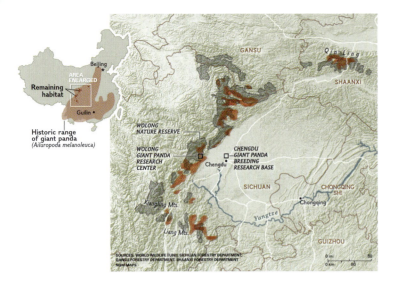

Historic range
of giant panda
(*Ailuropoda melanoleuca*)

Why is accommodating these bears so expensive? At most zoos, these animals get the best of everything: state-of-the-art
45 habitats, the best doctors and keepers, the tastiest food, and a variety of toys to play with. In the U.S. alone, this level of care costs millions of dollars a year. Every year, each zoo also sends China a million dollars for
50 the protection of pandas and their remaining habitat. China uses these funds to create education programs for schools near protected areas, and to restore the panda's bamboo forests.

55 Given the enormous cost of caring for these animals, what exactly are the benefits of raising pandas in captivity? For one thing, it has led to a number of successful births. In recent years, the captive-panda population has increased
60 dramatically. Record numbers of cubs have been born, with much better chances for survival rates. A decade ago, at the Wolong Nature Reserve in China, at least half the twins and many of the single cubs died as babies. Today,
65 new care and feeding techniques have improved the chances for survival of captive pandas in zoos in China and around the globe. All those cubs have pushed the captive population closer to a magic number: 300. With that
70 many pandas, says population biologist Jon Ballou, "we can have a self-sustaining[1] captive population and maintain 90 percent of known giant panda genetic variation for a century."

With panda numbers now on the rise,
75 China's goal is to release captive pandas into special nature reserves[2] and to eventually boost the numbers of these animals in the wild. Scientists hesitate to do this just yet, though. As National Zoo biologist David Wildt says,
80 "There may be as many wild pandas out there now as the habitat can support." However, many pandas born in captivity are being trained to be more self-sufficient and not to rely on their human keepers.

85 One day, we may be able to eliminate altogether the need to raise pandas in captivity. Though this hasn't happened yet, the work being done in China, the U.S., and other countries worldwide is helping to make the
90 goal a reality, one panda at a time.

[1] If something is **self-sustaining**, it is able to support itself without help from others.
[2] A **nature reserve** is an area of land where animals and plants are officially protected.

▼ Wolong Nature Reserve zookeeper Hu Haiping carries a four-month-old panda cub back to its mother after a checkup.

Reading Comprehension

A. Multiple Choice. Choose the best answer for each question.

Gist

1. What is this reading mainly about?
  a. the reasons panda numbers are decreasing
  b. the problems faced by pandas in zoos
  c. the differences between wild and captive pandas
  d. the expense of caring for pandas in captivity

Detail

2. What is NOT stated in the passage as a way China spends the money it receives in donations?
  a. educating children about wild pandas
  b. care of captive pandas in zoos
  c. building up the bamboo forests in China
  d. protection of pandas

Main Idea

3. What is the main idea of paragraph 5 (line 55)?
  a. The standard of care has improved in recent years.
  b. Successful captive panda births have increased.
  c. The number of wild pandas has increased.
  d. Training for carers has improved.

Vocabulary

4. In line 76, the word *boost* can be replaced with _____.
  a. increase
  b. reduce
  c. halve
  d. double

Paraphrase

5. Which of the following is closest in meaning to "many pandas born in captivity are being trained to be more self-sufficient and not to rely on their human keepers" (lines 82–84)?
  a. Human keepers are training many pandas born in zoos to rely on them.
  b. Pandas in the wild are self sufficient.
  c. A lot of pandas in zoos today are learning to be more independent of their human keepers.
  d. A lot of pandas in zoos today rely on their human keepers to survive.

Critical Thinking

With many starving people in the world, do you think so much money should be spent on saving the panda from extinction?

B. Summarizing. Complete the summary using words from the passage.

Baby panda Tai Shan could be seen by the public soon after his birth. In the first **1.** _____ months after his birth, the number of **2.** _____ to the zoo increased by half. However, caring for pandas in zoos is **3.** _____. It can cost over $2.5 million a year to look after the adult pandas alone. But the expenditure seems to be paying off. As a result of improvements in care over the last **4.** _____, the captive panda **5.** _____ has risen rapidly—to almost 300 pandas today.

☐ Vocabulary Practice

A. Completion. Complete the information below using the correct form of the words in red.

With its black-and-white coloring, cuddly shape, and sad-looking face, the giant panda is a precious animal to the people of China. Sadly, with the loss of the bamboo forests in which they live, the panda is becoming scarce. To restore the

▲ Wu Dai Fu, from the Wolong Nature Reserve, is teaching a new mother panda to look after her cub.

dwindling[1] number of pandas, various projects are in progress. One of these is the Wolong Panda Reserve in Sichuan Province, which is the best-known panda reserve in China. The center was founded in 1980 to accommodate captive pandas for the purposes of research and producing baby pandas. The success of the program has been dramatic, and has resulted in pandas being given or loaned to zoos around the world.

However, on May 12, 2008, disaster struck when the area in which the reserve is located was hit by a powerful earthquake. Two pandas died as a result of the earthquake, but fortunately most of the others escaped injury.

[1] If something **dwindles** it becomes smaller, weaker, or less in number.

1. In order to preserve the history and culture of a country, the _____ of old buildings is important.
2. During the _____ events following the 2008 earthquake, a number of pandas escaped from the reserve, but they were soon found.
3. Conservationists agree that endangered animals are a(n) _____ resource that we should protect.
4. For tourists who want to volunteer at Wolong Panda Reserve, _____ is available at a nearby hotel.
5. An animal species may become extinct if its food becomes _____.

B. Words in Context. Complete each sentence with the best answer.

1. On most highways, you exceed the speed limit if you drive at _____.
   a. 40 kph (25 mph)   b. 160 kph (100 mph)
2. Animal lovers _____ hesitate to help an animal in pain.
   a. would   b. would not
3. If you eliminate something, it is because you _____.
   a. want it   b. don't want it
4. An example of a zoo's revenue is _____.
   a. the money it brings in from tourists
   b. the money it pays its keepers and other workers
5. Wolong Reserve offsets the cost of doing research by _____.
   a. bringing in tourists   b. constructing more buildings

> **Word Partnership**
>
> Use **exceed** with:
> exceed **a limit**, exceed **expectations**, exceed **an estimate**, exceed **a budget**, exceed **(a million dollars a year)**

Cats in Crisis

① Compared to other cats, **lions** are unusually social; they live in groups (called *prides*) that consist of adult males, related females (called *lionesses*), and cubs. Once widespread, lions today exist only in Sub-Saharan Africa and in a small area of northwest India.

② **Jaguars** are found only in remote regions of South and Central America. The name is derived from the Native American word *yaguar*, which means "he who kills with one leap." Unlike many other cats, jaguars are quite good swimmers; their prey often includes fish and turtles.

③ **Leopards** can be found in Africa, Central Asia, India, and China. However, many populations are now endangered. Like jaguars, most are light colored with distinctive rose-shaped dark spots called *rosettes*.

④ Most wild **cheetahs** are found in eastern and southwestern Africa. A quiet and deadly daylight hunter, the cheetah is the world's fastest mammal on land, and can be easily identified by its spotted coat and dark eye marks. Perhaps only 12,000 remain in the wild.

⑤ Out of the original eight sub-species of **tigers**, three are now extinct. Today, this powerful predator can be found in places such as Indonesia, India, and Russia. No two tigers have the same pattern of stripes.

☐ Before You Read

A. Quiz. How much do you know about big cats? Circle true (**T**) or false (**F**) for each sentence. Then read the information below to check your ideas.

1. Each tiger's stripy pattern is unique.   **T F**
2. Lions are found only in Africa.   **T F**
3. Jaguars are good swimmers.   **T F**
4. The cheetah is the fastest land mammal.   **T F**
5. Leopards can be found in South America.   **T F**

B. Predict. Look quickly at the photos, captions, and first and last paragraphs of pages 40–41. Check (✔) the information you think you'll read about.

❐ The number of snow leopards left in the wild
❐ Methods of protecting snow leopards
❐ How baby snow leopards survive in the wild
❐ Conflicts between snow leopards and herders

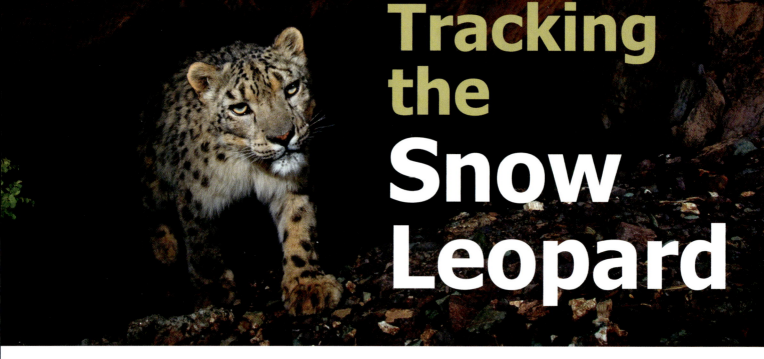

Tracking the Snow Leopard

▲ Because snow leopards usually hide from humans, photographer Steve Winter used camera traps to take this photo and the one on the next page. The traps automatically took a number of photos whenever the animal came near.

1 "When a snow leopard stalks[1] its prey among the mountain walls, it moves . . . softly, slowly," explains Indian biologist Raghunandan Singh Chundawat, who has studied the animal for years. "If it knocks a stone loose, it will reach out a foot to stop it from falling and making noise." One might be moving right now, perfectly silent, maybe
5 close by. But where? And how many are left to see?

Best known for its spotted coat and long distinctive tail, the snow leopard is one of the world's most secretive animals. These elusive[2] cats can only be found high in the remote,
10 mountainous regions of Central Asia. For this reason, and because they hunt primarily at night, they are very rarely seen.

Snow leopards have been officially protected since 1975, but enforcing this law has proven
15 difficult. Many continue to be killed for their fur and body parts, which are worth a fortune on the black market.[3] In recent years, though, conflict with local herders has also led to a number of snow leopard deaths.
20 This is because the big cats kill the herders' animals, and drag the bodies away to eat high up in the mountains.

As a result of these pressures, the current snow leopard population is estimated at only
25 4,000 to 7,000, and some fear that the actual number may already have dropped below 3,500. The only way to reverse this trend and bring these cats back from near extinction, say conservationists, is to make
30 them more valuable alive than dead.

Because farming is difficult in Central Asia's cold, dry landscape, traditional cultures depend mostly on livestock (mainly sheep and goats) to survive in these mountainous
35 regions. At night, when snow leopards hunt, herders' animals are in danger of snow leopard attacks. Losing only a few animals can push a family into desperate poverty. "The wolf[4] comes and kills, eats, and goes
40 somewhere else," said one herder, "but snow leopards are always around. They have killed one or two animals many times . . . Everybody wanted to finish this leopard."

To address this problem, local religious leaders have called for an end to snow leopard killings, saying that these wild animals have the right to exist peacefully. They've also tried to convince people that the leopards are quite rare, and thus it is important to protect them.

Financial incentives are also helping to slow snow leopard killings. The organization Snow Leopard Conservancy–India has established Himalayan Homestays, a program that sends visitors to the region to herders' houses. For a clean room and bed, meals with the family, and an introduction to their culture, visitors pay about ten U.S. dollars a night. Having guests once every two weeks through the tourist season provides the herders with enough income to replace the animals lost to snow leopards. In addition, Homestays helps herders build protective fences that keep out snow leopards. The organization also conducts environmental classes at village schools, and trains Homestays members as nature guides, available for hire. In exchange, the herders agree not to kill snow leopards.

In Mongolia, a project called Snow Leopard Enterprises (SLE) helps herder communities earn extra money in exchange for their promise to protect the endangered cat. Women in Mongolian herder communities make a variety of products—yarn for making clothes, decorative floor rugs, and toys—using the wool from their herds. SLE buys these items from herding families and sells them abroad. Herders must agree to protect the

▲ Stanzin Pulit, a yak farmer, has to guard his animals from snow leopard attacks.

snow leopards and to encourage neighbors to do the same.

The arrangement increases herders' incomes by 10 to 15 percent, and elevates the status of the women. If no one in the community kills the protected animals over the course of a year, the program members are rewarded with a 20 percent bonus in addition to the money they've already made. An independent review in 2006 found no snow leopard killings in areas where SLE operates. Today, the organization continues to add more communities.

Projects like the Homestays program in India and SLE's business in Mongolia are doing well. Though they cover only a small part of the snow leopard's homeland, they make the leopards more valuable to more people each year, and in doing so, they help preserve this endangered animal.

¹ If you **stalk** a person or animal, you follow them quietly.
² Something that is **elusive** is difficult to find.
³ If something is bought or sold on the **black market**, it is bought or sold illegally.
⁴ A **wolf** is a wild animal that looks like a large dog.

◀ Snow leopards' big eyes are so good in low light that they are able to hunt in near total darkness.

☐ Reading Comprehension

A. Multiple Choice. Choose the best answer for each question.

Main Idea

1. What is the main idea of paragraph 3 (line 13)?
- a. Local herders are uncooperative in attempts to save snow leopards.
- b. The snow leopard's endangerment is due in part to the black market.
- c. Snow leopards are killed for their fur and body parts.
- d. It is difficult to enforce the laws made to protect the snow leopard.

Reference

2. In line 21, the word *bodies* refers to _____.
- a. the big cats
- b. snow leopards
- c. local herders
- d. the herders' animals

Critical Thinking

Do you think any of the programs mentioned in the passage could be adapted to help other endangered animals?

Reference

3. In line 27, the word *trend* refers to _____.
- a. the fall in the cat population
- b. the pressures caused by the black market
- c. conflict with the herders
- d. the opinions of conservationists

Vocabulary

4. In line 44, the word *address* can be replaced with _____.
- a. solve
- b. locate
- c. discuss
- d. change

Detail

5. Why is the Mongolian women's status in the community "elevated"? (Paragraph 9)
- a. They can encourage their neighbors.
- b. They are saving the snow leopards.
- c. They are earning money for the community.
- d. They are living higher up in the mountain.

B. Classification. Match each answer (**a–g**) with the program it describes.

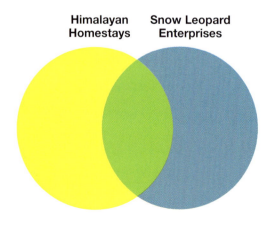

Himalayan Homestays   Snow Leopard Enterprises

- **a.** Local women sell home-made products.
- **b.** Herders provide accommodation to guests.
- **c.** Members become nature guides.
- **d.** Visitors provide income.
- **e.** Herders receive 20% extra if no protected animals are killed in the year.
- **f.** Herders receive help to build fences.
- **g.** Encourages herders to protect snow leopards.

☐ Vocabulary Practice

A. Matching. Read the information below and match each word in red with its definition.

The cheetah, an expert hunter, sits silently atop a hill and scans the herds of feeding animals looking for the perfect prey. Finding a target, it moves quietly through the grass until it is close enough to know it can get its reward—perhaps an antelope or a wildebeest.

The cheetah is perfectly built for the kill. Its coloring allows it to disappear into the landscape to avoid being seen. And its speed over a short distance, the fastest in the animal world, allows it to chase its target. Once the prey is killed, the cheetah drags the carcass[1] to a safe place, even pulling it up into a tree to stop other predators from stealing it.

▲ A cheetah and a vulture fight over prey in Serengeti National Park, Tanzania.

However, the cheetah is also a highly endangered animal. To reverse the fall in cheetah numbers, game wardens are working to enforce the anti-poaching laws[2] that should protect them. Also, conservation groups are providing incentives to local farmers to protect cheetahs that come on their land. It will be a sad day if this beautiful animal disappears from our planet.

[1] A **carcass** is the dead body of an animal.
[2] **Anti-poaching** laws are laws against the illegal hunting of animals.

1. the prize for doing something successfully _____
2. the reason to do something; the motive _____
3. to pull a heavy weight across the ground _____
4. to go backwards _____
5. to make sure people obey rules _____
6. the broad view that can be seen around you in the countryside _____

B. Words in Context. Complete each sentence with the best answer.

1. Someone who lives in poverty _____.
   a. is in poor health   b. doesn't have enough money
2. Conflict between two countries may result in _____ between them.
   a. war   b. increased trade
3. Workers who receive a bonus are usually _____.
   a. pleased   b. displeased
4. An example of a trend in recent years is _____.
   a. the 2008 earthquake in China
   b. the use of the Internet for shopping

> ### Word Link
>
> **en–** at the beginning of a word may mean *making* or *putting*. E.g. **en**able means *to make able*. Other examples include: **en**act, **en**force, **en**courage.

Leopard Under Threat

A. Preview. You will hear these words in the video. Use the words to complete the caption.

predator	branch	prey	jaws

B. Summarize. Watch the video, *Leopard Under Threat*. Then complete the summary below using the correct form of words from the box. Two words are extra.

drag	accommodate	estimate	hesitate
incentive	landscape	precious	dramatic
restore	reversal	reward	scarcity

▲ The leopard is a quiet and deadly nighttime
1. _____. This leopard is holding its
2. _____—an impala—in its powerful
3. _____, while standing on a tree
4. _____ in Mala Mala Game Reserve, South Africa.

It is nighttime in the Mala Mala Game Reserve in South Africa, and a quiet leopard can be seen hiding among the branches of a tree. Although there is normally no **1.** _____ of food in the reserve, hyenas and wild dogs will use any chance to take the leopard's **2.** _____ prey.

This gives leopards a great **3.** _____ to become expert tree-climbers. A tree is a useful place to hide its kill. But everyone makes mistakes. And in this case, the leopard falls and a lucky hyena runs off with the kill. Seeking a **4.** _____ of its fortune, the hungry leopard goes out and kills another impala, and, again, tries to **5.** _____ it up the tree. This time, a lioness comes along and chases the hyena away. But the lion wants the kill for herself. The leopard doesn't **6.** _____ to leap upward with its kill. The lioness follows.

Survival in this **7.** _____ often requires great skill. This time, the leopard has **8.** _____ the strength of the tree branches perfectly. The lioness gives up, peace is **9.** _____, and the leopard is **10.** _____ with a well-earned meal.

Mala Mala Game Reserve, South Africa

C. Think About It.

1. How are big cats like leopards similar and dissimilar to domestic cats?

2. Do you know any endangered species in your country? Why are they endangered?

To learn more about animals in danger, visit elt.heinle.com/explorer

A. Crossword. Use the definitions below to complete the missing words.

Across

1. to gradually change over time into something different
4. information, facts, or statistics that you can analyze
9. outside
10. partner
12. great eagerness and excitement
14. based on personal feelings and opinions rather than on facts
16. an idea or belief about something
17. to give something, like a prize
18. to change (something)
19. lasting forever

Down

1. very large
2. to grow weaker or paler
3. very great in strength or degree, e.g. _____ pain
5. important or essential
6. when you _____ something to a situation, you think it was caused by that situation
7. to remove completely
8. a substance used in a _____ reaction
11. extremely important
13. a change or development toward something new or different
15. to pull something across the ground

B. Notes Completion. Scan the information on pages 46–47 to complete the notes.

Field Notes

Site: Canaima National Park

Location: Venezuela

Information:

- Located at the frontier of three countries: Venezuela, Guyana, and _____
- Covers an area of about _____ hectares
- Canaima's table mountains are called _____ — the tallest are _____ kilometers high
- World's tallest waterfall was named _____ after an American pilot
- Native people of Canaima — the _____ — use poison from the skin of a _____ in their hunting darts
- Was the basis for Conan Doyle's novel _____

The Lost World

Sites: **Canaima National Park**

Location: **Venezuela**

Category: **Natural**

Status: **World Heritage Site since 1994**

Canaima National Park, Venezuela

Visitors who make the long journey to Canaima National Park—located deep in the Amazonian jungle near Venezuela's southeastern frontier with Guyana and Brazil—are rewarded with some of the most dramatic scenery in South America. Covering an area of three million hectares (7.5 million acres), the park is renowned predominantly for its steep cliffs and enormous "table mountains" (known as *tepuis*) that rise from the jungle like islands in a sea of green.

Meaning "house of the gods" in the native Pemon language, the tepuis rise to 2,700 meters above the surrounding forests, so high that each tepui seems wrapped in clouds. Formed out of **sandstone** over billions of years, their surfaces are scarred by canyons several hundred meters deep, and their vertical sides are continually being altered by water from heavy rainfalls. The rain helps to enhance the beauty of the landscape by creating hundreds of waterfalls, including the world's tallest—Angel Falls.

Glossary

plateau: a large area of high and fairly flat land
poisonous: able to kill or harm if swallowed or absorbed
sandstone: a type of rock that contains a lot of sand
vaporize: change from a solid or liquid into a gas, or vapor

A Dangerous Frog

Canaima is home to the yellow-banded poison dart frog, easily differentiated from other species by its brightly-colored body. The frog is precious to the Pemon—the native people of Canaima—as they traditionally use the chemicals in the frog's **poisonous** skin to cover the tips of their hunting darts.

The Tallest Waterfall

Although it was first discovered in the early 20th century by explorer Ernesto Sanchez La Cruz, Angel Falls was not known to the wider world until decades later, when American pilot Jimmie Angel became stuck in the mud while attempting to land on Auyan-tepui. During his 11-day hike back to civilization, Angel came across the waterfall that now has his name. Known as the "waterfall of the deepest place" to the Pemon, it falls through layers of cloud to a depth of 980 meters (2,940 feet). At the bottom, visitors to the park can barely feel the water at all: the height of the falls is so great that before it reaches the ground, the water is **vaporized** by intense winds.

Canaima's remote landscape

became the imaginary setting for Conan Doyle's famous fantasy novel *The Lost World*.

Land of Dinosaurs?

In 1912, Arthur Conan Doyle, author of the Sherlock Holmes stories, published a novel entitled *The Lost World*. The story follows four brave adventurers on an expedition to a **plateau** in South America where prehistoric animals (dinosaurs and other extinct creatures), and ape-men still survive. Various film and TV versions have since been made of this tale of adventure and discovery. Parts of Conan Doyle's story have been attributed to tales told by early explorers who visited Roraima, the oldest and highest table mountain in Canaima. Sadly, however, there is no truth in the notion that dinosaurs still exist—even in a place as remote as the tepuis.

Biodiversity

A Global View

Biodiversity is a critical factor for the planet's health. It refers to the number and variety of **species**, the genetic variety within a species, and the variety of ecosystems in which species live. Earth's air and water, its oceans and forests, all depend on healthy **ecosystems** (ecological systems). These, in turn, depend on a vast web of interacting species. As species are eliminated, the entire system weakens.

Many of the greatest threats to the planet's rich biodiversity can be attributed to human activity. Species' **habitats** are destroyed by deforestation, as people cut down forests for wood, fuel, and land. Pollution and climate change also lead to environmental instability, which generates additional pressure on species numbers.

"Within our lifetime, hundreds of species could be lost as a result of our own actions," says Julia Marton-Lefèvre, Director General of the International Union for the Conservation of Nature (IUCN). Scientists from many nations are working to understand and catalog the world's wealth of species, in order to plan for their—and our own—survival.

The Red List

In 1994, the IUCN established the Red List of Threatened Species, in which the world's species are assessed and categorized according to their risk of extinction. According to the IUCN's data, 109 species became "Critically **Endangered**" in 2008, meaning they face a real prospect of becoming extinct in the wild. In some cases, conservation efforts have helped to reverse the downward trend: in 2008, the African elephant and humpback whale were both taken off the "**Vulnerable**" list, as populations were restored to previous levels. However, more species will continue to be lost permanently unless additional conservation measures are enforced.

Experts estimate that species are becoming **extinct** at a dramatic rate—up to 1,000 times more than natural loss would cause. Though mankind has discovered, and named, about 1.75 million species of animals and plants, we know that tens of millions of additional species— predominantly unknown species of insects—have yet to be identified. In time, a significant number of these may disappear before we even notice their existence.

Our planet has hundreds of ecoregions, each represented by a different color on this map. For information on each one, see http://worldwildlife.org/wildworld.

Blue-throated Macaw
Location: Bolivia
Status: Critically Endangered
Est. pop.: 120

Threatened Species, by Continent

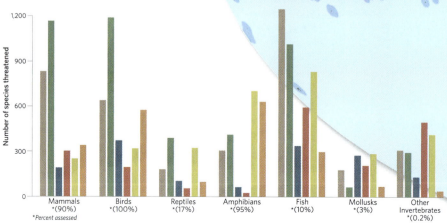

Africa Australia/Oceania North America
Asia Europe South America

Number of species threatened

| | Mammals *(90%) | Birds *(100%) | Reptiles *(17%) | Amphibians *(95%) | Fish *(10%) | Mollusks *(3%) | Other Invertebrates *(0.2%) |

*Percent assessed

Iberian Lynx
Location: Spain and Portugal
Status: Critically Endangered
Est. pop.: 143

Polar Bear
Location: Arctic region
Status: Vulnerable
Est. pop.: 20,000

Word Link

We can change some adjectives into nouns by changing –*able* to **–ability**, e.g., vulnerable—*vulnerability*; stable—*stability*; capable—*capability*; reliable— *reliability*; probable— *probability*; available—*availability*.

Siberian Tiger
Location: Russia
Status: Endangered
Est. pop.: 331–393

Ethiopian Wolf
Location: Ethiopia
Status: Endangered
Est. pop.: 239

Père David's Deer
Location: China
Status: Extinct in the Wild
Est. pop.: 53

ARCTIC OCEAN

EUROPE

ASIA

ATLANTIC OCEAN

AFRICA

SOUTH AMERICA

INDIAN OCEAN

AUSTRALIA

ANTARCTICA

Critical Thinking

Can it ever be acceptable to allow species to go extinct? What factors should determine which species are saved from extinction?

A Global View **49**

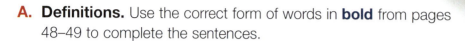

Vocabulary Building 1

A. Definitions. Use the correct form of words in **bold** from pages 48–49 to complete the sentences.

1. A(n) _____ is a category of plant or animal whose members have the same main characteristics.

2. To _____ something or someone means to put them in a situation where they might be harmed or destroyed.

3. If something (e.g., a type of animal or plant) becomes _____, it no longer exists.

4. A(n) _____ is all the plants and animals that live in a particular area, together with the complex relationship between them and their environment.

5. If someone or something is _____ to something, they are more likely to be harmed or affected by it.

6. The _____ of an animal or plant is the natural environment in which it lives or grows.

B. Word Link. We can add **–ability** to some adjectives to form nouns that refer to a particular state or quality. Complete each chart with the missing adjective or noun form of the word. Then use the correct form of the words to complete the passage.

Adjective	Noun
1. available	availability
2. capable	
3.	disability
4. probable	

Adjective	Noun
5.	stability
6. vulnerable	
7.	responsibility
8. likeable	

▲ Cheetahs, such as this young King Cheetah from Namibia, are among the most endangered of all big cats.

The fastest land animal on Earth is running the most critical race of its life—the race for survival. The cheetah—_____ of reaching speeds of 100 kilometers per hour (60+ mph)—is finding it harder to outrun pressure from humans and its shrinking habitat. According to the Cheetah Conservation Fund (CCF), it is _____ that fewer than 15,000 cheetahs remain in the wild.

Conservationists are particularly worried about the _____ of cheetahs in the world, as they live mainly in unprotected areas. Namibia has the largest number of cheetahs in the world, but as farmland spreads, the _____ of land that cheetahs can live on has been reduced. Cheetah populations declined significantly in the 1980s, but through the CCF's conservation efforts, it is hoped that the number of wild Namibian cheetahs will become more _____.

UNIT4
Violent Earth

WARM UP

Discuss these questions with a partner.

1. What kinds of natural disasters can you think of?
2. Do natural disasters occur in your country?
3. Have any natural disasters been in the news recently?

▲ A scientist in a protective suit collects volcanic samples on Mount Etna, Sicily.

51

4A The Ring of Fire

The Ring of Fire, an area circling the Pacific Ocean, is the most volcanically **active** area in the world. Three quarters of all the world's volcanoes (a total of 452) are located around the ring. Eighty percent of the world's largest **earthquakes** also occur here.

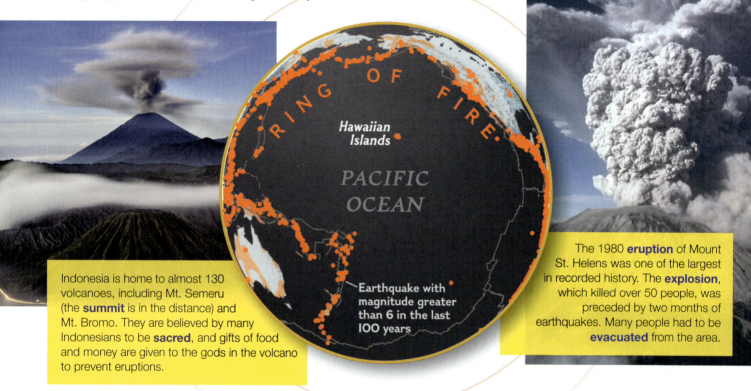

Indonesia is home to almost 130 volcanoes, including Mt. Semeru (the **summit** is in the distance) and Mt. Bromo. They are believed by many Indonesians to be **sacred**, and gifts of food and money are given to the gods in the volcano to prevent eruptions.

Hawaiian Islands

PACIFIC OCEAN

RING OF FIRE

Earthquake with magnitude greater than 6 in the last 100 years

The 1980 **eruption** of Mount St. Helens was one of the largest in recorded history. The **explosion**, which killed over 50 people, was preceded by two months of earthquakes. Many people had to be **evacuated** from the area.

☐ Before You Read

A. Definitions. Read the information above and match the words in **blue** with their definitions below.

1. used to describe a volcano that could erupt at any time _____
2. a shaking of the ground caused by the Earth's movement _____
3. (for a volcano) throwing out melted rock and smoke _____
4. to send people away from a dangerous place _____
5. a sudden, violent burst of energy _____
6. the top of a mountain _____
7. believed to have a connection to God, and given respect _____

B. Predict. Look quickly at the title, headings, photos, and captions on pages 53–54. Which volcanoes are talked about in the passage? Check the information you think you'll read about.

❒ When the volcanoes last erupted
❒ Why scientists are concerned about the volcanoes
❒ The size of the volcanoes
❒ How the volcanoes were named
❒ Other natural disasters in the two countries

SACRED MOUNTAINS

▲ Climbers normally begin their ascent of Mount Fuji around noon, so they can stand at the top of Japan's highest mountain at sunrise the next morning.

1 Volcanoes are both creators and destroyers. They can shape lands and cultures, but can also cause great destruction and loss of life. Two of the best-known examples are found at opposite
5 ends of the world, separated by the Pacific Ring of Fire.

FUJI: JAPAN'S SACRED SUMMIT

It's almost sunrise near the summit of Japan's
10 Mount Fuji. Exhausted climbers, many of whom have hiked the 3,776 meters (12,388 feet) through the night to reach this point, stop to watch as the sun begins its ascent,[1] spreading its golden rays across the mountain.
15 For everyone, this is an important moment: they have witnessed the dawn on Mount Fuji—the highest point in the Land of the Rising Sun.

Located in the center of Japan, Mount Fuji
20 (whose name means "without equal") is a sacred site. Japan's native religion, Shintoism, considers Fuji a holy place. Other people believe the mountain and its waters have the power to make a sick person well. For
25 many, climbing Fuji is also a rite of passage. Some do it as part of a religious journey; for others, it is a test of strength. Whatever their reason, reaching the top in order to stand on Fuji's summit at sunrise is a must for many
30 Japanese—and every July and August, almost 400,000 people attempt to do so.

Fuji is more than a sacred site and tourist destination, however. It is also an active volcano around which four million people
35 have settled, and sits just 112 kilometers (70 miles) from the crowded streets of Tokyo. The last time Fuji exploded, in 1707, it sent out a cloud of ash[3] that covered the capital city and darkened the skies for weeks.

40 Today, new data have some volcanologists concerned that Fuji may soon erupt again. According to Motoo Ukawa and his associates at the National Research Institute for Earth Science and Disaster Prevention, there has
45 been an increase in activity under Fuji recently, which may be caused by low-frequency earthquakes. Understanding what causes these quakes may help scientists predict when Fuji, the biggest of Japan's 86 active volcanoes,
50 will come back to life. In the meantime, locals living near Fuji hold special festivals each year to offer gifts to the goddess of the volcano— as they have for generations—so that she will not erupt and destroy the land and its
55 people below.

[1] An **ascent** is an upward movement.

[2] Japan is sometimes called **the Land of the Rising Sun**.

[3] **Ash** is the gray or black powder left when something is burnt.

▲ Near El Popo's summit, locals offer gifts to the volcano.

POPOCATÉPETL: MEXICO'S SMOKING MOUNTAIN

Halfway across the globe from Fuji, Popocatépetl—one of the world's tallest and
60 most dangerous active volcanoes—stands just 60 kilometers (37 miles) southeast of Mexico City. Although the volcano (whose name means "smoking mountain") has erupted many times over the centuries, scientists
65 believe its last great explosion occurred around 820 A.D. In recent years, however, El Popo, as Mexicans call the mountain, has been threatening to explode once more; in December 2000, almost 26,000 people were
70 evacuated when El Popo started to send out ash and smoke. As with all active volcanoes, the question is not *if* it will erupt again (an eruption is inevitable); the question is *when* it will happen.

75 "Every volcano works in a different way," explains Carlos Valdés González, a scientist who monitors El Popo. "What we're trying to learn here are the symptoms signaling that El Popo will erupt." These include earthquakes,
80 or any sign that the mountain's surface is changing or expanding. The hope is that scientists will be able to warn people in the surrounding areas so they have enough time to escape. A powerful eruption could displace
85 over 20 million people—people whose lives would be saved if the warning is delivered early enough.

For many people living near El Popo—especially the farmers—abandoning their land
90 is unthinkable. As anyone who farms near a volcano knows, the world's richest soils are volcanic. They produce bananas and coffee in Central America, fine wines in California, and enormous amounts of rice in Indonesia. For this
95 reason, people will stay on their land, even if they face danger.

Today, many people who live near El Popo continue to see the mountain as their ancestors did. According to ancient beliefs,
100 a volcano can be a god, a mountain, and a human all at the same time. To appease[4] El Popo and to ensure rain and a good harvest, locals begin a cycle of ceremonies that start in March and end in August. Carrying food
105 and gifts for the volcano, they hike up the mountain. Near the summit, they present their offerings, asking the volcano to protect and provide for one more season.

[4] If you **appease** someone, you try to stop them from being angry by giving them something they want.

▼ Children play on swings within sight of the smoking Popocatépetl.

Reading Comprehension

A. Multiple Choice. Choose the best answer for each question.

Main Idea

1. What is paragraph 3 (from line 19) mainly about?
   a. why Mount Fuji is a sacred place
   b. the healing properties of Mount Fuji
   c. reasons people climb Mount Fuji
   d. the visitors to Mount Fuji

Detail

2. Which of these statements about Mount Fuji is NOT true?
   a. It is the largest volcano in Japan.
   b. Scientists believe it may erupt soon.
   c. It has erupted quite recently.
   d. Locals have traditions concerning the mountain.

Vocabulary

3. In line 78, the word *symptoms* could be replaced with _____.
   a. earthquakes   c. sounds
   b. signs   d. lessons

Inference

4. Scientists can date the last eruption of El Popo _____.
   a. by talking to witnesses
   b. from videos of the eruption
   c. from investigating the geological evidence in the earth
   d. from religious books

Detail

5. What was the reason for evacuation from El Popo in 2000?
   a. ash and smoke were seen coming from the mountain
   b. a large explosion was heard
   c. a change in the mountain's surface was noticed
   d. a powerful eruption took place

> **Critical Thinking**
>
> Why do you think farmers would rather risk their lives than move and set up their farms away from a volcano?

B. Classification. Are the following related to Mount Fuji, to El Popo, or to both? Write each answer (**a–g**) in the correct place in the chart.

Mount Fuji   El Popo

a. last explosion A.D. 820
b. less than 100 km from city
c. more than 100 km from city
d. active
e. locals present gifts to the volcano for protection
f. provides rich soil for the production of bananas and coffee
g. last explosion 1707

Vocabulary Practice

A. Completion. Complete the information with the correct form of words from the box. One word is extra.

ancestor	disaster	monitor	holy
dawn	inevitable	abandon	

Many legends (stories passed down from **1.** _____) surround volcanoes. One famous legend, *The Legend of Popo*, is about the two volcanoes of Popocatépetl and Iztaccíhuatl in Mexico. These volcanoes lie side by side, and the latter is said to have the shape of a sleeping woman's body. So perhaps it was **2.** _____ that a story grew to explain this. In the story, Iztaccíhuatl, an Aztec princess, and a soldier called Popocatépetl, fell in love—with **3.** _____ consequences. In one version, Iztaccíhuatl dies of grief after she is told by her father that Popocatépetl has been killed in battle. When Popocatépetl returns from war to find her dead, he carries her body to the top of a nearby volcano and waits to die. Eventually, snow covers them both and they become two mountains.

▲ According to Hawaiian legend, Pele, the goddess of fire and volcanoes, lives in the top crater of Mt. Kilauea, and the formations made by cooling lava were given names like Pele's Tears and Pele's Hair.

It could be said that Mt. Popocatépetl is a(n) **4.** _____ place. The gods were touched by Popocatépetl's sacrifice of refusing to **5.** _____ Iztaccíhuatl's body until he died. Smoke can often be seen at **6.** _____ rising from the summit of the volcano. According to legend, this is the torch of Popocatépetl, who still stands guard over his beloved's body.

B. Completion. Complete the passage with the correct form of words from the box. One word is extra.

disaster	displace	expand	monitor	witness

The islands of Hawaii rose out of the sea as a result of volcanic activity on the ocean floor. One of the volcanoes on the islands, Mt. Kilauea, is still active—currently it is the most active volcano on Earth—and Hawaiians have **1.** _____ its evolving shape over hundreds of years. Often, sections of earth are **2.** _____ by a sudden jolt, or pressure builds up under the surface as the hot molten rock **3.** _____ , causing an eruption. Nowadays, the shape of the volcano is closely **4.** _____ by scientists, who hope one day to be able to predict when the next eruption might occur.

Word Link

The prefix **ex–** can refer to *away, from,* or *out,* e.g., **ex**ceed, **ex**it, **ex**plode, **ex**port.

When the Earth Moves

Before You Read

A. True or False. Look at the map and read the sentences below (**1–4**).
Circle **T** (True) or **F** (False).

1. Many of the world's most serious earthquakes occur in Europe and Asia.　**T　F**

2. Quakes generally occur along the boundaries between plates in the earth's crust.　**T　F**

3. There is a major fault line that passes through Greenland.　**T　F**

4. Many of the costliest earthquakes in the last century have occurred in China.　**T　F**

B. Scan. Quickly scan the reading on pages 58–59 to answer the question below. Then read again to check your answer.

Does the author of this passage think that predicting earthquakes is possible?

Predicting Earth quakes

The waves of an earthquake come in two forms. P waves (yellow) arrive fastest and compress and punch the rock. S waves (red) are slower but more destructive. They move from side to side to shake and destroy buildings. The building features in blue, such as deep foundations, can protect a building from earthquakes.

1 Never before have so many people packed into cities—places such as Los Angeles, Istanbul, Tokyo, and Lima—that are regularly affected by earthquakes. Located near the edge of Earth's
5 huge, shifting plates, these cities face the risk of death and economic disaster from large quakes—and from the tsunamis, fires, and other destruction they often cause.

We understand earthquakes better than we did
10 a century ago. Now, scientists would like to predict them, but is this possible? Today, some of the simplest questions about earthquakes are still difficult to answer: Why do they start? What makes them stop? Perhaps the most important
15 question scientists need to answer is this: Are there clear patterns in earthquakes, or are they basically random and impossible to predict?

In Japan, government scientists say they have an answer to the question. "We believe that
20 earthquake prediction is possible," says Koshun Yamaoka, a scientist at the Earthquake Research Institute at the University of Tokyo. Earthquakes follow a pattern; they have observable signs,

Yamaoka believes. In fact, Japan has already
25 predicted where its next great earthquake will be: Tokai, a region along the Pacific coast about 161 kilometers (100 miles) southwest of Tokyo. Here, two plate boundaries have generated huge earthquakes every 100 to 150 years. But the
30 section along Tokai hasn't had a major quake since 1854. The theory is that strain[1] is building up in this region, and that it's time for this zone to reduce its stress. Unfortunately, this is more a forecast than a prediction. It's one thing to say
35 that an earthquake is likely to happen in a high-risk area. It's another to predict exactly where and when the quake will occur.

The desire for a precise prediction of time and place has lead to another theory: the idea of "pre-
40 slip." Naoyuki Kato, a scientist at the Earthquake Research Institute, says his laboratory experiments show that before a fault in the Earth's crust finally breaks and causes an earthquake, it slips[2] just a little. If we can detect these early slips taking
45 place deep in the Earth's crust, we may be able to predict the next big quake.

[1] **Strain** is force or pressure that causes something to break or become damaged.

[2] If something **slips** it slides out of place.

▲ A car is flattened by a falling building during an earthquake in Turkey. Scientists hope one day to be able to predict earthquakes such as this.

Scientists working in Parkfield, California, in the U.S. are also trying to see if predicting earthquakes is possible. They've chosen the town of Parkfield not only because the San Andreas Fault runs through it, but because it's known for having earthquakes quite regularly—approximately every 22 years. In the late 1980s, scientists in Parkfield decided to study the fault to see if there were any warning signs prior to a quake. To do this, they drilled deep into the fault and set up equipment to register activity. Then they waited for the quake.

Year after year, nothing happened. When a quake did finally hit on September 28, 2004, it was years off schedule, but most disappointing were the lack of warning signs. Scientists reviewed the data but could find no evidence of anything unusual preceding the September 28th quake. It led many to believe that perhaps earthquakes really are random events. Instead of giving up, though, scientists in Parkfield dug deeper into the ground. By late summer 2005, they had reached the fault's final depth of three kilometers (two miles), where they continued collecting data, hoping to find a clue.

And then they found something. In an article published in the July 2008 journal *Nature*, the researchers in Parkfield claimed to have detected small changes in the fault shortly before an earthquake hit. What had they noticed? Just before a quake, the cracks in the fault had widened slightly. Scientists registered the first changes ten hours before a 3.0 quake[3] hit; they identified identical signs two hours before a 1.0 quake—demonstrating that perhaps the "pre-slip" theory is correct. In other words, it may in fact be possible to predict an earthquake.

Although there is still a long way to go, it appears from the research being done all over the world that earthquakes are not entirely random. If this is so, in the future we may be able to track the Earth's movements and design early-warning systems that allow us to predict when a quake will happen and, in doing so, prevent the loss of life.

◀ The San Andreas Fault cuts through the desert of southern California.

[3] The **Richter scale** is a scale used for measuring how severe an earthquake is. Higher numbers are more severe.

⬜ Reading Comprehension

A. Multiple Choice. Choose the best answer for each question.

Gist **1.** What is the reading mainly about?
a. earthquake prediction failures
b. the Japanese government's work on earthquakes
c. efforts to predict when an earthquake will happen
d. the Parkfield investigations

Reference **2.** In line 56, what does *do this* refer to?
a. wait for an earthquake
b. study the fault
c. predict an earthquake
d. set up equipment

Critical Thinking

How much time do you think an earthquake early-warning system would need to give people to be useful?

Vocabulary **3.** In line 64, the word *reviewed* could be replaced with _____.
a. recorded
b. deleted
c. saw
d. studied

Inference **4.** Which of the following statements is NOT true?
a. A major earthquake occurs in Tokai roughly every century.
b. Scientists believe that "pre-slip" theory can help predict earthquakes.
c. Data supporting "pre-slip" theory was found in Parkfield.
d. The last San Andreas earthquake was 22 years ago.

Detail **5.** Which of these statements is true?
a. Earthquake research happens mostly in Japan.
b. Earthquake research is happening all over the world.
c. Earthquake research is most successful in California.
d. Earthquake research has so far given no answers.

B. Sequencing. Sequence the events at Parkfield, California in the order they happened.

a. No change was registered before the quakes. ____
b. Scientists set up the equipment. ____
c. A change was registered before the earthquake. ____
d. Scientists drilled deeper into the fault, to depth of 3 km. ____
e. Scientists reviewed the data. ____
f. Scientists drilled into the fault. ____

Vocabulary Practice

A. Completion. Complete the sentences below using the correct form of words from the box. One word is extra.

identical	**precede**	**precise**	**drill**
schedule	**track**	**zone**	**random**

1. Scientists _____ holes into the ground near earthquake fault areas to learn what is happening under the surface.

2. One reason why earthquakes are so hard to predict is that they don't seem to follow any _____; they appear to occur _____.

3. Scientists _____ the movements of the earth's crust believe that a massive earthquake, known as "the Big One," will eventually occur in southern California.

4. Despite all the research done on earthquakes, seismologists still cannot tell the _____ time an earthquake will strike.

5. In 1975, in Haicheng, China, residents noticed dogs behaving strangely during the days _____ an earthquake. This enabled them to escape danger by moving to a safer place.

6. Research after the 2004 Asian tsunami found only two dead buffaloes and no other dead animal of any kind in a large wildlife conservation _____ in Sri Lanka. This led to renewed belief that animals are sensitive to the near arrival of earthquakes.

B. Completion. Complete the information with the words from the box. One word is extra.

detect	**identical**	**laboratory**	**schedule**

Research done by scientists—both in the **1.** _____ and in the real world—suggests that animals are much more aware of the world around them than we human beings. For example, if you watch a number of sleeping dogs, you will see them all show **2.** _____ behavior; notice how their ears often move, as they listen for any sounds or movement nearby. Dogs can also be trained using whistles that make sounds we humans can't hear.

Some scientists believe that dogs can be used to predict earthquakes. Mitsuaki Ota of Azabu University, Japan, claims that dogs can **3.** _____ big earthquakes about three hours before they happen. "Dogs and cats tell you a quake is going to happen with just enough time left over to make your escape," he says.

▲ A young girl and her pet dog at a temporary shelter after the 1995 earthquake in Kobe, Japan. Japanese researcher Mitsuaki Ota believes that 30% of cats and 20% of dogs in the area were able to detect the quake before it happened.

Word Partnership

Use **schedule** with: (*adj.*) **busy** schedule; **regular** schedule (*n.*) **change of** schedule; **work** schedule; **train** schedule (*prep.*) **according to** schedule; **ahead of** schedule; **behind** schedule; **on** schedule.

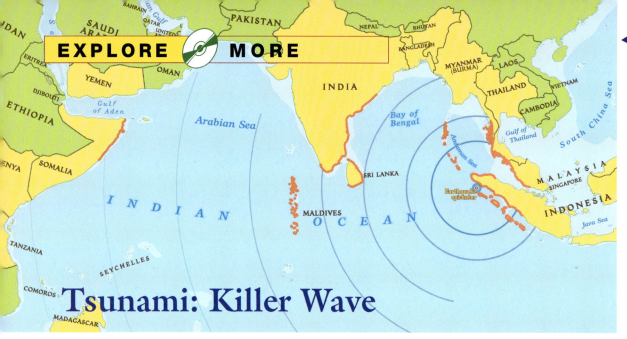

The path of the December 26, 2004 tsunami. Affected countries are marked in yellow, and severely affected shorelines are marked in red.

Tsunami: Killer Wave

A. Preview. A tsunami is a giant wave caused by an earthquake or volcanic eruption. A major tsunami occurred on December 26, 2004. Look at the map above. Do you remember that tsunami? Where did it start? How far did the waves travel?

B. Summarize. Watch the video, *Tsunami: Killer Wave*. Then complete the summary below using the correct form of words from the box. Two words are extra.

abandon	detect	disaster	displace	inevitable
laboratory	monitor	identical	witness	zone

When an undersea earthquake is very strong, it can generate a terrifying wall of water called a *tsunami*. The powerful movements send enormous amounts of energy up through the ocean, **1.** _____ huge amounts of water. The water advances toward the shore in giant waves that can rise to the height of a 10 story building.

In December 2004, **2.** _____ around the Indian Ocean stood by helplessly as the world's deadliest ever tsunami arrived on land. Few people within the strike **3.** _____ had any warning. The tsunami destroyed cities and took thousands of lives.

At the Pacific Tsunami Warning Center, scientists hope to prevent a similar **4.** _____ from happening again. The scientists **5.** _____ the Earth's movements 24 hours a day. If they **6.** _____ a quake big enough to cause a tsunami, they predict where the wave will head and warn people in its path.

In case of a tsunami warning, their advice is simple: **7.** _____ coastal areas and move to higher ground. Wait for news that the danger has passed. And be ready to deal with the destruction that is **8.** _____ left behind.

C. Think About It.

1. Which type of natural disaster mentioned in this unit concerns you the most? Why?

2. Where do you think is the safest place in the world to live? Which is the most dangerous? Why?

To learn more about violent earth, visit elt.heinle.com/explorer

Islands and Beaches

WARM UP

Discuss these questions with a partner.

1. What makes a good place for a vacation?

2. Can you name any famous beaches? What do you know about them?

3. Why do you think islands are so popular with tourists?

▲ A single palm tree casts a shadow on a white beach at the edge of the clear blue sea, Bora Bora, French Polynesia.

BRAZIL

Jericoacoara ①

Fernando de Noronha ②

Maceió

Salvador (Bahia)

Itacaré ● Prainha ③

ATLANTIC OCEAN

BRASÍLIA

Rio de Janeiro

Copacabana Ipanema ④

BRAZIL

5A

The Best of Brazil

☐ Before You Read

A. Discussion. Which of the beaches above would you most like to visit? Why?

B. Skim. Look quickly at the title, first paragraph, photos, and captions in the passage on pages 65–66. Then answer these questions:

1. Who is Stanley Stewart, and what is he doing in Brazil?

2. What is your idea of "the perfect beach"? Read the passage to see if Stewart visits a place like the one you've described.

The Perfect Beach

A sunset view of Ipanema beach and Two Brothers Peaks, Rio de Janeiro, Brazil. ▲

1 **In pursuit of the perfect beach, travel writer Stanley Stewart heads to Brazil, where he discovers some of the world's most beautiful sandy escapes.**

5 I'm standing on Rio de Janeiro's Copacabana beach, one of Brazil's—and the world's—most famous stretches of sand. As I watch life go by here in all its varied forms, I've come to realize that any understanding of Brazil really begins 10 on its beaches. In this vibrant, multicultural country, the beach is not just a place; it's a state of mind—a way of thinking and living. Rio alone, I'm told, has over 70 beaches, each with its own community: some are for 15 bodybuilders, others are for senior citizens, still others are popular with parents and children.

But Rio's beaches are just the starting point for my exploration of Brazil's Atlantic coastline, which at more than 8,000 kilometers (5,000 20 miles), and with more than 2,000 beaches, is the longest in the world. Every Brazilian has his or her own ideas of the perfect beach and is eager to tell you where to find it. I'm happy to take people's advice, but my ultimate goal is to 25 find my own dream beach.

I head to a place said to have some of Brazil's best coastline: the state of Bahia in the northeast. Portuguese settlers established themselves at Bahia's present-day capital, 30 Salvador da Bahia, in 1549. Over the centuries, people of many races have arrived and intermarried here, creating a distinctive cultural mix, which influences Bahia's language, religion, cuisine, music, and dance.

35 I'd been told that one of Bahia's best beaches—Prainha—lies just south of Salvador, near the town of Itacaré. On arriving at Prainha's beach, I discover its golden sand lined by a row of perfect palm trees, moving 40 softly in the ocean breeze. Under the moon, silver waves roll onto the sand. As I enter the water, I have the feeling of swimming through moonlight. Prainha's beauty is magnificent— its perfect curves and graceful lines are like 45 something you might see in a postcard. But for me, it's a little too perfect. The beach I'm searching for needs to be a little wilder . . .

◄ Copacabana beach is one of the most famous beaches in the world.

I continue my search, heading north to one of Brazil's legendary beaches: Jericoacoara.
50 Twenty years ago, only a handful of people were living in Jeri. Today it's an international destination, considered one of the best beach hangouts in the world (especially if you like windsurfing). It attracts visitors from Tokyo
55 to Toronto and has grown from a small village into a lively little town. Despite the changes, Jeri hasn't been spoiled by tourists, mostly because of its isolated location—it's at least five hours from any airport.

60 Everyone in Jeri rents a beach buggy,[1] which comes with a driver. I tell my driver to take me as far along the coast as he can. We drive for three hours, finally arriving at Maceió, a fisherman's beach. Boats lie on their sides
65 while nets hang out to dry on lines between fishermen's houses. We eat on the beach and later rest in hammocks near the table. It's a great day on an amazing beach. *How can it possibly get any better?* I wonder. But I have
70 one final place to visit.

Of the many beach destinations in this country, there is one that all Brazilians hold in high regard—the islands of Fernando de Noronha.

▼ Praia do Leão—one of the many beautiful stretches of coastline in Brazil's Fernando de Noronha.

More than a dozen beautiful beaches ring
75 the island of Fernando alone, three of which rank among the top ten in Brazil. The islands of Fernando de Noronha lie a few hundred kilometers out in the Atlantic. For years, people were prohibited from visiting these islands
80 because they were used as a prison and later by the army. Today the islands are a national park and UNESCO World Heritage Site, rich with diverse bird and sea life.

I visit a number of beaches on Fernando, but I
85 leave the best one for last. The beach at Praia do Leão is the perfect balance of sand, sea, and sky. The water is pale blue and warm, alive with colorful fish, turtles, and other marine[2] life; the sand is the color of honey. And in the rock
90 formations and strong winds that occasionally come in from the Atlantic, there is that hint of wildness I was seeking. Finally I've found the beach of my dreams. I dig my toes in the sand deeply and imagine I can hold on to this
95 place forever.

[1] A **beach buggy** is a small, open car with large wheels made for driving on a beach.

[2] **Marine** is used to describe things related to the sea.

◀ A surfer prepares to hit the waves at Prainha beach near Salvador, Brazil.

☐ Reading Comprehension

A. Multiple Choice. Choose the best answer for each question.

Gist **1.** What is the reading mainly about?
   a. Brazilian beach tourism
   b. an educational tour of South America's beaches
   c. the search for the author's dream beach
   d. little-known beaches of South America

Vocabulary **2.** In line 49, the word *legendary* could be replaced with
   _____.
   a. oldest
   b. isolated
   c. picturesque
   d. famous

Inference **3.** Which of these beaches is the most isolated?
   a. Copacabana
   b. Prainha
   c. Jericoacoara
   d. Maceió

Detail **4.** The islands of Fernando de Noronha are now
   used _____.
   a. as a prison
   b. as a national park
   c. by the army
   d. for fishing

Critical Thinking

What do you think can be done to preserve beautiful beaches from the negative effects of the tourist trade?

Reference **5.** In line 85, *the best one* refers to _____.
   a. the collection of Fernando beaches
   b. Praia do Leão
   c. the pale blue water
   d. the marine life

B. Matching. Number the beaches listed below **1–5** in the order Stewart visited them. Then match each beach to its description. One description is extra.

_____ Praia do Leão   **a.** beautiful but too crowded

_____ Copacabana   **b.** the author's perfect beach

_____ Maceió   **c.** remote village with beaches great for windsurfing

_____ Prainha   **d.** great place to fish, eat, and relax

_____ Jericoacoara   **e.** one of the most famous beaches in the world

                              f. picture perfect but not wild enough

Vocabulary Practice

A. Completion. Complete the information with the correct form of words from the box. One word is extra.

pursue	ultimate	eager	isolated	prohibited	destination

Writer seeks "wife" for a year on a tropical island. How many women do you think would answer this advertisement, which was placed by writer Gerald Kingsland in a London magazine in 1980? Well, 24 year-old British woman Lucy Irvine did. The opportunity to survive in a(n) **1.** _____ place provided her with the **2.** _____ challenge. In her own words: "The desert-island dream is one that has been seducing[1] people's imaginations for centuries, yet strangely, there seem to be very few people who have been willing to give it a go in real life." As an adventurer herself, Irvine was **3.** _____ to try living on an empty tropical island.

There were other applicants in **4.** _____ of the job, but Irvine eventually got it. And not long afterward, in May 1981, she was heading for a(n) **5.** _____ on the other side of the world . . .

Tuin

[1] If something **seduces** you, it is so attractive that it makes you do something you would not otherwise do.

B. Completion. Complete the information with the correct form of the words from the box. One word is extra.

eager	spoil	magnificence	diverse	rank	prohibit

The story continues . . . The island Irvine and Kingsland were to live on was Tuin, situated in the Torres Strait between the north coast of Australia and Papua New Guinea. As living there was **1.** _____ by law, they needed Australia's permission for this unusual experiment to take place. In addition, Australian law required the couple to be legally married in order to continue with their plan, and Irvine eventually agreed.

At first sight, the island looked like paradise, with white beaches lined with palm trees, and clear blue water in an untouched bay. Unfortunately, however, their experience was **2.** _____—as a source of drinking water **3.** _____ highest on their list of survival needs, the pair had to set up camp on a less attractive part of Tuin.

Over time, the stress caused by the enforced marriage, and the fact that their opinions on how to survive were so **4.** _____, caused deep problems in their relationship. Ultimately, the difficulties of working together proved too great, and despite the **5.** _____ of their surroundings, the adventure, although lasting a year, was unsuccessful.

Word Partnership

Use **rank** with:
(*adj.*) **high** rank, **top** rank; (*prep.*) rank **above**, rank **below**; (*adv.*) rank **high**

Island Explorations 5B

A

B

C

D

Before You Read

A. Matching. Match each description below with the island it describes.

1. ___ In 1704, Scottish sailor Alexander Selkirk's ship left him behind on Isla Más a Tierra, a small island hundreds of kilometers from land. Before being rescued, he lived on the small island completely alone for four years. His impressive story inspired the 1719 novel *Robinson Crusoe*, and in 1966 the island was renamed **Robinson Crusoe Island**.

2. ___ Also known as the Rock, **Alcatraz Island** is now a national park and popular tourist attraction. However, until 1963 it was one of the most famous prisons in the world—one from which no prisoner ever successfully escaped.

3. ___ **The World** is a spectacular group of 300 man-made islands that is literally shaped like a map of the world. Most of the islands have been sold for tens of millions of dollars each, mainly for tourist resorts or to the very wealthy.

4. ___ Although you might expect **Iceland** to be a very cold place, its temperature is actually quite mild. As well as dramatic natural beauty—including volcanoes, hot springs, and glaciers—the country has a lively and exciting capital city, making it a great destination for tourists.

B. Scan. Scan the article on the next page and answer the questions below.

1. Which island is the passage about? _____

2. Find numbers in the passage to match the following:
  a. population: _____ people
  b. area: _____ km²
  c. age of language: _____ years
  d. winter temperature: _____ degrees
  e. daylight hours in summer: _____ hours

Land of Fire and Ice

Never mind its chilly name—as a travel destination, Iceland is hot!

A rainbow adds color to a mountain landscape in Iceland.

1 Located in the North Atlantic Ocean, Iceland is Europe's westernmost country, with the most northerly capital city in the world. Viking explorers migrated here from northern Europe
5 in 930 A.D., when they established the world's first parliament.[1] The country's national language can still be traced to the one spoken by the Vikings over 1,000 years ago.

Today, Iceland has a population of just
10 over 310,000, spread over 100,000 square kilometers (about 40,000 square miles). Despite its small size, there are many reasons to visit this remarkable country.

City of Culture

15 Most visitors' first port of call is the country's capital, Reykjavík, a small and clean city known for its colorful and stylish architecture. The city's downtown area is lined with shops, art galleries, cafés, and bookstores. In 2000,
20 Reykjavík was awarded the title of Europe's City of Culture, thanks to its impressive art and museum scenes, and lively nightlife.

The good news for visitors is that Iceland's temperatures are fairly mild, even in the winter
25 when they stay at around four degrees (40°F). During winter months, nights are long, and the Northern Lights[2] become visible, lighting up the night sky with a spectacular natural display. In summer, the country gets almost 22 hours of
30 daylight, and native Icelanders and visitors alike enjoy partying outdoors until dawn.

Hot Springs

Iceland is one of the most volcanically active nations in the world, and there are a number
35 of thermal (hot water) springs around the island. All are heated naturally by underground volcanic activity. In fact, Iceland converts energy generated by these springs into electricity, which powers and heats people's
40 homes and businesses. As a result, Iceland burns very little fossil fuel, such as oil and gas, and has some of the cleanest air in the world.

[1] A **parliament** of a country is the group of elected people who make or change laws.

[2] **The Northern Lights** (also called the "aurora borealis") are colored lights often seen in the night sky in places near the Arctic Circle.

Visitors to Reykjavik's Blue Lagoon relax in its bright blue waters.

One of Iceland's most popular hot springs is the Blue Lagoon, a huge lake of bright blue seawater just outside Reykjavík. Surrounded by volcanoes and lava fields, the Blue Lagoon receives more than 300,000 visitors a year. After a long day's sightseeing or a long night of partying, visitors can relax their muscles and release their tension in the lagoon's steaming hot water, which has an average temperature of about 38 degrees (100°F). Some believe the waters are able to cure certain illnesses and improve skin quality.

Caves and Monsters

Most of the inner part of Iceland is uninhabited[3] and accessible only by truck or other vehicle. Nevertheless, there is a range of outdoor activities to enjoy elsewhere in the country, particularly along the coasts: "Iceland is an adventure," said Sol Squire, whose Icelandic company organizes adventure trips around the country. "We have Europe's biggest glaciers, active volcanoes, cave explorations, and skiing."

One of Iceland's most popular attractions is caving. Exploring Iceland's unusual lava caves, most of which formed more than 10,000 years ago, requires only basic caving knowledge and equipment. Ice caves, however, are more challenging and require special clothes and hiking tools. The best-known ice caves are in Vatnajökull—a vast layer of ice which, at 8,000 square kilometers (3,000 square miles), is Iceland's—and Europe's—largest glacier. It also happens to be situated just above an active volcano!

If exploring caves and glaciers doesn't interest you, head south, just outside the town of Vík, to check out[4] the huge rock formations that were once believed to be monsters turned into stone. These are a dramatic part of the scenery on one of Iceland's most impressive black-sand beaches.

[3] If a place is **uninhabited**, no one lives there.
[4] If you **check out** something, you look at it or try to find out more about it.

▲ Tourists look down on the mid-Atlantic fault that runs through Thingvellir National Park.

The Golden Circle

And finally, no trip to Iceland would be complete without a visit to the Golden Circle, a pathway northeast of Reykjavík that connects Gullfoss (a huge "Golden Waterfall"), the hot springs region of Geysir, and Thingvellir National Park. The mid-Atlantic fault that runs through Iceland is literally pulling the island apart. Nowhere is this more evident than in the Thingvellir Valley, where the land is actually separating and the stony ground beneath your feet frequently shifts. Hold on while you hike!

☐ Reading Comprehension

A. Multiple Choice. Choose the best answer for each question.

Paraphrase

1. Which of the following is closest in meaning to:
   "Despite its small size, there are many reasons to visit this remarkable country" (line 12)?
   a. There are many reasons why this country is too small to visit.
   b. There are a lot of attractions in this interesting country, even though it is so small.
   c. It is an unusual country because it is so small.
   d. Small countries are usually boring, but Iceland is different.

Detail

2. Where is the mid-Atlantic fault most noticeable?
   a. Reykjavík   c. Thingvellir Valley
   b. The Blue Lagoon   d. Geysir

Detail

3. The hot springs of the Blue Lagoon are heated by _____.
   a. solar energy   c. electrical power
   b. volcanic activity d. fossil fuels

Inference

4. Where is the best place to go if you like to party?
   a. Vatnajökull   c. The Blue Lagoon
   b. Reykjavík   d. Thingvellir Valley

Inference

5. Who is this passage probably written for?
   a. tourists   c. business travelers
   b. scientists   d. Icelanders

Critical Thinking

Do you think the author did a good job of promoting Iceland? Does it make you want to visit the country?

B. Labeling. Label the map with the activities from the list below (**a–f**) that visitors can do at each location.

a. go caving

b. view the mid-Atlantic Fault

c. see a large waterfall

d. look at art

e. visit huge rock formations on a black-sand beach

f. relax in steaming hot water

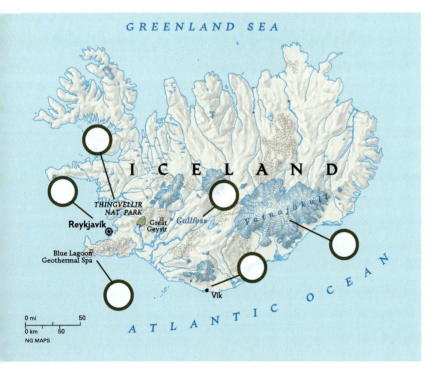

▲ Iceland

Vocabulary Practice

A. Completion. Complete the information with the correct form of words from the box. Two words are extra.

architecture	convert	cure	migrate	vast	vehicle	visible

Taroko National Park is about four hours southeast of Taipei, and is probably the island of Taiwan's most magnificent tourist destination. The **1.** _____, towering cliffs on each side of the deep gorge were created, and are still being created, when two volcanic plates collided, pushing the earth upward. The extremely high pressure **2.** _____ some of the volcanic rock into marble.

The journey there by **3.** _____ is an exciting ride. The highway that runs through the gorge is truly a(n) **4.** _____ wonder, passing through long tunnels and across high bridges. Once you leave your car, you can go on foot along a narrow walkway built into the sides of the cliffs, and if you are lucky, you may see some monkeys, just **5.** _____ in the trees on the other side of the gorge. This amazing area also features waterfalls and pools of spring water, as well as caves. Overall, it's a place that no tourist should miss.

B. Definitions. Read the information below. Then complete the definitions using the correct form of the words in red.

1. The islands of Okinawa, Japan, have a subtropical climate. Their mild winters never drop below 10°C (50°F).

2. The rainforests on the island of Madagascar have many plants and animals found nowhere else on Earth. Some scientists think it is possible that some of these plants could contain cures for diseases like cancer.

3. A strange creature with legs, flippers, and a beak-like mouth, now referred to as the "Montauk monster," washed up on the beach in Montauk, New York, on July 30, 2008.

4. The island nation of Singapore was built by the hard work of people who migrated there from other countries.

5. A few relaxing days on a beautiful beach would relieve the tension most of us feel from the stress of our everyday lives.

   a. something that restores health _____
   b. a beast-like animal _____
   c. gentle, not severe or harsh _____
   d. mental strain, stress _____
   e. move to a new or different country _____

▲ Taroko National Park

Thesaurus

vast Also look up: (*adj.*) broad, endless, massive

Island Paradise

A. Preview. Read the quote below about a group of Pacific Islands. What do you think the man means? Why do you think the islands might disappear?

"It struck me[1] the other day, when my children arrived from Tahiti and they saw an atoll[2] for the first time, that actually in their lifetime these [islands] could disappear."

—*Frank Murphy, marine biologist*

[1] If an idea or thought **strikes you**, it suddenly comes into your mind.

[2] An **atoll** is a group of coral islands.

B. Summarize. Watch the video, *Island Paradise.* Then complete the summary below using the correct form of words from the box. One word is extra.

destination	diversity	eager	isolate	visible
pursuit	migrate	tension	ultimate	vast

The Tuamotus

The small, **1.** _____ islands of the Tuamotus are like precious jewels hidden among the waters of the **2.** _____ Pacific Ocean. The islands enjoy mild tropical weather and are surrounded by living, breathing reefs filled with a rich **3.** _____ of sea life.

But this ideal vacation **4.** _____ is not without its **5.** _____. The groups of islands (called atolls) that make up the Tuamotus are made of thin coral reefs. Some are only just **6.** _____ above the water. As global warming causes sea levels to rise, these tiny but magnificent islands will become smaller, and may **7.** _____ disappear.

Time may be running out for these beautiful islands. Many holiday-makers come here in **8.** _____ of a taste of paradise. They are **9.** _____ to experience the islands' sights, before they are gone forever.

C. Think About It.

1. What do you think will happen to these islands? Do you think they can still be saved?

2. Where is "paradise" for you, and why?

To learn more about islands and beaches, visit elt.heinle.com/explorer

UNIT 6

Ancient Mysteries

Discuss these questions with a partner.

1. Do you know any mysterious places? Why are they mysterious?

2. What are the oldest places in your country? How old are they?

3. Who were the first people in your country? Where did they come from?

▲ Stonehenge, England, was abandoned 3,500 years ago, leaving how and why it was built a mystery.

75

Silent Stones

Visit Mysterious Britain

From monster legends to mysterious stones, Britain has more strange places and unexplained phenomena than perhaps anywhere in the world.

Loch Ness Monster ①

For years, people have claimed to have seen a huge monster in the waters of Scotland's Loch Ness. The mystery still **puzzles** investigators, as no **evidence** for the monster has yet been found.

Stonehenge ②

One of the most famous ancient **artifacts** in the world, this mysterious circle of standing stones in southern England has stood for more than 4,000 years. No one knows for sure who built it—or why.

Excalibur ③

Many places in Britain are closely **associated** with the **legends** of King Arthur. Some people believe the king's magical sword, Excalibur, lies hidden near Pembroke in south Wales, waiting to be rediscovered.

⬜ Before You Read

A. Matching. Read the information above. Use the correct form of words in blue to complete the definitions.

1. If you _____ something with another thing, the two are connected in your mind.
2. If something _____ you, you do not understand it.
3. A(n) _____ is an object made by human hand that is culturally or historically interesting.
4. A(n) _____ is a very old and popular story that may be true.
5. _____ is anything that makes you believe that something is true or has really happened.

B. Predict. There have been many theories about the original purpose of Stonehenge. Which of the following do you think are most likely? Read the passage to check your ideas.

❏ a temple to the sun or moon   ❏ a stone representation of the gods

❏ an astronomical calendar   ❏ a place where sick people were cured

❏ a cemetery   ❏ a site built by visitors from space

THE SECRETS OF STONEHENGE

▲ The oldest stones at Stonehenge were placed more than 4,500 years ago. Today, mystery still surrounds this ancient monument.

1   All over the globe are historical mysteries left to us by the ancient world—lost civilizations, abandoned cities, and puzzling monuments. One unexplained mystery that has both inspired and mystified modern man for centuries is Stonehenge. Though it is one of the best-known artifacts in the world, we have no definitive idea of why it was built and what it was actually used for. Today,
5   however, two new investigations may offer some answers.

A PLACE OF THE DEAD?

The first theory begins with findings being unearthed not at Stonehenge, but at a location nearby. Archeologist Mike Parker Pearson and
10   his colleagues[1] have been studying an area about three kilometers (two miles) northeast of Stonehenge. Here stands Durrington Walls—a structure similar to Stonehenge but about 20 times larger. In and around Durrington Walls
15   were three circular structures made of wood. Evidence suggests that these wooden circles were holy places, or perhaps the residences of important officials who cared for Durrington. Outside Durrington Walls, Parker Pearson and
20   his colleagues have also recently discovered a village of up to 300 houses which date back more than 4,500 years.

What do the findings at Durrington Walls have to do with Stonehenge? Parker Pearson
25   believes there is a connection between the two places, and he cites his recent studies of the Malagasy culture in Madagascar to help explain his theory. In Malagasy culture, stone is a symbol of hardened bones and death. Wood,
30   in contrast, is associated with life.

Using this model, Parker Pearson sees associations between the wooden structures of Durrington and the hard monument of Stonehenge. Durrington, in this new theory, is
35   the domain of the living, while Stonehenge is a place of the dead.

Parker Pearson goes on to explain that the houses near Durrington Walls were probably occupied at certain times of the year when
40   people gathered for the summer and winter solstices (the longest and shortest days of the year) to celebrate certain religious ceremonies. And in fact, large amounts of pottery[2] and animal bones have been found near Durrington,
45   suggesting that this site was used as a place for eating and drinking. In contrast, very little pottery has been found at Stonehenge. In addition, almost no human remains[3] have been found at Durrington, but a number of graves
50   have been uncovered at Stonehenge.

Paths from Stonehenge and Durrington Walls to the nearby River Avon also suggest that the two sites were linked. At certain times of the year, most of the dead would have been carried
55   down the road from Durrington and put in the river. Later, remains of the society's rulers would have been brought down the river, carried up the long avenue, and deposited at Stonehenge.

[1] Your **colleagues** are the people you work with.
[2] **Pottery** is pots, dishes, and other objects made from clay.
[3] Human **remains** are all or part of a dead body.

6A Silent Stones   **77**

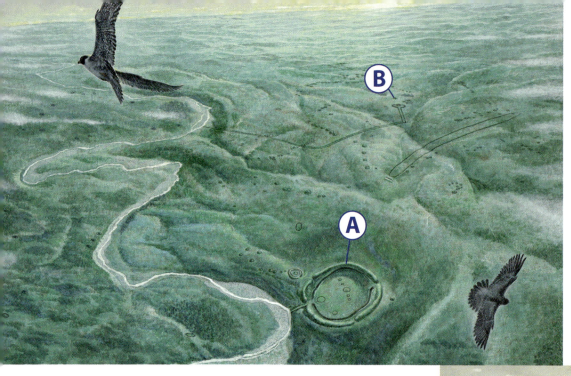

◄ Some archeologists believe that Durrington Walls Ⓐ and Stonehenge Ⓑ were linked.

▼ Evidence suggests that Durrington Walls—which had perhaps 300 houses—was a place for the living, whereas Stonehenge was a place for the dead.

A PLACE FOR HEALTH AND HEALING?

60

In Wales, about 400 kilometers (250 miles) west of Stonehenge, archeologists have another theory about why the monument

65 was built and what it was used for. In this region of Wales are the Preseli Mountains. Archeologists have traced the origin of Stonehenge's oldest stones (often referred to as "bluestones" because of their appearance when wet) to this site.

70

One question that has puzzled archeologists for years is why did ancient Britons transport these huge stones—which weighed up to 3,600 kilos (four tons)—and use them

75 to build Stonehenge? Some archeologists believe that early people saw the Preseli hills, with their giant blue stones, as a holy place. There is also a local belief, which is still common today, that the waters coming from

80 the Preseli Mountains can cure illness. It is possible that the motive for moving these stones the great distance to Salisbury Plain was to create a center for health and healing.

85 How exactly the stones were transported—without the use of wheels—remains a mystery. Perhaps they were pulled by teams of men and animals, or moved on giant rollers of wood. However it was done,

90 transporting such enormous stones was a remarkable achievement for the time.

Stonehenge was one of the last great monuments built in ancient England. It was abandoned about 3,500 years ago, and

95 because its creators wrote no texts to explain it, they have left us forever with one of history's great puzzles to solve.

Reading Comprehension

A. Multiple Choice. Choose the best answer for each question.

Gist 1. What is the reading mainly about?
   a. Stonehenge as a burial site
   b. the healing powers of blue stones
   c. how Stonehenge was built
   d. the mystery surrounding the purpose of Stonehenge

Inference 2. Which of these statements would Mike Parker Pearson most likely agree with?
   a. Stonehenge was designed by Malagasy people.
   b. Durrington Walls and Stonehenge were used by the same people.
   c. Stonehenge was inhabited all year round.
   d. Durrington Walls was used as a graveyard.

Detail 3. What is NOT mentioned in the passage as a feature of the summer solstice?
   a. People gathered to celebrate religious ceremonies on this day.
   b. It is the longest day of the year.
   c. People prayed to the dead on this day.
   d. Eating and drinking was an important part of the day.

Inference 4. The lack of human remains at Durrington suggests _____.
   a. Stonehenge was the local burial site
   b. no-one lived there
   c. people didn't bury the dead there
   d. the archeologists are not digging deep enough

Detail 5. How were the stones transported from Preseli?
   a. on wheels
   b. by boat along the River Avon
   c. on rollers of wood
   d. It is not known.

Critical Thinking

Which of the two theories in the passage do you think is most likely? Why?

B. True or False. Which of these statements about Stonehenge are True (**T**) and which are False (**F**)?

1. Historical records about Stonehenge exist.   **T F**

2. Archeologists don't agree on the reason Stonehenge was built.   **T F**

3. A lot of pottery has been found at the Stonehenge site.   **T F**

4. The blue stones of Stonehenge are local to the area.   **T F**

5. Few monuments of ancient England were built after Stonehenge.   **T F**

Vocabulary Practice

▲ The Royal Tombs of Petra were carved into sandstone cliffs by ancient Nabataeans.

A. Completion. Complete the information with the correct form of words from the box. One word is extra.

> deposit   domain   grave   transport   inspire

The lost city of Petra is a magnificent World Heritage Site in Jordan. Originally, it was the **1.** _____ of the Nabataeans, the people who ruled the area between 400 B.C. and A.D. 106, and was an important crossroads on the **2.** _____ routes between Arabia, Egypt, and other countries. However, over time, Petra become "lost" to the world, due in part to numerous earthquakes that continued to **3.** _____ more and more dirt and rocks on the city, until in A.D. 363 a large earthquake caused the city to be mostly abandoned.

The city remained hidden from the rest of the world until it was rediscovered in 1812 by Swiss explorer Johann Ludwig Burckhardt. Today, it is a major archeological site. Modern researchers and scientists are analyzing the many tombs and **4.** _____ that exist throughout the area; many more clues to the religion and lifestyle of the original residents are still buried beneath the present surface of the ground.

B. Completion. Complete the sentences below using the correct form of the words in red. One word is extra.

The ancient city of Ephesus on Turkey's western coast is cited as being a "lost" city, having remained hidden for centuries. Excavations on the site, which only began in the 1920s, have already uncovered fantastic archeological riches, inspiring archeologists to keep looking for more artifacts.

For some of their discoveries, such as the Temple of Artemis, the original purpose and use is definitively known. But for others, archeologists are less sure of the builders' motives. For example, the avenue leading up to the Temple of Artemis is very wide; perhaps rather than just being a beautiful road, it was built wide enough to allow thousands of people to walk to the temple together. Historians and scientists continue their research to not only discover more secrets, but also to trace the lifestyle of the people who lived in the city at that time.

▲ An ancient Roman amphitheater in Ephesus.

1. Using very modern technology, scientists are able to _____ the history of the Earth.
2. From studying Tutankhamen's body, archeologists have _____ proven that he was just a teenager when he died.
3. While most archeologists have excavated sites to learn more about ancient people, the _____ of some was greed—they wanted to sell the ancient artifacts they found.
4. Scientists often _____ the importance of their research as a reason for being allowed to explore historical areas.
5. The Greeks' love of drama _____ the creation of the amphitheater, a kind of large outdoor theater.

> ## Word Link
>
> The word roots **dom** and **domin** often mean *to rule or master*, e.g., *domain, dominate, predominant.*

▲ Artist John Gurche reconstructs the head of a prehistoric man.

Based on analysis of fossil remains in East Africa, Asia and other parts of the world, anthropologists have attempted to piece together a timeline of human history. Their discoveries suggest that modern humans (*Homo sapiens sapiens*) were preceded by other human-like species such as *Homo habilis* (Handy Man) and *Homo erectus* (Upright Man). According to scientists, the recent finding of an 18,000-year-old skeleton suggests that another type of human, *Homo floresiensis* (Man of Flores) once existed. Researchers have determined that the skeleton was an adult—one that was similar to us, but also, in some ways, very different.

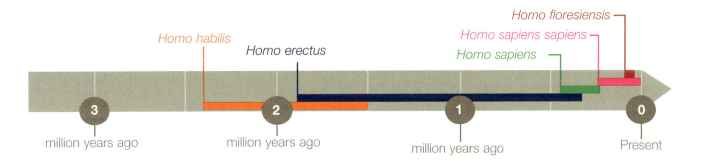

Homo floresiensis

Homo sapiens sapiens

Homo sapiens

Homo habilis

Homo erectus

| 3 | 2 | 1 | 0 |
| million years ago | million years ago | million years ago | Present |

⬜ Before You Read

A. Discussion. Read the information and timeline above, paying attention to the words in blue. Then answer the questions below.

   1. What kinds of *remains* does an *anthropologist* study?
   2. What are some human-like *species* that scientists have discovered?
   3. What have scientists *determined* about the recent skeleton *finding*?

B. Skim. Look at the title, photos, and captions on pages 82–83, and answer the questions below. Then read the passage to check your ideas.

   1. Who are "the people that time forgot"? Circle them on the timeline above.
   2. Where did these people live?
   3. What was unusual about them?

The People That Time Forgot

▲ A reconstruction brings to life an 18,000-year-old skull from Indonesia. Could this be the face of a lost human species?

1 While excavating a cave on the Indonesian island of Flores, archeologists made an astonishing and unexpected find:

5 a very unusual human skeleton. "At first we thought it was a child," says Mike Morwood, one of the archeologists involved in the project. The remains were

10 definitely human, but the body was only about one meter (three feet) long—about the size of a modern three-year-old.

The team transported the skeleton back to Jakarta (the capital of Indonesia) for closer

15 inspection. There, Peter Brown, an anthropologist from the University of New England in Australia, analyzed the skeleton. He determined that the human was a female, and contrary to what archeologists

20 first thought, that she was an adult, not a child. Additional studies also showed that she had lived about 18,000 years ago, the same time that modern humans (*Homo sapiens*) were walking the Earth. Her

25 forehead and jaw were similar to those of an earlier type of human, *Homo erectus*, but her size was unique—unlike any other human archeologists had ever seen. But it wasn't just her height and weight that made her unusual.

30 She also had a very small brain—about a third of a modern human's, even smaller than a chimpanzee's.

Perhaps, scientists suggested, this was a modern human who had suffered from a rare

35 disease which caused her body to develop abnormally. But when archeologists returned to the cave where they had made their original discovery, they unearthed[1] several other adult skeletons. All shared the same characteristics

40 as the first female. Scientists began to realize that an entire population of tiny beings had once lived on Flores. Had they discovered a new species of modern human?

Immediately, scientists had a number of

45 questions about these people—which they now called *Homo floresiensis*. One of the first was, where did this species come from? According to Peter Brown, these little people (who lived on Flores from about 95,000 until

50 at least 13,000 years ago) may have evolved from a population of *Homo erectus*, which crossed from Asia to Indonesia at least 1.5 million years ago.

But how could those early humans have reached the remote island of Flores? Located between mainland Asia and Australia, Flores was never connected by land bridges to either continent. Even when the sea level was low, traveling to Flores involved sea crossings of up to 24 kilometers (15 miles). People could only have reached Flores if they had the brain power to design and sail boats. Scientists had believed that *Homo erectus* had a fairly limited intelligence. But with these new findings, they are now asking whether *Homo erectus* was smarter than first thought.

Which raises another question: *Homo erectus* was probably several centimeters taller than *Homo floresiensis*. What caused the change in size? Scientists believe thousands of years of isolation on Flores could have caused the people to shrink—especially if they had no natural predators,[2] which would make physical size and strength less important. In addition, having a larger body requires more food, and on Flores, resources were scarce. Minimizing food consumption and adapting in size were necessary for *Homo floresiensis* to survive—a phenomenon often seen in nature.

Despite their smaller brains, the little people were apparently skilled toolmakers and clever hunters. Near the spot where archeologists found the bones of *Homo floresiensis*, they also unearthed pointed stone tools and the remains of a stegodont—an extinct relative of the elephant, which could weigh 400 kilos (800 pounds). The stone tools were probably used to hunt animals that were many times larger than the little people.

There is no sign of modern humans on Flores before 11,000 years ago. Nevertheless, it is possible that people like us (who were already living in Australia and parts of Asia 40,000 years ago) met their tiny human cousins. Some scientists have suggested that a conflict between the two human species may have caused *Homo floresiensis* to die out. More likely, though, is that the tiny humans became extinct as a result of a major volcanic eruption. Today, though, local stories are still told about little people who once walked the island. It's amazing to think that modern humans may still have a memory of sharing the planet with another species of human—one who was like us but also very different.

[1] If you **unearth** something, you take it out of the ground.
[2] A **predator** is an animal that kills and eats other animals.

◄ Archeologists Wahyu Saptomo and Mike Morwood look for signs of early humans in a cave known as Liang Bua, on the island of Flores.

◻ Reading Comprehension

A. Multiple Choice. Choose the best answer for each question.

Inference

1. Scientists probably assumed *Homo floresiensis* was not very intelligent because _____.
   a. they were very small
   b. they lived in isolation
   c. their brains were very small
   d. they lived so long ago

Detail

2. Why do scientists now think *Homo erectus* was smarter than originally thought?
   a. They made tools from bones.
   b. They may have designed and sailed boats.
   c. They built bridges.
   d. They were able to travel large distances.

Critical Thinking

What do you think is most interesting about scientists discovering this new species? Why?

Reference

3. In line 42, the word *they* refers to _____.
   a. modern humans
   b. tiny beings
   c. females from Flores
   d. scientists

Main Idea

4. What is paragraph 6 (starting line 71) mainly about?
   a. the reason for the small size of *Homo floresiensis*
   b. scarcity of food on Flores
   c. the lack of natural predators on Flores
   d. *Homo floresiensis*' isolation on Flores

Detail

5. According the passage, which of these is an adaptation to limited resources?
   a. a reduced body size
   b. the use of tools
   c. a high intelligence
   d. a smaller population

B. Completion. Complete the anthropologist's notebook on the discoveries made about *Homo floresiensis*.

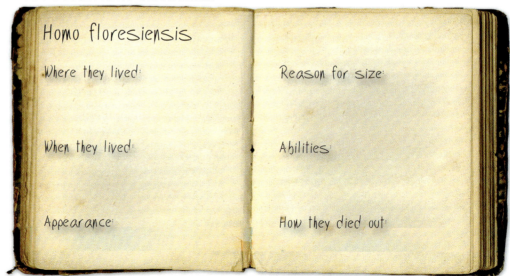

Homo floresiensis

Where they lived:

When they lived:

Appearance:

Reason for size:

Abilities:

How they died out:

Vocabulary Practice

A. Completion. Complete the information with the correct form of words from the box. One word is extra.

| abnormal | contrary | cousin | inspect | minimize | phenomenon | unique |

The pygmies of the Kalahari are not **1.** _____ in their small size—they seem to be **2.** _____ with other small peoples around the world. There are similarities between these groups of short people; not only are they **3.** _____ short in height (under 150 cm, or 4 foot 11 inches), but they share reasons for being so. The **4.** _____ of their extremely short height was initially thought to be due to lack of nutritious food. But according to Andrea Migliano, the author of a study on three separate tribes of pygmies, there is a problem with this theory. From **5.** _____ of their poor diet, you would expect the Masaai and Samburu peoples of Kenya and Tanzania to also be short. But, **6.** _____ to this expectation, they are extremely tall.

So why are pygmies short? Migliano found that pygmies have a very brief life, often dying at the age of 16, and her theory is that therefore they need to have babies at a younger age. She states: "The idea is that pygmies have to stop growing earlier, because when you start reproducing—at least for women—all the energy you would put in growth is put into reproduction."

B. Words in Context. Read the passage. Then circle the correct answer for each choice.

The population of nomadic[1] tribes like the Kalihari Bushmen of southern Africa is **1.** shrinking/increasing. There are several reasons for this. One reason is that they can easily die from diseases that come to them from the outside world, and for which they have no resistance. Another reason is that they find it difficult to **2.** enhance/adapt to a different way of life when they are forced to move to a more modern lifestyle.

Outsiders who observe these people are amazed by their **3.** astonishing/external ways of surviving by understanding perfectly the environment in which they live. Researchers believe that the importance of preserving cultures like this should not be **4.** minimized/inspected, and that losing them would be a loss to humankind.

[1] **Nomadic** people travel from place to place, rather than staying in one place all the time.

◀ A young San Bushman hunter with a spear looks out on the savanna of Namibia.

Word Link

We can add *-ize* to words to make them mean *become something*, e.g., *visualize, minimize, normalize, standardize, incentivize*.

Ancient Little People

▲ Paleoanthropologist Lee Berger

A. Preview. Paleoanthropologists such as Lee Berger (pictured) examine the remains of ancient humans. What questions do you think they are hoping to answer?

B. Summarize. Watch the video, *Ancient Little People*. Then complete the summary below using the correct form of words from the box. Two words are extra.

astonish	contrary	shrink
cousin	definitive	deposit
grave	avenue	inspect
inspire	phenomenon	unique

Lee Berger studies and searches for the fossil remains of ancient humans. On a visit to the island of Palau, he was **1.** _____ to find the **2.** _____ of some of the earliest humans ever discovered in the area. On a later expedition, he found even older bones under something called a "flowstone." A common **3.** _____ in caves, a flowstone is formed where water flowing over the ground **4.** _____ minerals which harden into stone.

After **5.** _____ the bones, Berger found that they had some **6.** _____ features unlike any others so far discovered: a small chin, large teeth and a small brain size. This has **7.** _____ Berger to reconsider his notion of what early humans looked like.

Berger's results may also have significance for the discovery of a tiny human that researchers call "the hobbit." **8.** _____ to some researchers who say the hobbit could be a separate species, Berger instead believes that it might be our ancestral **9.** _____—a variation of the same human species. Berger plans to return to Palau to continue his search for more **10.** _____ answers to our human past.

C. Think About It.

1. Do you think the "hobbit" is just a small human, or a completely different species?

2. Which ancient mystery would you most like to see solved?

To learn more about ancient mysteries, visit elt.heinle.com/explorer

A. Crossword. Use the definitions below to complete the missing words.

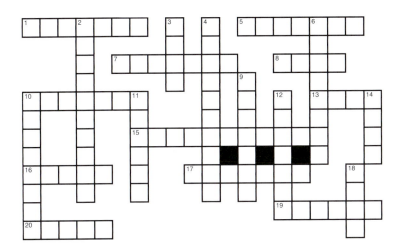

Across

1. a machine with an engine, like a car, bus, or truck that carries things and people from place to place.
5. an attempt to achieve or reach something; an activity
7. a feeling of worry and anxiety that makes it difficult to relax
8. to quote or mention something, especially as an example or proof of what you saying
10. damaged or harmed
13. not very strong or severe
15. extremely good, beautiful, or impressive
16. to make a hole in something
17. to _____ something somewhere is to put or leave it there
19. to become larger
20. if you are _____ to do something, you want to do it very much

Down

2. if something is _____, it is certain to happen and cannot be avoided or prevented
3. extremely large
4. not allowed or made illegal
6. an adjective describing the final result or aim of a long series of events
9. to regularly check the development or progress of something
10. a list of events and the times at which each should happen
11. a particular area of land, or field of thought, that someone has control and influence over
12. exact
14. the time of day when the sun begins to rise; the beginning of something
18. position or grade compared to others

B. Notes Completion. Scan the information on pages 88–89 to complete the notes.

Field Notes

Site: Serengeti National Park and Ngorongoro _____ Area

Location: _____, Africa

Information:

- Serengeti National Park covers more than _____ hectares
- Site of one of world's natural wonders—a vast migration of wildebeest and _____ that occurs from October to _____
- Serengeti's native people—the _____—are skilled at tracking animals
- Close to Serengeti is _____, a deep valley where scientists have made important discoveries
- In 1959, Louis and Mary _____ found a type of human later named homo habilis, which means _____

The Serengeti

Site: **Serengeti National Park and Ngorongoro Conservation Area**

Location: **Tanzania, Africa**

Category: **Natural**

Status: **World Heritage Sites since 1981/1979**

The Serengeti

In October, as the rain clouds shrink and disappear, and drought settles over the Tanzanian grasslands, the great animal migration begins. Up to 200,000 zebras and more than a million wildebeest abandon their usual feeding grounds and, in massive herds, travel over 1,200 miles in pursuit of water and greener lands. In April, as if according to a precise schedule, the animals return, across what the native Maasai people call the "place where the land runs on forever"—the vast **plains** of the Serengeti.

The 1.5 million-hectare Serengeti National Park is part of the Serengeti-Ngorongoro Biosphere Reserve, which preserves one of Africa's most complex and least spoiled ecosystems. The region sustains the world's greatest concentration of large mammal species, an astonishing range of biodiversity that includes big cats, elephants, and rhinoceroses, besides the migrating **herds**.

The Serengeti's migration of wildebeests and zebras is one of the most magnificent in the world, and provides an inspiring sight for those fortunate to witness it. The largest and longest overland migration on Earth, this unique natural phenomenon has been ranked one of the Ten Natural Wonders of the World.

▲ A giraffe's outline is visible against the rising sun on the Serengeti Plains.

Glossary

cradle: a baby's small bed with high sides
gorge: a deep, narrow valley with steep sides
herd: a large group of animals that live together
nomads: people who move from place to place, rather than living in one place all the time
plain: large flat area of land with very few trees

People of the Plains

The Maasai—native people of the Serengeti who spend part of the year as **nomads**—are a people ideally adapted to their landscape. They can walk for days across the plains, protecting their cattle from predators, and many are skilled at tracking wild animals. Recently, however, increasing poverty and demand for scarce resources has created tension between the area's human population and the wild creatures with which they share their lands. Populations of Maasai have been displaced several times in the past and, as they try to adjust to the 21st century, the Maasai's future remains uncertain. "I know where I am from," says one, Jombi Ole Kivuyo. "But I don't know where I am going. I am like a blind man feeling his way."

The Dawn of Humans

In Ngorongoro, southeast of the Serengeti, is a region commonly known as the "**Cradle** of Mankind"—the Olduvai Gorge, renowned for the astonishing archeological finds made there. Around 500,000 years ago, volcanic activity in this area displaced a nearby stream which began to cut into the ground, ultimately revealing in the walls of the **gorge** precious deposits of long-buried history. In 1959, Louis (below) and Mary Leakey, a husband and wife team of British scientists, discovered a 1.8 million-year-old grave, and traced the remains of various extinct creatures, including a very unusual skull. On closer inspection, it was shown to belong to an ancestral cousin that preceded modern-day mankind—a prehistoric species that became known as "handy man," or *homo habilis*, because of the stone tools found with it.

Earth in Motion

A Global View

About 240 million years ago, all the land on the Earth's surface was joined together in one vast supercontinent that extended from pole to pole. But by 18,000 years ago, the Earth had been transformed; the continents as we know them today had been created and had moved into their present positions. But the Earth's surface has not stopped moving, and the process continues today.

Why does this movement occur? Deep within the Earth, **pressure** and **heat** cause rocks of the mantle to become partly molten, but near the surface a thin **layer** of solid rock forms the crust. As currents of heat **rise** and fall within the mantle, the crust breaks up into large pieces, called plates, which move about very slowly on Earth's surface.

The movement of the plates creates powerful forces that continually create and destroy land features and reshape the Earth's surface. Most of the action takes place at the plate edges, or boundaries, where plates move against or over each other, or **dive** back below the surface. As the plates move, mountains are uplifted, the sea floor **cracks** and **spreads**, volcanoes erupt, and new land is **formed**.

Distance from the Earth's surface to its center: 6,370 km (3,963 miles)

Volcanoes form when molten rock—called magma—rises to the Earth's surface. Some volcanoes occur as one plate pushes beneath another plate. Other volcanoes result when a plate passes over a "hot spot," an area of magma rising from the mantle.

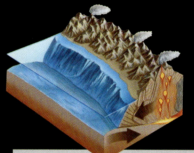

Subduction occurs when an oceanic plate dives under a continental plate and often results in volcanoes and mountains, as well as disastrous earthquakes. When a subduction earthquake occurred near Sumatra in December 2004, the resulting energy was converted into powerful tsunami waves that killed many thousands of people.

Faulting happens when two plates rub against each other, creating cracks along the plate edges. The San Andreas Fault in California, where the Pacific and North American plates meet, ranks as one of the most destructive earthquake zones in the world.

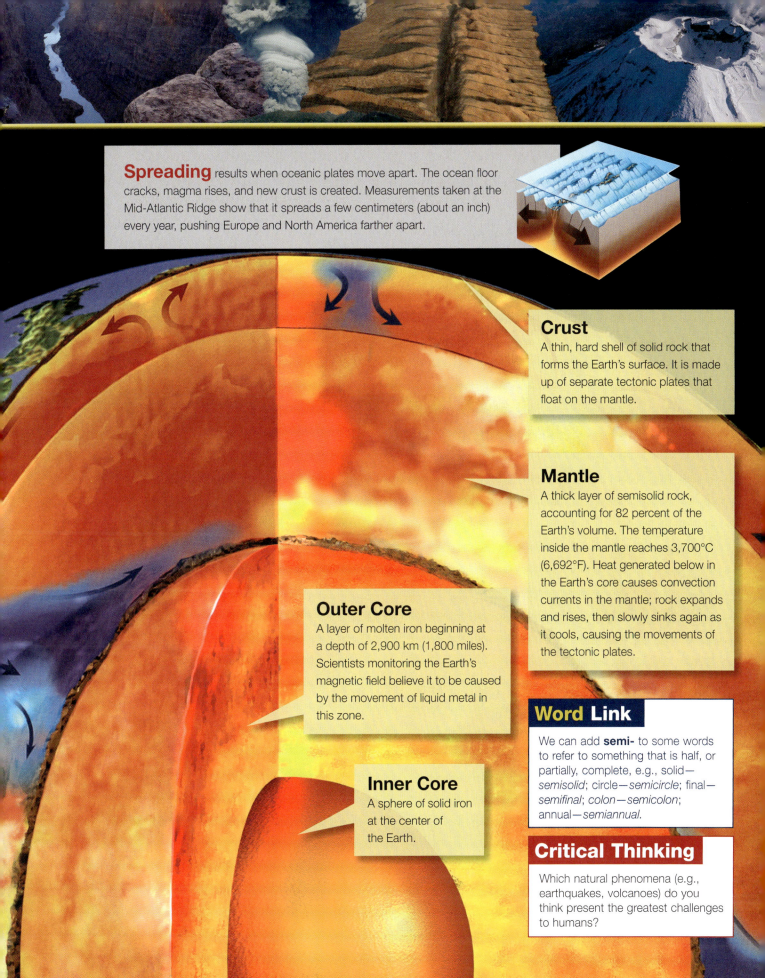

Spreading results when oceanic plates move apart. The ocean floor cracks, magma rises, and new crust is created. Measurements taken at the Mid-Atlantic Ridge show that it spreads a few centimeters (about an inch) every year, pushing Europe and North America farther apart.

Crust
A thin, hard shell of solid rock that forms the Earth's surface. It is made up of separate tectonic plates that float on the mantle.

Mantle
A thick layer of semisolid rock, accounting for 82 percent of the Earth's volume. The temperature inside the mantle reaches 3,700°C (6,692°F). Heat generated below in the Earth's core causes convection currents in the mantle; rock expands and rises, then slowly sinks again as it cools, causing the movements of the tectonic plates.

Outer Core
A layer of molten iron beginning at a depth of 2,900 km (1,800 miles). Scientists monitoring the Earth's magnetic field believe it to be caused by the movement of liquid metal in this zone.

Inner Core
A sphere of solid iron at the center of the Earth.

Word Link
We can add **semi-** to some words to refer to something that is half, or partially, complete, e.g., solid— *semisolid*; circle— *semicircle*; final— *semifinal*; colon— *semicolon*; annual— *semiannual*.

Critical Thinking
Which natural phenomena (e.g., earthquakes, volcanoes) do you think present the greatest challenges to humans?

Vocabulary Building 2

A. Definitions. Use the correct form of words in **bold** from pages 90–91 to complete the sentences.

Inside the Earth's mantle, rock is **1.** _____ to an extremely high temperature. This, combined with very intense **2.** _____, causes the rock to become semimolten. As this magma **3.** _____ toward the surface, **4.** _____ appear in the crust (a thin **5.** _____ of solid rock above the mantle), creating the oceanic and continental plates.

The Earth's movement is both constructive and destructive. In places where two ocean plates **6.** _____ apart, new land is **7.** _____. In places where one plate **8.** _____ under another—a process known as subduction—volcanoes and earthquakes often result.

▲ Movements deep inside the Earth caused this volcano in Quito, Ecuador, to explode on October 7, 1999.

B. Word Partnership. Many common expressions include the verbs *break* or *take*, e.g., *take place* and *break apart*. Use the correct verb to complete each expression below. Then match phrases from the list to the definitions (**a–e**).

1. _____ a bath (or shower)
2. _____ a break
3. _____ a chance
4. _____ a look
5. _____ a promise
6. _____ a (world) record
7. _____ a photograph
8. _____ a seat
9. _____ a taxi
10. _____ advantage (of something)
11. _____ an exam
12. _____ care of (something or someone)

13. _____ charge (of something)
14. _____ into pieces
15. _____ measurements
16. _____ notes
17. _____ (one's) time
18. _____ (someone's) heart
19. _____ (someone's) place
20. _____ (someone's) temperature
21. _____ the ice (e.g., at a party)
22. _____ the law
23. _____ the news (to someone)
24. _____ the rules
25. _____ up (with someone)

a. _____ temporarily stop an activity; have a rest
b. _____ relax a tense or formal situation
c. _____ look after (something or someone)
d. _____ separate (from someone)
e. _____ gain control or command

UNIT 7

Global Addictions

Discuss these questions with a partner.

1. What are some things that people can become addicted to?

2. Is it OK to be addicted to certain things? If so, what?

3. Some people say that humans are addicted to fossil fuels. Do you agree?

Are there any other things that humans in general are addicted to?

▲ South Belridge oilfield, in California, U.S.A., has produced over a billion barrels of oil since 1911.

7A The World's Favorite Drug

☐ Before You Read

A. Matching. Look at the information below. How many milligrams (mg) of caffeine do you think is in each item? Match the items and the numbers. Then check your answers below.

25 mg	50 mg	57 mg	80 mg	130 mg	200 mg	294 mg

1. Espresso coffee, 28 g (1 oz)   _40 mg_
2. Milk chocolate bar, 170 g (6 oz)   _____
3. Brewed tea, 227 g (8 oz) cup   _____
4. Can of energy drink, 235 g (8.3 oz)   _____
5. Brewed coffee, 340 g (12oz) cup   _____
6. Bottle of cola drink, 567 g (20 oz)   _____
7. Large soda drink, 1814 g (64 oz)   _____
8. Pain relief medicine (2 tablets)   _____

B. Discussion. Why do you think caffeine is common in everyday foods and drinks? Do you think caffeine is good for you? Read the passage to check your ideas.

► Caffeine is a naturally-occurring substance that can affect a person's nervous system. Most people associate caffeine with coffee, but it can also be found in many other familiar items.

2. 25 mg; 3. 50 mg; 4. 80 mg; 5. 200 mg; 6. 57 mg; 7. 294 mg; 8. 130 mg

Caffeine

◄ Steamed milk decorates the top of an espresso in what coffee fans call "latte art." "I drank this cappuccino," says photographer Bob Sacha, "and it tasted even better than it looked."

It's 1:45 a.m., and 21-year-old Thomas Murphy is burning the midnight oil,[1] studying for an important engineering exam he has at 2:00 in the afternoon later today. To stay awake and focused, he's had two cups of coffee in the last three hours and is now downing a popular energy drink—one that has two to three times the amount of caffeine as a similar sized can of soda. Many students like Murphy, as well as marathon runners, airline pilots, and long-distance travelers, owe their energy—and sometimes their efficiency—to one of mankind's oldest stimulants: caffeine. Many say they couldn't live without it.

The power to counter physical fatigue and increase alertness is part of the reason caffeine ranks as the world's most popular mood-altering drug. It is found not only in sodas, energy drinks, coffee, and tea, but also in diet pills, pain relievers (like aspirin), and chocolate bars. Many societies around the world have also created entire rituals around the use of caffeine: afternoon tea in the U.K., the café culture of France, tea ceremony in Japan, and the morning cup of coffee or tea that in many cultures marks the start of the day.

Caffeine is in many of the foods or drinks we consume, but is it really good for us? Charles Czeisler, a scientist and sleep expert at Harvard Medical School, believes that caffeine causes us to lose sleep, which he says is unhealthy. "Without adequate sleep—the typical eight hours—the human body will not function at its best, physically, mentally, or emotionally." Too often, Czeisler says, we consume caffeine to stay awake, which later makes it impossible for us to get the rest we need.

Health risks have also been tied to caffeine consumption. Over the years, studies have attributed higher rates of certain types of cancer and bone disease to caffeine consumption. To date, however, there is no definitive proof that caffeine actually causes these diseases.

[1] If someone is **burning the midnight oil**, they are staying up very late in order to study or do some other work.

People from Finland drink more coffee per person than anyone else. The average Finn consumes an estimated 145 grams of caffeine a year.

▲ Allowed just three hours of sleep in 52 hours of exercise, a Canadian soldier chews caffeine gum to help stay awake. Chewed caffeine is absorbed directly into the mouth, and works three times faster than caffeine in coffee or pills.

A number of scientists, including Roland Griffiths, a professor at the Johns Hopkins School of Medicine in the U.S., believe that regular caffeine use causes physical dependence.
50　Heavy caffeine users, Griffiths says, exhibit similar behaviors: their moods fluctuate from high to low; they get mild to severe headaches; or they feel tired or sad when they can't have a coffee, soft drink, energy drink, or cup of tea.
55　To minimize or stop these feelings, users must consume caffeine—a behavior Griffiths says that is characteristic of drug addiction.[2]

Despite these concerns, the general opinion in the scientific community is that caffeine is
60　not dangerous when consumed moderately— for example, by having one or two small cups of coffee (about 300 milligrams of caffeine) per day. Furthermore, a lot of current research contradicts long-held negative beliefs
65　about caffeine, and suggests that it may, in fact, have health benefits. For instance, studies have shown that caffeine can help ease pain by reducing muscle inflammation.[3] Because it is a

stimulant, caffeine can also help improve one's
70　mood. Research has also shown that some caffeinated drinks—specifically certain teas— have disease-fighting chemicals that can help the body fight a number of illnesses, including certain types of cancer.

75　In addition, as a type of mental stimulant, caffeine increases alertness, memory, and reaction speed. Because it fights fatigue, it facilitates performance on tasks like driving, flying, and solving simple math problems. And
80　while it is true that caffeine can increase blood pressure, the effect is usually temporary and therefore not likely to cause heart trouble— especially if caffeine is consumed in moderation.

85　And despite its nearly universal use, caffeine has rarely been abused. "With caffeine, overuse tends to stop itself," says Jack Bergman, a specialist at Harvard Medical School. If you consume too much, "you get . . .
90　uncomfortable, and you don't want to continue."

Caffeine's behavioral effects are real, but most often, mild. Getting that burst of energy, of course, is why many of the most popular
95　drinks on Earth contain caffeine. Whether it's a student drinking coffee before class or a businessman enjoying tea with lunch, mankind's favorite stimulant is at work every day, all over the world.

[2] An **addiction** to something is a very strong desire or need for it.
[3] An **inflammation** is a painful redness of part of your body as a result of infection, illness, or injury.

▼ Tea, green tea, and oolong tea are all made from the same plant; the differences in taste and color come from the way in which they are processed.

☐ Reading Comprehension

A. **Multiple Choice.** Choose the best answer for each question.

Gist
1. What is this reading mainly about?
   a. the popularity of coffee
   b. the effects of caffeine on the body
   c. Thomas Murphy's need for caffeine
   d. the health risks associated with caffeine intake

Reference
2. In line 31, *which* refers to _____.
   a. adequate sleep   c. food containing caffeine
   b. losing sleep   d. consuming caffeine

Vocabulary
3. In line 32, the word *adequate* could be replaced with _____.
   a. deep   c. relaxed
   b. long   d. enough

Detail
4. Which of the following is NOT listed as a possible side effect of drinking caffeine?
   a. addiction   c. painful headaches
   b. mood swings   d. heart disease

Paraphrase
5. Which of the following is closest in meaning to: "And despite its nearly universal use, caffeine has rarely been abused." (line 85)?
   a. Even though caffeine is consumed almost the world over, there aren't many instances of misuse.
   b. Even though caffeine is often misused, it is consumed almost the world over.
   c. Despite caffeine's popularity, addiction isn't a problem.
   d. Caffeine is used all over the world, so it is commonly misused.

B. **Completion.** Complete the information below with the pros and cons of caffeine consumption.

Caffeine Consumption

Pros	Cons
Increased alertness	1. _____
2. _____	Possible risk of certain cancers and bone disease
Improves mood	Can be addictive
3. _____	Causes mood swings
Increases memory	4. _____
5. _____	Going without it causes tiredness and sadness
Improves performance	Increases blood pressure temporarily
No risk of overuse	

Critical Thinking

What is your opinion of using caffeine to improve your performance?

Vocabulary Practice

A. Completion. Complete the information below with the correct form of words from the box. Two words are extra.

depend	abuse	severe	contradictory	fluctuate
facilitate	furthermore	temporary	awake	exhibit

Chocolate News

Did you know that growing trees to produce chocolate is saving a rain forest?

At first, the idea sounds **1.** _____; you would expect that to grow cacao trees you would first have to clear the forest. But, in the Dominican Republic, local people who **2.** _____ on the land for their income have **3.** _____ to the brilliant idea that they can plant and grow cacao on land that was previously cleared for cattle. Their secret is to grow organic cacao, which can be sold for a much higher price than that grown with the use of chemicals. So, growing organic cacao provides a permanent income for farmers, and, **4.** _____, does it without destroying any more forest.

Did you know that you are 5. _____ **your dog if you feed it chocolate?**

Many dogs love chocolate snacks, but too much chocolate can be harmful for dogs. Chocolate contains "theobromine," a chemical found in cocoa beans that can cause a variety of medical problems for dogs. Some of these are quite **6.** _____, and could possibly lead to death. So if your dog **7.** _____ symptoms such as a(n) **8.** _____ heartbeat, or vomiting, it's possible that a chocolate "treat" was the cause.

▲ A cacao tree in the Dominican Republic

B. Words in Context. Complete each sentence with the best answer.

1. If you facilitate something, you _____.
   a. make it easier   b. make it more difficult
2. Something that is temporary continues _____.
   a. forever   b. for a limited time
3. You are most likely to find exhibits _____.
   a. in a bank   b. in a museum
4. If you contradict someone, you _____ with him or her.
   a. agree   b. disagree
5. Fluctuating prices _____.
   a. are going up   b. go up and down

Addicted to Fossil Fuel?

▲ Five members of the Foster family from Ohio, U.S.A., are photographed on their lawn, surrounded by household items that are ultimately derived from oil. Many everyday items—from beach balls to bicycle helmets—depend on oil during their production.

☐ Before You Read

A. Discussion. Look at the photo and caption, and answer the questions below.

1. What items can you recognize in the photo? Which do you own?
2. In what other ways do humans depend on fossil fuels[1]?

B. Scan. The passage on pages 100–101 discusses energy sources that are alternatives to fossil fuels. Quickly scan the reading to answer the questions below. Then read again to check your ideas.

1. What are the three alternative sources of energy discussed in the passage?
2. Worldwide, which of these three currently produces the most energy?

[1] **Fossil fuel** is fuel such as coal or oil that is formed from the decayed remains of plants and animals.

Powering the Future

1 Despite modern society's heavy dependence on fossil fuels for energy, most people are aware that the supply of these fuels is finite. As oil, in particular, becomes more costly
5 and difficult to find, researchers are looking at alternative energy sources, including solar, wind, and even nuclear power. But which substitute—if any—is the right one?

Solar

10 Solar panels catch energy directly from the sun and convert it into electricity. One of the world's largest solar power stations is located near Leipzig, Germany, where more than 33,000 solar panels generate enough energy
15 to power about 1,800 homes. But unlike the burning of fossil fuels, the process used to create all that solar energy produces no emissions.

Today, however, solar provides less than
20 one percent of the world's energy, primarily because the cost of the panels is still very high. And price is only one issue. Clouds and

▲ A helicopter lowers a worker to do repairs on a wind farm in Denmark. In Denmark, wind generates about 20 percent of all electricity. Globally, wind supplies less than one percent of electric power, but it's the fastest growing energy source.

darkness also cause solar panels to produce less energy, which requires one to have
25 additional power sources (such as batteries) available.

Some scientists think the solution to this problem can be found in space—which they say is the ideal place to gather energy from
30 the sun. With no clouds and no nighttime, a space-based solar power station could operate constantly. These stations would send the power back to Earth, which could then be turned into electricity for consumption.

35 Advocates of solar space stations say this technology would require a lot of money initially, but eventually it could provide continuous, clean energy that would be cheaper than other fuels. Also, unlike other
40 energy sources, solar power from space will last as long as the sun shines, and will be able to guarantee everyone on Earth all the energy they need.

A solar park near Leipzig, Germany, with ▶ more than 33,000 panels, is one of the world's largest.

Wind

45 Wind—the fastest-growing alternative energy source—is another way of collecting energy from the sun. Unlike solar power, however, it works well on cloudy days.

50 All over Europe, incentives designed to decrease the dependence on oil and coal have led to a steep increase in wind-powered energy. Today, Europe leads the world in wind power, with almost 35,000 megawatts,[1] the equivalent of 35 large coal-powered plants. North
55 America remains a distant second, with just over 7,000 megawatts.

Despite its successes, some oppose wind-power development, saying the turbines[2] are both noisy and ugly. Just outside England's Lake
60 District, a protected national park, 27 wind towers are planned, each about 40 meters (130 feet) tall. Many locals are protesting. "This is a high-quality landscape," says one local home owner. "They shouldn't be
65 putting those things in here."

There are other challenges too. If the wind doesn't blow, the turbines don't have the capacity to produce sufficient energy. As a result, other power sources are needed. In
70 contrast, a strong wind can create too much power. In cases like this, the energy company must sell the extra power at a much-reduced rate, which is not good for business.

What's needed for both wind and solar is a
75 way to store a large energy surplus[3] so that it can later be turned into electricity. However, most systems are still decades away from making this a reality. On the plus side, both wind and solar enable people to generate their
80 own energy where they live: people can have their own windmills or solar panels, with batteries for calm days.

Nuclear

In the 1970s, nuclear was the energy
85 alternative. Nuclear power produces vast amounts of electricity more cheaply than gas or coal, with no carbon emissions. For a number of years in the 1980s and '90s, however, use of nuclear power declined due
90 to accidents, concerns about nuclear waste storage and disposal, and high construction costs.

Today, though, times are changing. Worldwide about 440 plants now generate 16 percent of
95 the planet's electric power, and some countries have invested heavily in nuclear energy. France, for instance, gets 78 percent of its electricity from nuclear power. China has started to build one or two new plants a year, and Japan
100 and India have also begun to utilize nuclear energy on a large scale. Though there are still concerns about the safety of nuclear power, many now believe it may be one of the future's greenest energy alternatives.

105 In the end, are any of these sources alone the answer to our current energy problems? The short answer is no, but used in some combination—along with other power sources—we may find ways to reduce and
110 eventually eliminate our dependence on fossil fuels.

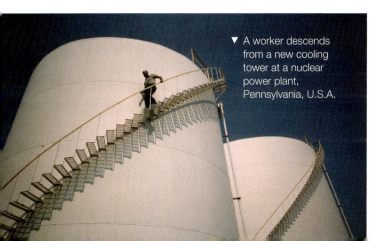

▼ A worker descends from a new cooling tower at a nuclear power plant, Pennsylvania, U.S.A.

[1] A **megawatt** is a unit of power.
[2] A **turbine** is a machine that uses water, steam, or wind to turn a wheel to produce electricity.
[3] If you have a **surplus** of something, you have more of it than you need; you have extra.

Reading Comprehension

A. Multiple Choice. Choose the best answer for each question.

Gist **1.** What is this reading mainly about?
- a. possible replacements for fossil fuels for energy
- b. the causes of the energy crisis
- c. the benefits of solar power
- d. over dependence on fossil fuels

Critical Thinking

Which of the three energy sources in the article do you think is most likely to replace fossil fuels? Why?

Vocabulary **2.** In line 18, the word *emissions* is closest in meaning to _____.
- a. panels
- b. electricity
- c. pollution
- d. accidents

Detail **3.** Which of these statements about solar energy is stated in the text?
- a. Solar is the biggest contributor to the world's energy.
- b. Solar energy is cheap to produce.
- c. Solar space stations could be the solution to the energy crisis.
- d. Solar panels are coming down in price.

Detail **4.** What is NOT mentioned as a disadvantage of wind power?
- a. The turbines are uneconomical.
- b. The turbines don't work well on cloudy days.
- c. The turbines are noisy.
- d. Local residents think the turbines are ugly.

Detail **5.** Which of these statements is NOT true about nuclear energy?
- a. It is cheaper to produce than coal or gas.
- b. Nuclear energy produces no carbon waste.
- c. Safety concerns made nuclear energy unpopular for several decades.
- d. Nuclear energy is becoming less popular than other energy sources.

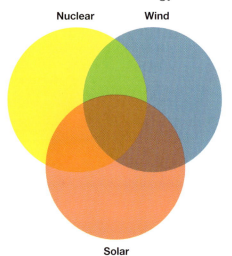

B. Classification. Match each description (**a–g**) with the energy source it describes.

- **a.** fastest growing energy source today
- **b.** expensive to produce
- **c.** produces no carbon emissions
- **d.** there are safety concerns
- **e.** no constant power supply
- **f.** requires a way to store surplus energy to be effective
- **g.** unpopular with nearby residential communities

☐ Vocabulary Practice

A. Completion. Complete the information using the words from the box. Three words are extra.

utilize	dispose	equivalent	finite
guarantee	steep	substitute	utilize

The Singapore government, recognizing that fossil fuels are a(n) **1.** _____ resource, is keen to **2.** _____ traditional energy production with "renewable energies." It has decided to turn Pulau Ubin, a small, undeveloped, but inhabited island off the coast of Singapore, into a "green island." It will be powered entirely by clean and renewable energy, providing the **3.** _____ amount of electricity as it does now, but without using fossil fuels. Residents on the island who presently **4.** _____ old, inefficient diesel-run generators to supply their power will be pleased to **5.** _____ of them when the new system starts running in 2010.

▲ Diesel generators, in addition to using fossil fuels, produce pollution and can be very noisy.

B. Words in Context. Choose the best answer for each question.

1. Advocates of an idea _____.
   a. are for it   b. are against it
2. If a country's energy capacity increases, it means _____.
   a. it needs more energy   b. it can produce more energy
3. A country that utilizes nuclear power probably _____ nuclear power plants.
   a. has   b. doesn't have any
4. Over the last 100 years _____ has been declining.
   a. environmental quality   b. the world's population
5. A steep price rise takes place over a _____ period of time.
   a. short   b. long
6. If you guarantee that something will happen, you _____ that it will occur.
   a. promise   b. doubt

Word Partnership

Use **steep** with:
steep **hill**, steep **slope**, steep **driveway**,
steep **drop**, steep **rise**, steep **fall**

Solar Power

A. Preview. You will hear these words in the video. Match each word with its definition.

1. utility company   ___ **a.** a building, piece of equipment, or service that is provided for a particular purpose

2. facility   ___ **b.** a long hollow object that is usually round, like a pipe

3. meter   ___ **c.** to measure how much of something (e.g. water or gas) people use, in order to determine how much they should pay

4. tube   ___ **d.** a business that provides electricity, water, or gas

▲ Solar panels generate energy in a field on Samso Island, Denmark.

Sacramento, California

B. Summarize. Watch the video, *Solar Power*. Then complete the summary below using the correct form of words from the box. Two words are extra.

advocate	capacity	dependable	equivalent
finite	fluctuate	abuse	contradict
furthermore	guarantee	substitute	utilize

Earth's most powerful source of energy is actually out in space. It's our sun. Many people already **1.** _____ some solar energy, but for solar power to be a real **2.** _____ for other more **3.** _____ and disappearing resources, it has to be both affordable and **4.** _____.

Sacramento, the state capital of California, is a major **5.** _____ for solar energy. Its people can save or even make money using solar power through "net metering." This system allows people who produce extra power to sell it back to the utility company, for the **6.** _____ price they would normally pay for it.

In California's Mojave Desert there is a huge solar generating plant. At full **7.** _____, Kramer Junction solar power facility creates a total of 150 megawatts—enough power for the residential needs of about half a million people. Each section of the facility also has a natural gas generator, so that it can **8.** _____ a supply of power even during periods of unpredictable and **9.** _____ weather. **10.** _____, it can do all this while producing very little carbon dioxide or pollution.

C. Think About It.

1. Do you think California's solar energy policies could work in your country?

2. What do you think can be done to help solve the world's energy problems?

To learn more about global addictions, visit elt.heinle.com/explorer

Legendary Voyages

Discuss these questions with a partner.

1. What great historical voyages do you know about?

2. If you could recreate a famous voyage, which one would you choose? Why?

3. Are there any great voyages that haven't been made yet?

▲ The rusted front of the *Titanic*, which sank on April 14, 1912, on its first voyage across the north Atlantic Ocean.

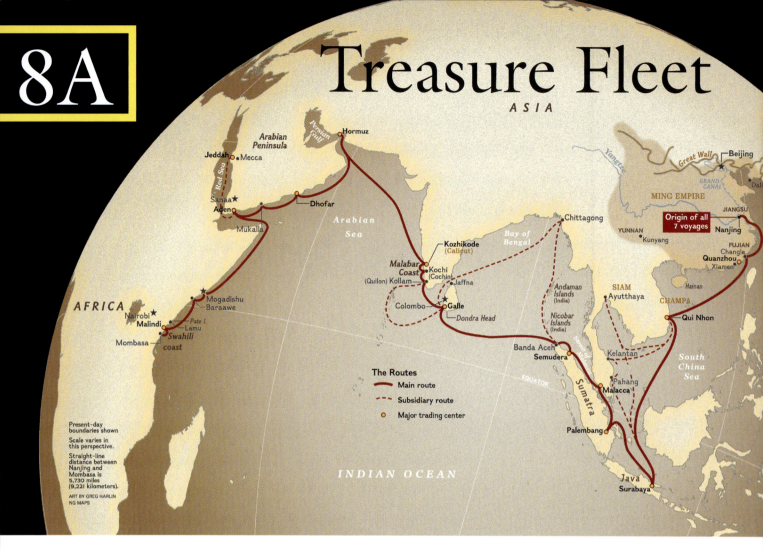

8A

Treasure Fleet
ASIA

▲ Nearly a century before Christopher Columbus arrived in the Americas, a Chinese admiral named Zheng He led one of the most powerful trading fleets the world has ever known. From 1405 to 1433, he and his armada sailed seven voyages that spanned over 16,000 kilometers (10,000 miles), 30 countries, and three decades. By establishing trading ports throughout Asia and as far as Africa, Zheng He's voyages established China as the world's major sea power.

☐ Before You Read

A. Matching. Read the information and match the words in blue with their definitions.

1. a very large group of ships _____

2. towns where ships load or unload goods or people _____

3. groups of ships that are organized to buy and sell goods _____

4. a very senior officer who is in charge of a large number of ships _____

B. Skim for the Main Idea. Quickly read the passage on pages 107–108. Which questions are addressed in the passage?

❏ Who exactly was Zheng He?   ❏ Did Zheng He reach America?

❏ How and why did the voyages end?   ❏ What is Zheng He's significance today?

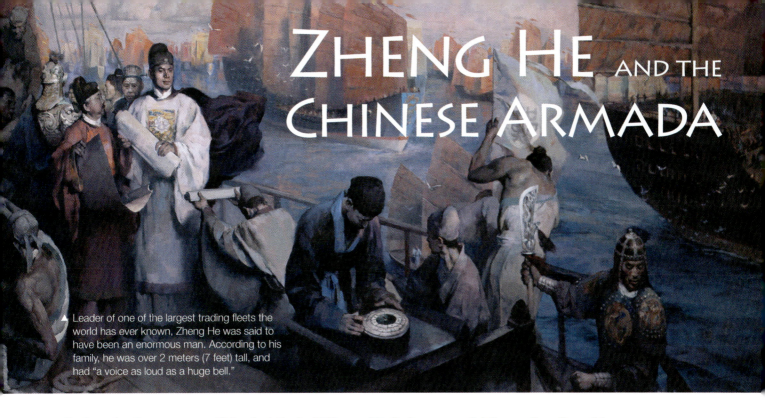

ZHENG HE AND THE CHINESE ARMADA

▲ Leader of one of the largest trading fleets the world has ever known, Zheng He was said to have been an enormous man. According to his family, he was over 2 meters (7 feet) tall, and had "a voice as loud as a huge bell."

1 Six hundred years ago, China's Admiral Zheng He led a powerful fleet of trading ships on seven voyages that changed China and many parts of the world forever. On each of his journeys, Zheng He commanded more than 300 ships of 30,000 sailors, accompanied as well by hundreds of government officials, doctors, cooks, merchants, and interpreters. The fleet accumulated knowledge and wealth and spread Chinese influence all across Asia to Africa. And yet, today, Zheng He—one of the world's greatest explorers—is scarcely known in many places around the world.

Born into a Muslim family in 1371 and given the name Ma He at birth ("Ma" is the Chinese translation of the name "Muhammad"), Zheng He was captured as a young boy by the Chinese army. By the time he was 31, in 1402, Ma He had become one of the military's most powerful soldiers and an advisor to China's leader, who gave him a new name—Zheng He— and an important new job: Admiral of China's Imperial Navy.

In the summer of 1405, Zheng He departed on the first of his seven voyages from the city of Nanjing, then the capital of China. His goal was to mix exploration with business and diplomacy,[1] and to that end, he carried Chinese silk, coins, and other goods to be exchanged for foreign commodities such as spices, animals, cloth, and other products.

By the end of 1405, Zheng He's fleet had arrived in present-day Vietnam. Later, he traveled to the islands of Java and Sumatra (in Indonesia), and then west toward India via Sri Lanka. On subsequent voyages, Zheng He's ships traveled further west to places such as Iran, Oman, and Yemen and ultimately to the eastern coast of Africa. By the end of his last voyage 28 years later, Zheng He had established major trading centers at ports all along the way, and China was importing and exporting goods in ports from East Asia to Africa.

Throughout their travels, Zheng He and his men were introduced to different foods, languages, customs, architecture, and scientific and religious beliefs. "How can there be such diversity in the world?" said one of the admiral's men at one point. Though he was constantly faced with the unfamiliar, Zheng He was fascinated by the cultures he visited, and he spoke often of the need to "treat distant people with kindness."

▲ A mural of Zheng He painted on a wall in his hometown of Kunyang, China.

focus on China only. This reversal "changed history, and stopped short what might have been a very different future for Asia and the world," says professor Liu Ying-sheng of Nanjing University. As China ended foreign exploration, European powers such as Spain and England rose to take its place, and by 1492 Columbus had arrived in the Americas.

Before his fleet was grounded forever, though, Zheng He's armada made one final voyage in 1431—back to Africa's east coast. Along the way, the admiral, a lifelong Muslim,[2] also made a personal visit to Mecca, Islam's most holy site. On the return journey to China in 1433, Zheng He died, and it is believed that he was buried at sea just off India's southwestern coast.

Over 600 years after his first voyage, Zheng He's legacy[3] lives on. Mosques[4] in Indonesia are named after him. In some places in Southeast Asia, he is considered a god, and there are festivals that celebrate his life. Perhaps most important, says scholar Roderich Ptak, is that today, "China is again engaging the world [and] Zheng is a symbol of that opening."

[1] **Diplomacy** is the activity of creating good relations between the people and governments of different nations.
[2] A **Muslim** is someone who believes in Islam and lives according to its rules.
[3] A person's **legacy** is something that continues to live on or that people remember after the person dies.
[4] A **mosque** is a building where Muslims go to worship.

In addition to promoting trade and diplomacy, Zheng He's seven voyages also resulted in the spread of Chinese people and culture throughout Asia and beyond. Malaysia and Indonesia, for example, had important ports that Zheng He's fleet returned to often. Eventually, thousands of Chinese migrated to and settled in these places, and maintain a strong presence there today. In a later voyage to eastern Africa, legend says that some of Zheng He's ships were caught in a storm and sank. The men swam to an island off the coast of Kenya, where they ultimately married local women and had children. Their descendants in Africa are said to have Asian features and family names, such as Famao and Wei.

The end of Zheng He's sixth voyage in 1422 coincided with a new emperor coming to power. The country's new leader wanted to terminate all foreign exploration and to

▼ Zheng He's treasure ships, the largest wooden ships ever built, make those of Portuguese explorer Vasco da Gama seem tiny in comparison.

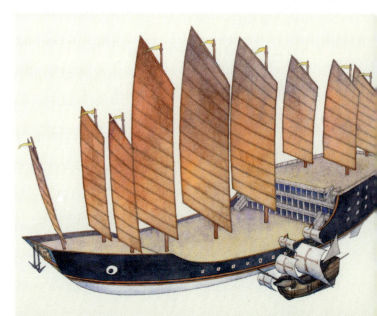

☐ Reading Comprehension

A. Multiple Choice. Choose the best answer for each question.

Main Idea

1. What is paragraph 4 mainly about?
   a. Zheng He's time in the Middle East
   b. Zheng He's last voyage
   c. a summary of Zheng He's voyages
   d. the trading routes to China

Detail

2. How many voyages did Zheng He make in his lifetime?
   a. 4   c. 28
   b. 7   d. It was never recorded.

Vocabulary

3. In line 59, the word *ultimately* could be replaced with _____.
   a. quickly   c. eventually
   b. all   d. somehow

Detail

4. Why did China's foreign exploration stop in 1422?
   a. A new ruler came to power.
   b. Zheng He died.
   c. Zheng He's fleet sank.
   d. Zheng He had completed his explorations.

Paraphrase

5. Which of the following is closest in meaning to: "The end of Zheng He's sixth voyage in 1422 coincided with a new emperor coming to power." (lines 63–65)?
   a. In 1422, a new emperor came to power and ended Zheng He's sixth voyage.
   b. When Zheng He finished his sixth voyage in 1422, he became China's emperor.
   c. Zheng He completed his sixth voyage in 1422 because China gained a new emperor.
   d. A new emperor came to power in China in 1422 at the time that Zheng He's sixth voyage came to an end.

B. Completion. Complete the timeline of key events in the life of Zheng He.

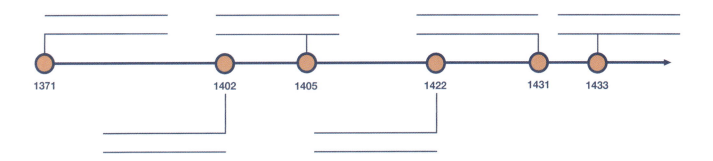

Critical Thinking

How do you think the world would be different today if China hadn't stopped foreign exploration in 1422?

Vocabulary Practice

A. Completion. Complete the information using the correct form of words from the box. Two words are extra.

accompany	accumulate	coincide	command	commodity
depart	fascinate	subsequent	terminate	via

▲ Norwegian explorer Thor Heyerdahl stands in front of the Pyramid of Chephren, Egypt, on December 6, 1987. In 1969, he and a crew built a reed boat, *Ra II*, on this exact spot. They later sailed it across the Atlantic.

As a young man, Norwegian explorer Thor Heyerdahl had long been **1.** _____ by Pacific cultures and island life. Heyerdahl developed an innovative theory for how the Pacific islands of Polynesia were first settled. He believed it was possible for humans, even in very basic craft, to travel from South America to Polynesia **2.** _____ the strong ocean currents near the Equator. **3.** _____, he claimed, it was South American Indians who first settled in Polynesia, not Southeast Asians as was commonly believed. Despite all the evidence he **4.** _____, however, few people took his viewpoint seriously.

To prove his theory, Heyerdahl decided to build a basic raft himself—called the *Kon-Tiki*—and sail it from South America to Polynesia. In 1947, he **5.** _____ from Callao, Peru on a 101-day voyage, **6.** _____ by a team of only five men. Later he remembered how he felt when he arrived on the Polynesian island of Raroia: "I crawled up on the dry sand and counted the men around me. That feeling can never be matched. We had really made it and we were all alive!"

In April 2002, Thor Heyerdahl's life of adventure was **7.** _____ as a result of a brain tumor. The year **8.** _____ with the 55th anniversary of his historic voyage in the *Kon-Tiki*, a voyage that changed forever the way we view one of humanity's greatest journeys.

B. Words in Context. Choose the best answer for each question.

1. Generally, you give commands to people who are _____ in rank.
   a. below you   b. your equal
2. Examples of commodities include _____.
   a. bread and coffee   b. love and happiness
3. Accumulating wealth usually happens _____.
   a. suddenly   b. over a period of time
4. To terminate something means to _____.
   a. start it   b. finish it
5. Two things that coincide happen _____.
   a. at the same time   b. one after the other

> ## Word Link
> The prefix **sub–** before some words can mean *below*. E.g., **sub**way, **sub**marine, **sub**heading, **sub**title, **sub**-zero temperatures.

Arabian Tales

The famous folk tale *The Seven Voyages of Sindbad the Sailor* forms part of the *Tales of the Arabian Nights* (or, *One Thousand and One Nights*), a collection of ancient and medieval stories from Arabic, Persian, Indian, and Egyptian literature.

Other stories in the *Arabian Nights* include *Aladdin's Wonderful Lamp* and *Ali Baba and the Forty Thieves*, although, like Sindbad, these were not part of the earliest versions of the collection.

The story of Sindbad the Sailor concerns the fictional adventures of a merchant living during the Abbasid period (750–1258), when much of the Islamic world was ruled by a powerful dynasty in Baghdad (present-day Iraq).

It is believed that many of the voyages and places in Sindbad's story are based on real trade routes that sailors used between the Middle East and other parts of Asia and east Africa.

Sindbad's tales have inspired several TV and film versions, including a 1970s Japanese TV anime series, and a 2003 U.S. animated movie.

⬚ Before You Read

A. Discussion. Read the information about Sindbad. Is this story, or are any other tales of the *Arabian Nights*, famous in your country? Do you know any other similar legends?

B. Scan. You are going to read about a modern-day recreation of Sindbad's voyages. Scan the reading to answer the questions below. Then read again to check your answers.

  1. Who is Tim Severin, and what was the purpose of his journey?
  2. How did Severin travel, and how far did he go?
  3. What places does he mention in the reading? Circle them on the map.

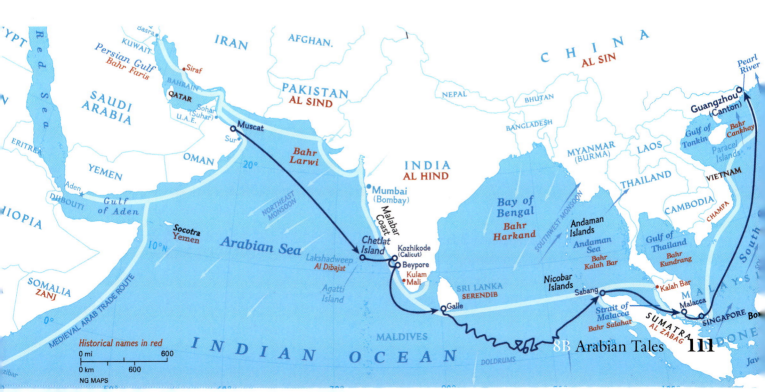

The Travels of Sindbad

1 Explorer Tim Severin steps back a thousand years to recreate Sindbad's legendary voyages. The selections below detail Severin's voyages.

An idea forms

5 To recreate Sindbad's voyages, I'll need to research, design, and build an early medieval Arab ship and use it to sail from the Persian Gulf to China. Searching for more data about traditional Arab ships, I visit the 10 country of Oman, which has a long history of shipbuilding. I am welcomed to Muscat (the country's capital) by the Minister of National Culture, who tells me that Oman will pay for the entire project—the ship, the crew, the 15 voyage—all on behalf of the Omani people and the Arab world.

The voyage begins

With a team comprised of 17 Omanis and 10 Westerners, our ship *Sohar* departs Muscat on 20 November 23 and heads east into the Arabian Sea toward India.

By December, we reach India's coast, and after a short stay, we sail to Sri Lanka, or Serendib, as early Arabs called it. The name has given 25 us the word "serendipity" (meaning "a lucky chance") in English, and it's easy to see why early visitors to this beautiful island gave it this name. On his second voyage, Sindbad was carried by a giant bird to "the valley of the 30 diamonds"—a place possibly in Sri Lanka, a country famous for its precious gems.[1]

Later, during his sixth voyage, Sindbad claimed Serendib's king held magnificent parades during which huge, decorated elephants 35 marched in the streets. In fact, what visitors to Sri Lanka may have seen during Sindbad's time (and can still see today) was *Perahera*—a parade held every year in which people and elephants, dressed colorfully, march through 40 the streets to honor the Buddha.[2]

Adrift at sea

In early February, we depart Sri Lanka, hoping to catch strong winds that will carry us eastward toward the Indonesian island of 45 Sumatra. The winds are light, however, and after three weeks at sea we are still 1,127 kilometers (700 miles) away. I begin to worry about our fresh water and food supplies. And then we get lucky. In early March, a storm 50 passes over and we catch fresh water. About a week later, the crew also catches 17 sharks and replenishes[3] the food supply.

---

[1] A **gem** is a jewel or stone (such as a diamond) that is used in jewelry.
[2] **Buddha** is the title given to Gautama Siddhartha, a religious leader and founder of Buddhism.
[3] If you **replenish** something, you make it full or complete again.

▲ Arab *dhows* being built at Sur, the shipyard where *Sohar* was built. For centuries, large oceangoing ships that sailed to Africa and Asia were built here.

The Land of Gold

On April 5, two months after leaving Sri Lanka, the winds accelerate and we make progress. Finally, by April 18, we reach Sumatra, known during Sindbad's time as the Land of Gold—a place of great wealth and beauty, but also believed to be home to terrible dangers.

Here, during his fourth voyage, Sindbad's crew met island natives who fed them food that made them sleepy. Once drugged, the crew was to become part of the natives' dinner menu. Fortunately, Sindbad refused to take the food, and as a result was able to escape before he could be eaten. Hashish, a drug derived from a plant and used in northern Sumatra as a flavoring in food, may have been the source for this story.

While visiting Sumatra again during his fifth voyage, Sindbad was captured this time in a forest by a short, old man with dark skin and red hair who could not talk. Sindbad called this strange person the Old Man of the Sea.

More likely it was the great ape of Sumatra: the orangutan—a highly intelligent animal who is a close relative of humans and is now an endangered species in the forests of Indonesia.

Stormy weather

After a brief stay in Sumatra, we sail quickly to Singapore and then on to our final destination: Guangzhou, China. In the South China Sea, we're hit by a violent storm. Our main sail is broken, and as the crew struggles to repair the damaged sail, the ship nearly capsizes.[4] During his sixth voyage, Sindbad spoke of the terrible weather in this region, and for the next five days, *Sohar* is hit regularly by storms. The weather finally improves, and by July 11 we reach the port of Guangzhou. We have been at sea for seven and a half months, and have covered 9,656 kilometers (6,000 miles).

Our Chinese hosts treat us to a huge celebration, though at one point, I can't help but feel sad. We have traced Sindbad's route, and now our great adventure is ending. But inside me, there is happiness too: the generosity of the Omani people, and the determination of the men who built and sailed *Sohar*, made the voyage a reality. Now this journey, like Sindbad's seven voyages, will become another tale to be told.

[4] If a boat or ship **capsizes**, it falls and turns upside down in the water.

◄ Five years before his Sindbad voyage, explorer Tim Severin led another expedition to sail across the North Atlantic. The team traveled from Ireland to Canada in a traditional Irish boat made from wood and leather.

Reading Comprehension

A. Multiple Choice. Choose the best answer for each question.

Gist

1. What is this reading mainly about?
a. the author's recreation of Sindbad's voyages
b. the adventures of Sindbad
c. the author's experiences in Sri Lanka
d. Sindbad's voyages with Severin

Detail

2. What nationality were Severin's crew?
a. Indonesian and Chinese
b. Omani
c. Omani and Western
d. Chinese

Inference

3. Severin's ship relies on what to move?
a. a modern ship engine
b. wind in its sails
c. the crew with oars
d. the passage doesn't say

Vocabulary

4. Who or what is *Hashish* (line 67)?
a. one of Sindbad's sailors
b. a type of food
c. a place the author visited
d. a plant-based drug

Detail

5. Where did *Sohar* experience the worst weather?
a. in the Arabian Sea
b. between Sri Lanka and Indonesia
c. between Sumatra and Singapore
d. in the South China Sea

> **Critical Thinking**
>
> How much of the story of Sindbad do you think is true, and how much do you think is just legend?

B. Classification. Match each statement (**a–g**) with the person it describes.

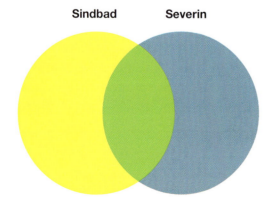

Sindbad   **Severin**

a. journey paid for by Omani government
b. visited Sri Lanka
c. saw "valley of the diamonds"
d. visited Sumatra
e. crew drugged by locals
f. captured by an old man
g. experienced terrible storms

☐ Vocabulary Practice

A. Matching. Match the words in the box to the words in red (**1–5**) with the same meaning.

> ___ **ministry**   ___ **on behalf of**   ___ **comprising**   ___ **tales**   ___ **brief**

A cultural festival took place in Seoul in June 2008 to celebrate cultural links between South Korea and the Arab world. The "Arabian Nights in Seoul" festival, named after the famous collection of Arabian (**1**) stories, featured music, dance, and poetry from a group of Arab countries (**2**) consisting of Libya, Morocco, Algeria, Saudi Arabia and Jordan.

Despite covering only a (**3**) short 4-day period, the festival was packed with events, including exhibitions, food-tasting, and dance performances. "Cultural understanding is one of the key channels of communication," said Bae Jae-hyun, speaking (**4**) for the Korean government's foreign affairs (**5**) department which helped to organize the event.

B. Completion. Complete the information below using the correct form of words from the box. One word is used twice.

> | accelerate | brief | comprise | crew |
> |---|---|---|---|
> | struggle | tale | violent | generous |

In 1873, author Jules Verne wrote *Around the World in Eighty Days*, a fictional **1.** _____ about a British man who attempts to travel around the world within eighty days. Over a century later, Michel Palin, a British adventurer, attempted to make the same journey, using only land and sea transport. Palin was accompanied by a TV **2.** _____ which **3.** _____ five people including a cameraman and director.

Palin **4.** _____ through a number of challenges in the early stages of the journey, including missed connections and often **5.** _____ weather. After crossing Europe and the Middle East overland, he stopped in Dubai, where he met a boat **6.** _____ who **7.** _____ agreed to take him to Bombay. Once in India, however, he realized he would have to **8.** _____ if he was going to get home in time. Palin made **9.** _____ stops in Singapore and Hong Kong before departing for North America. After racing across both the Pacific and Atlantic Oceans, he finally arrived back in London, England—79 days and 7 hours after his journey began.

▲ Adventurer and TV presenter Michael Palin

Thesaurus

tale Also look up: (*n.*) story, fable, anecdote, lie

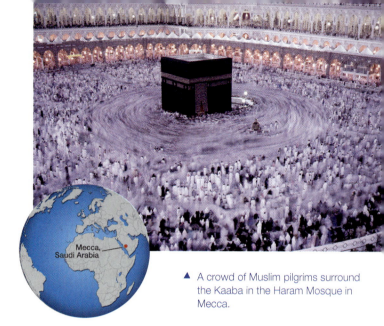

▲ A crowd of Muslim pilgrims surround the Kaaba in the Haram Mosque in Mecca.

Mecca

A. Preview. Read the definition below. What kinds of pilgrimages do people go on? Where do they go?

> **pil•grim•age** | ˈpɪlgrɪmɪdʒ |
> **1.** (*n.*) If you make a **pilgrimage** to a holy place, you go there for a religious reason.
> **2.** (*n.*) A **pilgrimage** is a journey that someone makes to a place that is very important to them.

B. Summarize. Watch the video, *Mecca*. Then complete the summary below using the correct form of words from the box. One word is extra.

accompany	accumulation	brief	command	comprise
depart	struggle	subsequent	tale	via

Every year, during the last month of the Islamic calendar, thousands of Muslim pilgrims arrive in the holy city of Mecca for the annual pilgrimage known as the Hajj. The pilgrimage **1.** _____ a series of rituals, and begins with the pilgrims circling the Kaaba, located in the center of a great mosque called Al-Masjid Al Haram.

The pilgrims **2.** _____ continue on to a place called the Plain of Arafat. They travel **3.** _____ the town of Mina, where crowds of pilgrims stop to rest at a vast campsite. At sunrise, a(n) **4.** _____ of up to 50,000 vehicles may be seen on the busy roads, all heading toward Arafat.

At sunset the same day, the pilgrims return to Mina. Muslim tradition states that it was here that God **5.** _____ Abraham to sacrifice his son, but Satan[1] challenged him not to. According to the **6.** _____, Abraham attacked Satan with stones, chasing him away. At a place called Muzdalifah, pilgrims join in a symbolic **7.** _____ with Satan, picking up small stones to stone Satan.

The pilgrims then return to Mecca for the last part of their journey. After completing their **8.** _____ visit, they finally **9.** _____ for home. Those who complete the pilgrimage earn themselves a special title—Hajji for men, Hajja for women.

[1] **Satan** is the devil, a powerful evil being.

C. Think About It.

1. Have you ever gone on a journey to a place that had a special meaning for you?

2. Which of the places mentioned in this unit would you most like to visit, and why?

To learn more about legendary voyages, visit elt.heinle.com/explorer

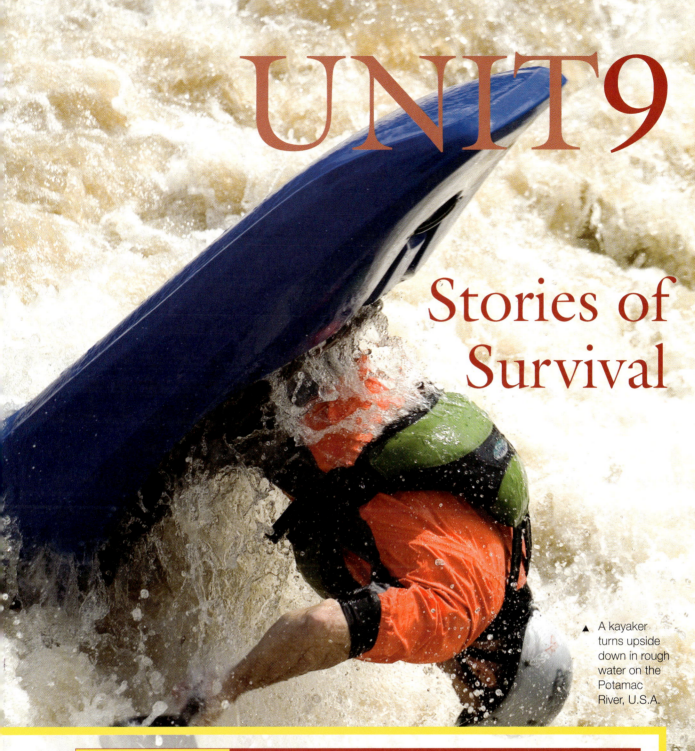

UNIT 9

Stories of Survival

▲ A kayaker turns upside down in rough water on the Potamac River, U.S.A.

Discuss these questions with a partner.

1. Have you ever been in a life-threatening situation?

2. Do you know any stories of people who survived accidents or another dangerous event?

3. Why do you think some people survive certain events while others don't?

117

9A An Ill-Fated Flight

BREAKING NEWS

Thursday, October 12, 1972: A plane carrying Uruguay's championship rugby team takes off from Montevideo, Uruguay, heading to Santiago, Chile. On board are 45 people: the crew, the Uruguayan players, and their friends and relatives.

Shortly after takeoff, the plane makes a stop in Mendoza, Argentina, due to bad weather.

Friday, October 13, 2:18 p.m.: Flight 571 takes off again, heading for Santiago.

October 13, 3:20 p.m.: About an hour into the flight, the pilots begin the descent into Santiago, not realizing the plane is still close to the high peaks of the Andes mountains…

▲ The Andes mountains near Santiago, Chile

⬜ Before You Read

A. Discussion. Read the information above about a real-life story. Who are the people in the story, and where are they? Where are they going? What do you think happens next?

B. Scan. You are going to read the story of what happened to the passengers on Flight 571. Quickly scan the reading to check your predictions from **A**.

Survival in the Andes

◀ Two climbers place a Uruguayan flag at the crash site to remember the 29 passengers who did not survive.

1   On Friday, October 13, 1972, a small plane flying from Uruguay to Chile with 45 people on board accidentally flew too low and crashed into a mountain in the Andes. How some of the passengers managed to live is one of the greatest survival stories ever told.

Thirteen people died in the impact, and in
5   the weeks that followed, 16 more would as
well, including eight who were killed by an
avalanche.[1] The survivors were dressed only
in street clothes and had no supplies that
would allow them to endure the mountain's
10   temperatures, which, at night at an altitude
of 3,600 meters (12,000 feet), sometimes
dropped to 30 degrees below zero (-22°F).
The survivors stayed inside the remains of the
aircraft, using thin seat covers for blankets,
15   and waited for a rescue that never came.

Days turned into weeks. It was urgent, the
survivors knew, to find a way to escape before
others died. Three of the passengers—Roberto
Canessa, Nando Parrado, and Antonio
20   Vizintín—volunteered to journey through the
mountains to search for help. On the day of
their departure, each man wore similar clothes:
three pairs of socks, a plastic bag around each
foot to keep the water out, boots, four pairs of
25   pants, and four sweaters. Many of the clothes
came from those who had died in the crash.
The escape team also carried a crucial piece of
survival equipment: a sleeping bag they had
made and sewn together using wire[2] from
30   the plane. As they departed the crash site, the
three men promised the remaining survivors
that they would survive and bring back help.

And so their journey began. For part of the
first day, they made steady progress, thanks
35   to mild weather. But none of the young men
had mountain-climbing experience, and as
the land and weather changed, climbing
became tougher. By the second day, they were
climbing steep, icy peaks, hoping to reach
40   the mountain's summit. After several days,
exhausted and cold, they reached what they
thought was the top. There the men paused.
They had imagined this moment for days.
On the other side of the summit, they hoped,
45   would be a valley leading down and out of the
mountains. But instead of a valley, they saw
more of the same snow-covered peaks. They
weren't near the end of the mountains, they
realized; they were in the middle of them.

Roberto Canessa   Nando Parrado   Antonio Vizintín

▲ Two climbers approach the mountain where the aircraft crashed. The plane hit the ridge (A) and slid more than 1,000 meters (3,000 feet) into the valley, where it came to rest (B).

50 But all hope wasn't lost. Parrado was able to spot two low summits about 65 kilometers (40 miles) away that didn't have snow. If they could get there, he rationalized, they would be out of the high Andes. Reaching the two peaks
55 would require more days of walking. and they didn't have enough food and drink to sustain them. But Parrado had a solution: Vizintín could return to the plane, and he and Canessa would take his supplies. They agreed on the
60 plan, and Canessa and Parrado continued their journey.

Walking toward the two peaks was difficult. But as the two men continued their hike, little by little, the landscape began to change. The
65 men discovered a small stream of water; the sun was also warmer, and it stayed lighter for more of the day. Within a few days of walking, the snow had disappeared completely, and flowers were everywhere. "This is the valley,"
70 Canessa said. "This is the way out."

Within days of reaching the valley, the first signs of humanity started to appear—a few cans on the ground, some farm animals in a field. It was December 19, and they had been
75 walking for eight days. By December 21, the exhausted pair made it to the town of Los Maitenes in Chile, and a rescue team was sent to save their 14 fellow survivors who were still high in the Andes.

80 In the end, all of the remaining survivors were saved. The memories of the crash in the Andes would be with the friends forever, but for now, their ordeal[3] was over. They had made it out—alive.

---

[1] An **avalanche** is a large amount of snow that falls down the side of a mountain.
[2] A **wire** is a long, thin piece of metal. Sometimes it is also covered in plastic.
[3] An **ordeal** is a very difficult or stressful situation.

Reading Comprehension

A. Multiple Choice. Choose the best answer for each question.

Gist
1. What is this reading mainly about?
   - a. how survivors of a plane crash survived the wait to be rescued
   - b. how 13 people died in a plane crash
   - c. how survivors of a plane crash managed to get help
   - d. how a rescue team managed to find the site of a plane crash

Gist
2. What is paragraph 3 mainly about?
   - a. the account of the crash
   - b. the preparation to go for help
   - c. the three volunteers
   - d. the clothes the men wore

Vocabulary
3. In line 40, the word *summit* could be replaced with _____.
   - a. base
   - b. top
   - c. north side
   - d. valley

Detail
4. Why did Vizintín return to the crash site?
   - a. The weather had become too cold.
   - b. He had become ill.
   - c. He was too weak to climb.
   - d. There wasn't enough food for three people.

Inference
5. After the crash, a rescue team did not arrive because _____.
   - a. the plane could not be found
   - b. no one knew the plane had been flying
   - c. there were no rescue teams in the Andes
   - d. the rescue team knew where the plane was but couldn't reach it

> **Critical Thinking**
>
> What do you think you would do if you were the survivor of a plane crash in a remote area? Would you leave the plane?

B. Summary. Identify and correct the errors in the following summary.

On ~~Tuesday,~~ *Friday* October 13, 1972, a small plane flying from Brazil to Chile crashed into a mountain in the Andes. In total, 27 people died in the plane crash or before they were rescued. Three survivors chose to go for help. From the top of the mountain they spotted two peaks that weren't covered in snow, and the three of them headed for the two peaks. When they reached the town of Los Maitenes, they had been walking for 21 days. As a result of their brave efforts, the 16 fellow survivors left behind at the crash site were rescued.

Vocabulary Practice

A. Completion. Complete the information with words from the box. One word is extra.

rational	steady	rescue	urgent	sew
tough	aircraft	blanket	sustain	volunteer

In January 2000, photographer Alison Wright was injured in a bus accident while traveling in Laos. It was the start of her long struggle for a new life.

When the truck hit, the impact instantly broke my back and ribs; my left arm was cut open by broken window glass; my heart and stomach tore loose and ended up near my shoulder. Later, doctors told me that the injuries I **1.** _____ in the accident were so severe that I shouldn't be alive.

▲ Alison Wright with penguins in Antarctica.

Somehow I managed to get out of the bus and lay by the side of the road. I remember thinking about my situation in a very clear, **2.** _____ way. I knew I had to calm down, so I focused on making my breathing slow and **3.** _____. I heard people shouting, "My God, someone do something! This woman is bleeding to death!" I wondered who they were talking about. Then I realized it was me.

Eventually I was **4.** _____ by some people who were passing by. They took me to a nearby village. A teenager in a T-shirt poured alcohol on the cuts in my arm, and used a needle to **5.** _____ them up. There were no drugs to reduce the pain. Some hours later, an aid worker arrived. He realized it was **6.** _____ that I get to a hospital quickly, so he **7.** _____ to drive me to the capital, Vientiane. From there I was taken to Udon Thani, Thailand.

Three weeks later, I boarded an **8.** _____ to return to the U.S. There, I went through more than 20 operations. Although my body was weak, my mind was still strong and **9.** _____, and I never gave up. In December 2001, almost two years after the accident, I achieved my goal of hiking to the top of Mount Kilimanjaro, in Africa. It was the start of a new day, and, for me, a new life.

B. Matching. Match words from the box in **A** with the definitions.

1. based on reason, not emotion _____
2. a thick cloth usually put on a bed _____
3. strong; difficult to break _____
4. gradual; without quick changes _____
5. to save from danger _____
6. to do work without pay _____

Word Link

We can add **–eer** to describe someone who is associated with a certain activity, e.g., volunt**eer**, mountain**eer**, engin**eer**.

A Photographer's Quest

◄ In December 1984, *National Geographic* photographer Steve McCurry was in Pakistan doing a story on the war in neighboring Afghanistan. Because of the conflict, millions of Afghan people had fled[1] to Pakistan and were living in refugee[2] camps. On a visit to one of the camps, McCurry took a number of photos. "I remember the noise and confusion in that refugee camp… ," he wrote later about the experience. "I asked the teacher for permission to enter the girls' school tent and photograph a few of the students." One girl, a shy student with intense green eyes, agreed to have her photograph taken.

National Geographic featured her photo on its cover in June 1985, and her image became a symbol of the pain, as well as the strength and beauty, of the Afghan people. Questions about the "Afghan Girl" poured in: What was her name? What happened to her? But no one could answer these questions, not even the man who had taken the famous photograph.

[1] If you **flee** from something, you escape from it.

[2] A **refugee** is a person who has been forced to leave their home or country, usually because of war.

▢ Before You Read

A. Discussion. Look at the photo and information above, and answer the questions.

1. Where and when was this photograph taken?
2. Who took the photograph, and why?
3. How did the girl become famous?

B. Scan. You are going to read about the search for the "Afghan Girl." Quickly scan the reading to answer the questions below. Then read again to check your answers.

1. What do we now know about the "Afghan Girl"?
2. What clues helped to confirm her identity?

In Search of the Afghan Girl

1　She was one of the world's most famous faces, and yet no one knew who she was. Her image appeared on the front of magazines, books, and posters, but
5　she didn't know it. Who was this young girl, and what happened to her? After searching for nearly two decades, *National Geographic* once again found the Afghan girl with the unforgettable green eyes. This
10　is her story.

For almost 20 years, the young Afghan girl's identity—and her fate[1]—remained a mystery. After several unsuccessful attempts to locate her, *National Geographic* photographer Steve
15　McCurry, who had taken her famous photo, returned to Pakistan once more to see if he could uncover any information about the girl. She would now be a woman in her early thirties, and finding her, if she was indeed still
20　alive, would not be easy.

McCurry discovered that the refugee camp where he'd taken the original photo was still standing. He began his search there. He showed the girl's photograph to many
25　people. Most did not know the child. And then, a man who had also lived in the camp as a boy recognized the girl's picture. Yes, he told McCurry, she was alive. She had left the camp and was now living in the mountains
30　of Afghanistan. The man offered to find the woman and bring her to McCurry. It seemed a long shot, but McCurry agreed.

It took three days for the woman to arrive, but when McCurry saw her walk into the room,
35　he was convinced this was the right person. Time and hardship had erased her youth,

▲ Sharbat Gula in 1984

but the eyes had not changed—they were the same bright color, with the same intense stare. The woman, through an interpreter, was
40　introduced as Sharbat Gula. At last, the girl in the photo had a name and could tell her story.

In the winter of 1984, when Gula was just a child, bombs[2] exploded in her village, killing her parents. She, her grandmother, brother,
45　and sisters fled in terror across dangerous mountain roads to Pakistan. Once there, they stayed in various refugee camps along the border of the two countries, living in crowded surroundings at the mercy of other people. It
50　was in one of these camps that McCurry met and photographed young Sharbat Gula.

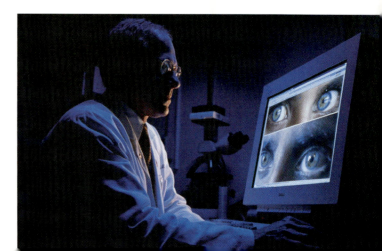

▲ Sharbat Gula in 2002

Gula had married at the age of 16. In the mid-1990s, during a pause in the fighting in Afghanistan, she and her husband returned
55 home. Once there, however, the couple's life remained difficult and unstable. One of their four daughters died as a baby. Following this tragedy, Gula's husband contracted a serious illness, and there were no medical clinics in
60 the region for him to go to. Although he survived the illness, money was scarce, and Gula's husband had to travel to Pakistan for work. His wages were just enough for the family to live on.

65 Though Gula received some schooling as a child, she was unable to complete her studies. Today she can write her name but cannot read; nevertheless, she has hopes for the future. "I want my daughters to have skills,"
70 she said. "I wanted to finish school but could not. I was sorry when I had to leave." Gula hopes her girls will get the education she was never able to complete.

She had also never seen the photograph
75 taken by McCurry, nor did she know that it had become a famous image and inspired thousands of people worldwide to aid refugees. "I don't think she was particularly interested in her personal fame,"[3] McCurry
80 said. But Gula was pleased when she learned she had become a symbol of the strength of her people.

Today Sharbat Gula and her story are once again mobilizing people to help, for
85 example, by inspiring people to assist in the development and delivery of educational opportunities for young Afghan women and girls. "She stood for an entire group of refugees, not just Afghan refugees," says
90 Boyd Matson of *National Geographic*. "She has helped us with our mission[4] of educating people about other cultures and regions—and she's helping us again by drawing attention to the lives of Afghan women and girls
95 in general."

[1] A person's **fate** is what happens to them in their lives.
[2] A **bomb** is a device that explodes and damages or destroys a large area.
[3] If a person achieves **fame**, he or she becomes very well known.
[4] A **mission** is an important task or activity.

◄ A family portrait shows, from left to right, three-year-old daughter Zahida, husband Rahmat Gul, Sharbart Gula, daughter Alia, and Sharbat's older brother, Kashar Khan.

Opposite page: Dr. Harry Quigley, an ophthalmologist (eye doctor), reviewed photographs of the eyes, and said, "It's the same person." Other experts agreed.

Reading Comprehension

A. Multiple Choice. Choose the best answer for each question.

Gist **1.** What is this reading mainly about?
   a. Sharbat Gula's early life
   b. the experiences of Afghan refugees
   c. the life of photographer Steve McCurry
   d. McCurry's quest to find the subject of his famous photo

Vocabulary **2.** In line 36, the word *erased* could be replaced with _____.
   a. changed
   b. made stronger
   c. rubbed away
   d. taken away

Detail **3.** What was still the same about Gula after 20 years?
   a. her clothes
   b. her hair
   c. her stare
   d. her home

Detail **4.** Why did Gula's husband have to travel to Pakistan?
   a. for medical help
   b. to see his family
   c. to fight
   d. for work

Critical Thinking

Why do you think Gula's picture inspired so many people?

Reference **5.** In line 91, *us* refers to _____.
   a. *National Geographic*
   b. Boyd Matson and Steve McCurry
   c. Afghan women and children
   d. refugees

B. Sequencing. Put the events below in order from **1–9**. Then retell Sharbat Gula's life story to a partner.

   a. ___ She married at the age of 16.
   b. ___ Her husband traveled to Pakistan to work.
   c. ___ She returned to Afghanistan.
   d. ___ Her parents were killed.
   e. ___ One of her daughters died as a baby.
   f. ___ Her husband became seriously ill.
   g. ___ She was photographed by McCurry.
   h. ___ She learned from McCurry how her picture has inspired people to help refugees.
   i. ___ She and her family fled to a refugee camp in Pakistan.

☐ Vocabulary Practice

A. Completion. Complete the information with words from the box. Two words are extra.

border	**clinic**	**convince**	**explosion**	**mercy**
mobilize	**stable**	**terror**	**tragic**	**wages**

John Dau was one of thousands of young African males caught in Sudan's civil war. This is his story of survival.

One night in 1987, 13-year-old John Dau was woken from his sleep by the sound of loud **1.** _____ close by his family's hut. Outside, he saw people running in **2.** _____ from armed soldiers. "The women and children were running and crying," he remembers. "I could hear bullets, zzzzing zzzing, whistling past us. I can still hear that sound."

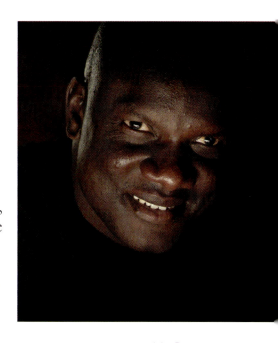

As his village burned, Dau joined thousands of other boys, now known as the "Lost Boys of Sudan," who escaped the war on foot. Together they faced dangerous wild animals, disease, and hunger, often depending on the **3.** _____ of villagers who offered them food. Fewer than half of the children completed the journey and crossed the **4.** _____ into Ethiopia.

▲ John Dau, a Sudanese refugee, now an immigrant in the United States.

Some years later, Dau found his way to Kenya, where he began rebuilding his life. In 2001, a volunteer organization arranged for Dau and some of his fellow Lost Boys to fly to the U.S.A. Dau began working 60 hours a week in New York, and used his **5.** _____ to cover the cost of studying at university. Dau has since established the American Care for Sudan Foundation, which has helped to build a health **6.** _____ in southern Sudan.

Dau remains hopeful and is **7.** _____ that one day his country will become **8.** _____ and peaceful again. "Hope must not be lost," he says. "All those miles in the desert, I always said, maybe tomorrow will not be like this."

B. Matching. Match words from the box in **A** with the correct definition.

1. to succeed in encouraging people to take (political) action _____
2. not likely to change or come to an end soon _____
3. extremely sad _____
4. a building where people go to receive medical treatment _____
5. the dividing line between two countries _____
6. make someone believe that something is true _____

Word Partnership

Use **mercy** with:
(v.) **beg for** mercy, **call for** mercy, **have** mercy **on someone**, **show** mercy; (prep.) **at the** mercy **of someone/something**

Coast Guard School

In the Atlantic, rough seas crash over the bow of the *N.G. Endeavor.* ▶

A. Preview. You will hear these words and phrases in the video. Match each word with its definition.

1. adrenaline   ___   **a.** a feeling of excitement about something pleasant you know is going to happen

2. pulse rate   ___   **b.** a substance that your body produces when you are angry, scared, or excited. It makes your heart beat faster and gives you more energy

3. anticipation   ___   **c.** something that prevents one extending beyond a particular boundary

4. limitation   ___   **d.** how frequently your heart beats

B. Summarize. Watch the video, *Coast Guard School*. Then complete the summary below using the correct form of words from the box. Two words are extra.

wage	**mercy**	**convince**	**endure**
mobilize	**rescue**	**steady**	**sustain**
terror	**border**	**tough**	**tragedy**

C. Think About It.

1. Why do you think people become lifeboat drivers?

2. Whose story of survival in this unit do you think is the most incredible, and why?

In the U.S. Coast Guard's national motor lifeboat school, trainee boat drivers often find themselves at the **1.** _____ of waves that can kill. They must face the **2.** _____ of some of the most violent and unpredictable seas. In an area known as the "Graveyard of the Pacific," drivers learn how to **3.** _____ the kind of rough conditions that they will frequently face in their job, battling against the elements.[1]

The training is important as these are the skills that will **4.** _____ them as they perform their dangerous and **5.** _____ life-saving missions. Instructor Aaron Ferguson is **6.** _____ that the motor lifeboat school gives the students the best kind of training, a strong base that they will later depend on.

The two-week class ends with the students **7.** _____ for the man overboard drill. For student Ralph Johnston, this is the chance to prove he can move the lifeboat through heavy surf while keeping it **8.** _____. The **9.** _____ attempt succeeds, and he passes the test.

Meanwhile, for the instructors, there is satisfaction in knowing that the skills students learn here might one day prevent a terrible **10.** _____.

[1] You can refer to weather, particularly wind and rain, as **the elements**.

To learn more about stories of survival, visit elt.heinle.com/explorer

A. Crossword. Use the definitions below to complete the missing words.

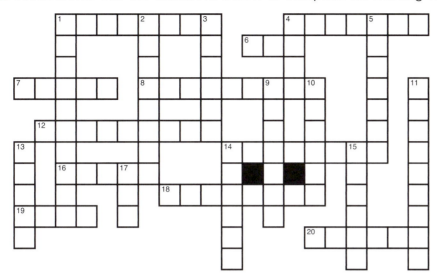

Across

1. to recommend a course of action publicly
4. a shocking or sad event
6. by way, or means, of
7. strong and difficult to destroy
8. to do something by choice and without being forced
12. to promise or make certain
14. to happen at the same time
16. to ill-treat or misuse
18. to organise people and resources for an urgent purpose
19. a group of people working together
20. very great fear, panic, or dread

Down

1. to gather together in an increasing quantity, collect
2. to persuade by argument or evidence
3. to experience, or put up with, something unpleasant, without giving up
4. story
5. to burst with great violence, blow up
9. to show
10. to save someone or something from danger or trouble
11. lasting only for a short time, not permanent
13. kind or forgiving treatment toward someone who is powerless
14. a place in which patients are given medical treatment or advice
15. to leave
17. to join together with thread

B. Notes Completion. Scan the information on pages 130–131 to complete the notes.

Field Notes

Site: Imperial Palaces of Ming and Qing Dynasties

Location: Beijing, China

Information:

- Center of power in China for nearly _____ centuries— from Emperor Yongle (who moved the capital from _____) to Emperor Puyi
- Opened to the public in _____; visitors can now see treasures including porcelain, timepieces, and thousands of _____
- Emperor's official seat of power was the _____, located in the Hall of _____
- Only the Emperor could walk or be carried along a path known as the _____
- To the south is Tiananmen Square, the world's biggest _____

The Forbidden City

Site: **Imperial Palace of the Ming and Qing Dynasties**

Location: **Beijing, China**

Category: **Cultural**

Status: **World Heritage Site since 1987**

Beijing, China

For nearly 500 years, from the early 15th century to the early 20th, 24 emperors of the Ming and Qing **dynasties** ruled China from a vast palace city in the heart of Beijing. Built like a treasure box with walls nearly ten meters tall, the **Forbidden** City served as the home and seat of command for China's ruling family, and as the scene for important religious and official ceremonies.

For centuries, only the emperor's family and officials could enter this fascinating hidden city. Since its opening in 1925, thousands of visitors have passed through its gates, drawn not only by the **imperial** city's historical importance but also by its huge size and magnificent architecture. The site also houses an astonishing range of imperial treasures—an accumulation that comprises nearly 50,000 paintings, 320,000 pieces of **porcelain**, and up to 1,000 precious timepieces, including historical pieces from Switzerland, Britain, and the U.S.A.

Glossary

dynasty: a series of rulers who belong to the same family
forbidden: not allowed
harmony: pleasing or peaceful arrangement of parts
imperial: referring to people or things connected with an empire
porcelain: a hard, shiny material made by heating clay
supreme: very great; at the highest level

1406

Ming emperor Yongle (Zhu Di) moves his capital from Nanjing to Beijing, where he builds the Forbidden City on the site of Kublai Khan's palace (described by explorer Marco Polo). The construction coincides with a period of sea exploration led by Zhu Di's commander Zheng He.

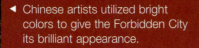
◄ Chinese artists utilized bright colors to give the Forbidden City its brilliant appearance.

An Imperial Wedding

In March 1889, more than 500 officials and male family members gathered at the Hall of **Supreme Harmony** for the ritual of announcing the marriage of the emperor Guangxu and empress Longyu. The event coincided with the start of the Qing dynasty's decline—an imperial wedding was never celebrated on such a vast scale again.

① The Hall of Supreme Harmony's steep **roof** is supported by painted beams connecting 72 columns nearly 12 meters (39 feet) tall.

② In the center of the building, the emperor sits on the **dragon throne**, the imperial seat of power.

③ In the **courtyard**, government ministers, accompanied by family members, line up according to rank; many began waiting before dawn.

④ The narrow avenue leading south is known as the **Imperial Way**; only the emperor can walk—or be carried—along this path.

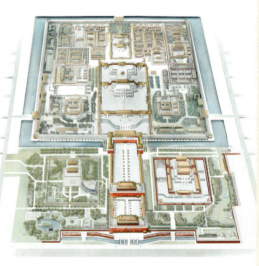

The layout of the Forbidden City is built precisely along a central north-south line. This line continues south to Tiananmen Square, the world's largest public square.

1644

The last Ming emperor kills himself as the capital erupts in violence; after a brief struggle for power the Qing (Manchu) gain control, beginning a new dynasty.

1912

The last Qing emperor, six-year-old Puyi, gives up his power; he is allowed to live temporarily in the Forbidden City until subsequently forced to depart in 1924.

1949

China's new leader Mao announces the establishment of the People's Republic of China from the Forbidden City's Tiananmen Gate.

The Forbidden City   **131**

Energy

A Global View

Almost everything people do requires energy. The world's chief sources of energy today are oil, coal, and natural gas. **Industrialization** and **urbanization** have resulted in widespread dependence on these three fossil fuels.

But fossil fuels—so called because they formed from the **fossilization** of plant and animal material over millions of years—are finite resources and will eventually run out. The American Petroleum Institute, for example, predicts that the world's oil supply will be gone by 2057. More people are turning instead to coal, of which there is at least 900 billion tons in reserve.

However, fossil fuels are problematic not just because of their scarcity. Fossil fuels are unevenly distributed, so only some countries have them, and only some can afford them. Supplying reliable energy at affordable prices has therefore become a major challenge for today's **globalized** world.

Furthermore, the burning of fossil fuel releases carbon dioxide and other pollutants into the atmosphere and is a major contributor to global warming. Subsequently, many governments and **organizations** are investigating ways to develop cleaner, renewable sources of energy.

Renewable Energy

As demand for energy grows, and fuel prices rise, many people have come to the **realization** that discovering alternative sources is more necessary than ever. Scientists are looking at ways to substitute nonrenewable fossil fuels with renewable sources such as water, wind, and solar power. These sources are sustainable; in other words, they can be replaced or reused and so will not run out.

◄ **World Energy Production**

Oil 38%
Coal 24%
Natural gas 24%
Nuclear 6%
Renewable Sources 8%

Solar 0.1%
Wind 1.9%
Geothermal 3.5%
Biomass 6.6%
Hydroelectric 87.9%

NORTH AMERICA

Toronto
New York
Los Angeles
Mexico City

PACIFIC OCEAN

ATLANTIC OCEAN

SOUTH AMERICA

Buenos Aires

Major Coal, Natural Gas, and Oil Deposits

- Coal
- Natural gas
- Oil

▲ Wadham Biomass Facility in the U.S. generates electricity by burning waste material from rice plants.

Hydroelectricity is produced from the energy of falling or flowing water. Water has been **utilized** for energy production for thousands of years, at least since the **civilizations** of ancient Greece and Rome. Modern hydroelectric facilities produce no direct waste and fewer greenhouse gases than energy plants powered by fossil fuels. The world's largest hydroelectric power station is the Three Gorges Dam across the Yangtze River in China.

Geothermal power is energy generated from heat stored in the Earth. The United States is the largest producer of geothermal electricity, but the Philippines and Iceland are the only countries to generate a significant percentage of their electricity (15–20 percent) from geothermal sources.

Biomass energy is derived from dead plants and waste (things we dispose of) converted into fuel. It is considered a renewable resource because people can grow new plants and will continually produce waste materials.

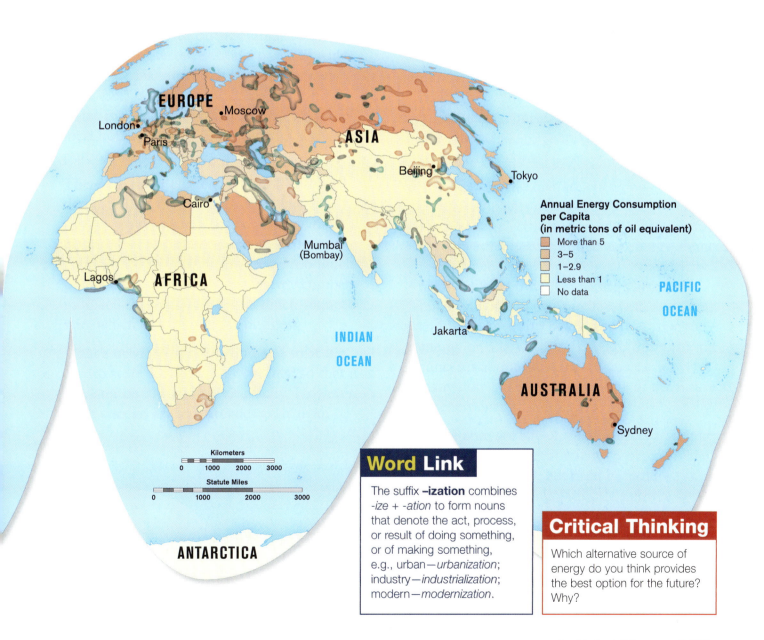

Annual Energy Consumption per Capita (in metric tons of oil equivalent)
- More than 5
- 3–5
- 1–2.9
- Less than 1
- No data

Kilometers
0 1000 2000 3000

Statute Miles
0 1000 2000 3000

Word Link

The suffix **–ization** combines -ize + -ation to form nouns that denote the act, process, or result of doing something, or of making something, e.g., urban—*urbanization*; industry—*industrialization*; modern—*modernization*.

Critical Thinking

Which alternative source of energy do you think provides the best option for the future? Why?

A. Completion. Use the correct form of words in **bold** from pages 132–133 to complete the sentences.

One of the first sources of power was running water, or *hydropower*, which was **1.** _____ by ancient **2.** _____ such as Greece and Rome.

Energy demand increased greatly during the **3.** _____ Revolution, as people changed from agricultural work; the same period also witnessed rapid **4.** _____ as people moved from rural areas to cities.

Today, oil, gas, and coal (produced by the **5.** _____ of ancient plants and animals) are the predominant sources of the world's energy.

As the world becomes more **6.** _____ —with more interconnections between countries and economies—decisions made by governments and energy **7.** _____ affect people all over the globe.

There is a growing **8.** _____ that we cannot rely on fossil fuels forever, and that renewable sources are essential for future energy demands to be met.

B. Usage. Cohesive markers like *furthermore* and *subsequently* help to connect ideas in a text. Read the passage and match each word or phrase in **blue** with a word or phrase below. Number the phrases 1–12.

_____ even though	_____ furthermore	_____ especially	_____ so as
_____ overall	_____ in conclusion	_____ for instance	_____ later
_____ nevertheless	_____ clearly	_____ definitely	_____ therefore

Movie Review:

There Will Be Blood

I should start this review by pointing out that, (1) on the whole, I have never been a big fan of director Paul Thomas Anderson's films. *Cigarettes and Coffee* (1993) and *Magnolia* (1999), (2) for example, I felt were disappointing. (3) For this reason, I was not expecting much from Anderson's latest offering, *There Will Be Blood*. (4) However, my low expectations proved to be very wrong.

There Will Be Blood—a violent and tragic tale of a tough oil man working in early 20th-century California—is a work that Anderson (5) obviously cared deeply about. The director exhibits his skill in every scene, including an astonishing opening which,

(6) although it is filmed without any dialogue, manages to establish the oil man's character without any words.

(7) Subsequently, as the film progresses, the main character becomes more and more terrifying. (8) In addition, the acting in the film—(9) in particular, Daniel Day-Lewis's intense and commanding performance as the oil man—is outstanding. Day-Lewis is said to have spent two years studying the historical period (10) in order to convincingly play the main character. (11) In summary, *There Will Be Blood* is a fascinating story, a remarkable piece of filmmaking, and (12) certainly one of the best movies of the year.

UNIT 10

All in the Mind

Discuss these questions with a partner.

1. Do you think you have a good memory? What are your earliest memories?

2. How many different human emotions can you think of?

3. Which animals do you think are the most intelligent?

Do you think that animals have the same emotions as humans?

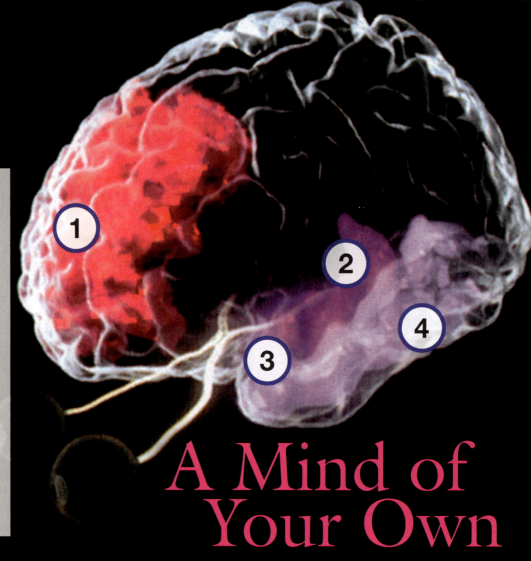

10A

The human brain contains roughly 100 billion cells (neurons), each having more than 10,000 connections. We now know that different parts of the brain specialize in different functions. This brain scan shows four areas. The **prefrontal cortex** (1) is key to an individual's **self-awareness**. The **hippocampus** (2) enables people to **recall** long-term memories. The **amygdala** (3) helps to process **emotional** memories, and may be related to social **behavior**. The **temporal lobe** (4) is associated with speech and **perception**.

A Mind of Your Own

☐ Before You Read

A. Matching. Read the information above. Use the words in **blue** to complete the definitions.

1. If you have _____ it means you are conscious of your own identity.

2. If you are in a(n) _____ mental state, you display strong feelings.

3. If you are able to _____ something, you can remember it.

4. _____ is the recognition of things using your senses, especially sight.

5. _____ is the way that someone acts, performs, or functions.

B. Skim. Read the headings below and quickly skim the passage on pages 137–138. Which heading is most suitable for each break in the text? Label the headings A–D.

_____ Who am I?   _____ How do I remember?

_____ Why do I have emotions?   _____ Can I control how I feel?

WHAT'S ON YOUR MIND?

Electrodes are used ▶ to measure the brain activity of a meditating Buddhist monk, Dru-gu Choegyal Rinpoche. According to scientist Richard Davidson, one monk they studied was proven to be "the happiest man in the world."

1   The ancient Egyptians thought so little of the brain that when a king died, they removed the brain from his body and threw it away. The Egyptians presumed, like many people before and
5   after them, that consciousness existed in the heart.

Today we know that the mind is a product of the brain, but how exactly does this 1.5-kilo (three-pound) piece of flesh create a mind which allows you to think about
10   yourself, experience happiness and anger, or remember events that happened 20 minutes or 20 years ago? This isn't a new question. Today, however, powerful new techniques for visualizing the sources of thought, emotion,
15   behavior, and memory are transforming the way we understand the brain and the mind it creates.

A. _____

Have you ever stopped and thought, "What's
20   wrong with me today? I just don't feel like myself"? Perhaps you were more tired or worried than usual—but somehow, you knew that something was different about *you*. This self-awareness—the ability to think
25   about yourself and how you're feeling—is an important part of being human.

This part of your mind has its origins in the prefrontal cortex—a region of your brain just behind your forehead that extends to about
30   your ears. Before this area began to function (around age two), you didn't understand that you were a separate entity with your own identity. In time, as this part of your brain developed, you then became more aware of
35   yourself and your thoughts and feelings.

B. _____

Perhaps one of the most important factors involved in shaping our identity is memory—the ability to retain and
40   remember facts, faces, and experiences. What exactly is a memory? Most scientists define it as a stored pattern of
45   connections between neurons in the brain. Every feeling you remember, every thought you think, alters the connections
50   within the vast network of brain cells, and memories are reinforced, weakened, or newly formed.

This 85-year-old man, who researchers call "EP," lives almost entirely ▲ in the present. A brain infection wiped out decades of memories, along with the capacity to create new ones.

Most people's earliest memories reach back to about age three or so. Very few people recall anything before this time because the part of the brain that helps form long-term memories (the hippocampus) was not yet mature. This doesn't mean earlier memories don't exist in your mind, though. Some scientists believe highly emotional memories—especially those associated with intense fear—might be stored in another structure in the brain (the amygdala) that may be functional at birth. Though these memories are not accessible to the conscious mind, they might still influence the way we feel and behave, even into adulthood.

C. _____

But where do our emotions come from, and how do they shape the people we are and the way we perceive the world? Forty years ago, psychologist Paul Ekman demonstrated that facial expressions used to exhibit certain emotions are recognized by people everywhere. Ekman suggested that these emotions and their corresponding facial expressions evolved to help us deal quickly with situations that can affect our welfare.

Though humans may share certain emotions and recognize them in others, we don't all have the same emotional response to every situation. In fact, most emotional responses are learned and stored in our memories. The smell of freshly cut grass, for example, will generate happy feelings in someone who spent enjoyable childhood summers in the countryside, but not in someone who was forced to work long hours on a farm. Once an emotional association like this is made, it is very difficult to reverse it. "Emotion is the least flexible part of the brain," says Ekman. But we can learn to control our emotions by becoming consciously aware of their underlying causes and by not reacting automatically to things in our environment.

► Glen McNeill spends six or seven hours a day learning the streets of London in order to become a taxi driver. After his training, which will last for years, his hippocampus, the part of his brain used for memory and learning, will be larger than that of other adults.

D. _____

But is it really possible to control our emotions? Researcher Richard Davidson has demonstrated that people who experience negative emotions display activity in their right prefrontal cortex. In those with a more positive perspective, the activity occurs in the left prefrontal cortex. Could we, Davidson wondered, control this activity and shift our mental state away from negative feelings toward a calmer state of mind?

To answer this question, Davidson worked with a group of volunteers in the United States. One group received eight weeks of training using different meditation and relaxation techniques, while another group did not. By the end of the study, those who had meditated had accomplished their goal: they showed a clear shift in brain activity toward the left, "happier" frontal cortex

For centuries people have studied the brain, but it is only in recent years that we have really started to learn how it works. Nevertheless, there is still a long way to go before we understand our minds' many complexities.

Reading Comprehension

A. Multiple Choice. Choose the best answer for each question.

Gist **1.** What is this reading mainly about?
a. how memory works
b. how the mind works
c. mind reading
d. how our emotions are processed in our brain

Reference **2.** In line 8, *piece of flesh* refers to the _____.
a. heart
b. mind
c. brain
d. body

Detail **3.** Which of these statements is NOT true?
a. The pre-frontal cortex affects a person's emotion's.
b. Self-awareness develops around the age of two.
c. The pre-frontal cortex is located at the back of the brain.
d. The pre-frontal cortex is not fully developed at birth.

Vocabulary **4.** The word *corresponding* in line 76 is closest in meaning to _____.
a. sending
b. changing
c. powerful
d. related

Detail **5.** Why do most people not remember what happened before they were three years of age?
a. The pre-frontal cortex is not developed at this stage.
b. Early memories disappear soon after they are formed.
c. The part of the brain that forms memory is not fully developed at this stage.
d. People tend to forget emotional memories.

Critical Thinking

What do you think would be the benefits of a better understanding of how the brain works?

B. Matching. Match each part of the brain (**1–5**) with its function (**a–e**), according to the passage.

Part of Brain	Description
1. ____ amygdala	**a.** helps in forming long-term memories
2. ____ hippocampus	**b.** responsible for self-awareness
3. ____ left pre-frontal cortex	**c.** stores very emotional memories
4. ____ right pre-frontal cortex	**d.** the activity center for positive emotions
5. ____ pre-frontal cortex	**e.** the activity center for negative emotions

☐ Vocabulary Practice

A. Completion. Complete the information below using the correct form of words from the box.

accomplish	**reinforce**	**flexible**	**visualize**	**perspective**
presume	**welfare**	**transform**	**underlie**	**entity**

Memorizing information is something that all of us need to do, but it is particularly essential for students. There are various ways to improve your memory, and one technique is known as "mind-mapping." This method is the invention of a British man called Tony Buzan. His **1.** _____ is that no matter how weak you are as a student, no matter how bad your exam results, the use of mind-mapping can **2.** _____ you and help you to **3.** _____ more in your life.

A mind map is like a diagram of thoughts, starting from a single idea, and spreading outward to new ideas, showing the connections between them (see example below). The **4.** _____ theory behind it is that by drawing the map on paper, you are made to **5.** _____ the information clearly. Later, as you look at the mind map again and again, you **6.** _____ your knowledge of the information and you memorize it.

B. Definitions. Use the correct form of words in the box in **A** to complete the definitions.

1. A(n) _____ object or material can be bent easily without breaking.

2. If you _____ that something is true, you think it is true, but are not certain.

3. A(n) _____ is something that exists separately from other things.

4. The _____ of a person or group is their health, comfort, or happiness.

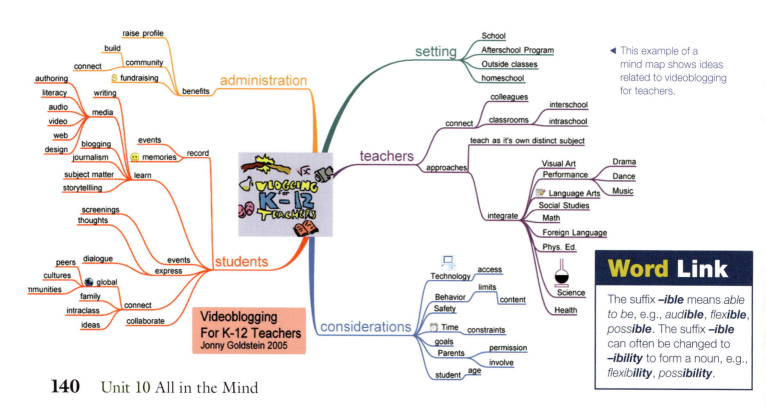

◄ This example of a mind map shows ideas related to videoblogging for teachers.

Word Link

The suffix *–ible* means *able to be*, e.g., *aud**ible**, flex**ible**, poss**ible***. The suffix *–ible* can often be changed to *–ibility* to form a noun, e.g., *flex**ibility**, poss**ibility***.

Logical reasoning ►
Male African cichlid fish observe other males fighting to identify which fish constitute the biggest challenge—a first step toward logical reasoning.[1] "They can do all this at eight weeks old," says researcher Russell Fernald, "with brains the size of a pea."

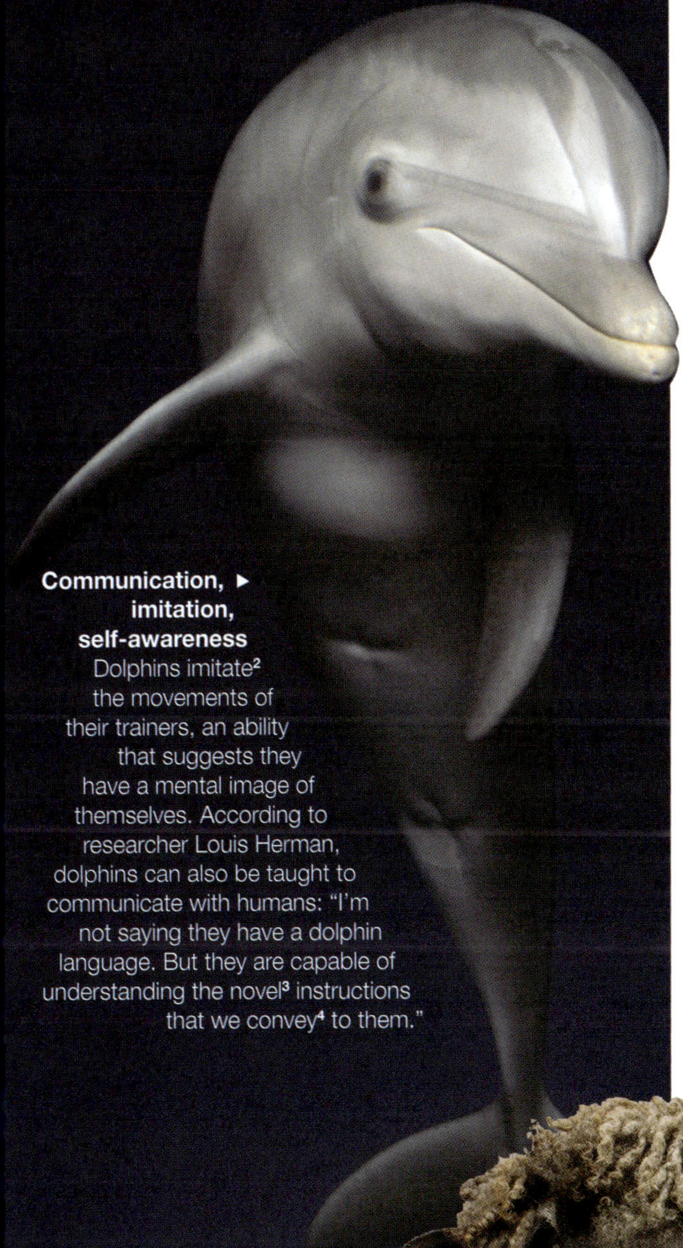

How Smart Are Animals?

▲
Problem solving and creativity
Crows can create and use tools to solve problems, such as using a metal wire to obtain food. This ability was previously thought to belong only to humans and apes.

**Communication, ►
imitation,
self-awareness**
Dolphins imitate[2] the movements of their trainers, an ability that suggests they have a mental image of themselves. According to researcher Louis Herman, dolphins can also be taught to communicate with humans: "I'm not saying they have a dolphin language. But they are capable of understanding the novel[3] instructions that we convey[4] to them."

▢ Before You Read

A. Discussion. Look at the photos and read the information. Do you think these animals can be called "intelligent"? How would you define "intelligence"?

B. Scan. You are going to read about animal intelligence. Quickly scan the reading to answer the questions below. Then read again to check your answers.

1. What animals are mentioned in the reading?
2. What kinds of "intelligence" does each animal display?

Memory and emotions ►
Sheep can recognize different faces (up to about 50 other sheep and ten humans); they can also recognize if the person—or sheep—is happy or angry.

[1] **Logical reasoning** is the process of using a rational series of steps to reach a conclusion.
[2] If you **imitate** something, you copy it.
[3] **Novel** things are new and different from anything done before.
[4] If you **convey** something (e.g., information or feelings), you cause them to be known or understood.

Alex, an African gray parrot, had a large vocabulary and was able to answer questions about his understanding of the world.

Inside Animal Minds

1 In 1977, Irene Pepperberg, a recent graduate of Harvard University, did something very unusual. She was interested in learning if animals could think, and the best way to do this, she reasoned,
5 was to talk to them. To test her theory, she bought an African gray parrot she named Alex and taught him to reproduce the sounds of the English language. "I thought if he learned to communicate, I could ask him questions about
10 how he sees the world," she explains.

When Pepperberg began her research with Alex, very few scientists acknowledged that animals were capable of thought. The belief was that animals reacted to things in their
15 environment but lacked the ability to think or feel. How, then, could a scientist demonstrate that animals might, in fact, possess intelligence? "That's why I started my studies with Alex," Pepperberg says.

20 Certain skills are considered key signs of higher mental abilities: a good memory, an understanding of symbols, self-awareness, understanding of others' motives, and creativity. Little by little, researchers have documented
25 these abilities in other species. Sheep and elephants can recognize faces. Chimpanzees— who are genetically similar to humans—use a variety of primitive tools for eating, drinking, and hunting; they also laugh when pleased
30 and spit[1] to show disgust with something. Octopuses in captivity[2] are known to amuse themselves by shooting water at laboratory staff. They may even exhibit basic emotions by changing color.

35 Alex the parrot was a surprisingly good talker. He learned how to use his voice to imitate almost 100 English words, including those for foods, colors, shapes, and numbers. Although imitation was once considered a simple skill, in
40 recent years cognitive scientists have revealed that it's extremely difficult. It requires the imitator to form a mental image of the other person's body and actions and then adjust his own body parts into the same position. It is a
45 behavior that shows an awareness of one's self.

Because Alex had mastered many English words, Pepperberg could ask him questions about a bird's basic understanding of the world. Alex could count, as well as describe shapes,
50 colors, and sizes for Pepperberg; he even had a basic understanding of the abstract concept of zero.

Betsy, a border collie, has a vocabulary of over 340 words, and knows at least 15 people by name.

Many of Alex's cognitive skills, such as his ability to understand the concepts of same and different, are generally attributed only to higher mammals, particularly primates (such as humans and apes). But parrots, like great apes (and humans), live a long time in complex societies. And like primates, these birds must monitor the changing relationships within the group. This may explain Alex's ability to learn a human language. "When we take [parrots] into captivity, what they start to do is treat us as their flock,"[3] explains Pepperberg. Parrots learn to pronounce and use our words so they can become a part of our group.

Researchers in Germany and Austria have also been studying language ability in dogs. One named Betsy has shown that she is able to learn and remember words as quickly as a two-year-old child. She has an extraordinary vocabulary of over 340 words (and counting), knows at least 15 people by name, and can link photographs with the real objects they represent. Like Alex, she's pretty smart.

This is the larger lesson of animal cognition research: it humbles us. We are not alone in our ability to invent, communicate, demonstrate emotions, or think about ourselves. Still, humans remain the creative species. No other animal has built cities, written music, or made a computer. In fact, a number of critics dismiss animals' ability to use tools or understand human language. They believe animals are just simulating human behavior.

Yet many researchers say that creativity and language in animals, like other forms of intelligence, have evolved. "People were surprised to discover that chimpanzees make tools," says Alex Kacelnik, an animal researcher at Oxford University. "But people also thought, 'Well, they share our ancestry—of course they're smart.' Now we're finding these kinds of behaviors in some species of birds. But we don't have a recently shared ancestry with birds. It means," Kacelnik continues, "that evolution can invent similar forms of advanced intelligence more than once—that it's not something reserved only for primates or mammals."

[1] If you **spit**, you force liquid out of your mouth.

[2] An animal in **captivity** lives in a zoo, a cage, or other enclosed place.

[3] A **flock** of birds is a group of birds.

◄ Kanzi, a bonobo, began learning language on his own by watching scientists trying to train his mother. At 27, he understands thousands of spoken words, and even plays the piano.

☐ Reading Comprehension

A. Multiple Choice. Choose the best answer for each question.

Gist **1.** What is this reading mainly about?
a. ways of teaching animals to become more intelligent
b. the discovery that intelligence is not limited to humans
c. animals that can communicate
d. how human and animal intelligence are different

Detail **2.** Which of the following is NOT mentioned in the passage?
a. how an octopus displays basic emotions
b. ways in which elephants can communicate
c. how birds and chimps evolved tool-making abilities
d. the language ability of dogs

Detail **3.** What could Alex do that showed self-awareness?
a. count
b. learn vocabulary
c. copy human sounds
d. understand the concept of zero

Critical Thinking

Which of the animals in the passage do you think is most intelligent? Why?

Reference **4.** In line 44, *it* refers to ____.
a. counting
b. talking
c. imitation
d. self-awareness

Vocabulary **5.** In line 75, the word *link* could be replaced with ____.
a. match
b. take
c. count
d. view

B. Summary. Complete the information with words from the reading.

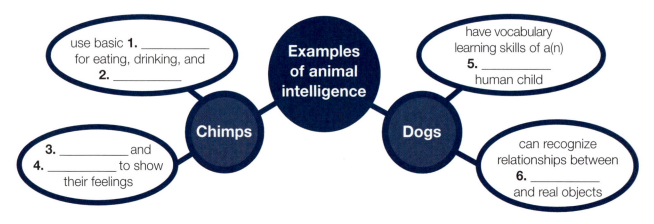

use basic **1.** _____ for eating, drinking, and **2.** _____

3. _____ and **4.** _____ to show their feelings

Chimps

Examples of animal intelligence

Dogs

have vocabulary learning skills of a(n) **5.** _____ human child

can recognize relationships between **6.** _____ and real objects

Senegal

Vocabulary Practice

A. Completion. Complete the paragraph with the correct form of words from the box. Three words are extra.

acknowledge	dismiss	abstract	extraordinary	master
humble	primitive	reveal	pronounce	simulate

Research into chimpanzees in the Fongoli region of Senegal has **1.** _____ behavior that could change the way we view our closest cousins.

The research suggests that the Fongoli chimps seem to have **2.** _____ the art of basic tool-making. Furthermore, a chimp was observed sharpening a stick with her teeth before using it as a(n) **3.** _____ tool for killing a bush-baby.[1]

Although few people **4.** _____ the findings completely, some researchers question their significance. Primatologist Craig Stanford, for example, while **5.** _____ that the behavior is fascinating, **6.** _____ that the research findings are only important enough to be ". . . a short note in a journal." However, researcher Jill Pruetz claims that the discovery is remarkable, as it shows that chimp behavior can be **7.** _____ human-like.

[1] A **bush-baby** is a small animal with large eyes.

B. Definitions. Complete the definitions using words from the box in **A**.

1. To _____ something means to become skilled in the use of it.

2. If you _____ an action or a feeling, you pretend to do it.

3. To _____ something means to show it, or make people aware of it.

4. A(n) _____ person is not proud, and does not believe they are better than other people.

5. If you _____ a fact or situation, you accept or admit that it is true.

6. A(n) _____ idea or way of thinking is based on general ideas rather than on real things and events.

▲ A recent study of Fongoli chimps such as this adult male has revealed behavior that is almost human-like.

Thesaurus

master Also look up: (*n.*) owner, artist, expert, professional; (*v.*) learn, study, understand

Shark vs. Octopus

A. Preview. In a fight between a shark and a giant octopus, which do you think would win, and why?

B. Summarize. Watch the video, *Shark vs. Octopus*. Then complete the summary below using the correct form of words from the box. One word is extra.

acknowledge	reveal
extraordinary	entity
humble	simulate
master	presume
flexible	transform
welfare	dismiss

▼ A giant Pacific octopus

One might **1.** _____ that sharks in an aquarium tank would be safe from being eaten. However, when dead sharks began to appear at the bottom of one tank, aquarium staff became worried about the sharks' **2.** _____.

Nobody really expected the **3.** _____ octopus to be responsible for the deaths, even the giant Pacific octopus who shared the tank with the sharks. The aquarium staff already knew that the giant Pacific octopus has some **4.** _____ abilities. For example, it uses camouflage to hide itself from predators, by **5.** _____ its skin color to **6.** _____ its surroundings.

But the giant Pacific octopus usually dines on fish and small sea creatures like shrimps, which it grabs using its **7.** _____ arms, known as tentacles. So the staff initially **8.** _____ the possibility that the octopus was a shark killer.

However, a video of a fight between the octopus and a shark clearly **9.** _____ that the octopus had **10.** _____ another skill: the ability to catch and kill sharks. The aquarium staff were forced to **11.** _____ that they had been wrong, and that the giant octopus was far more deadly than they had previously imagined.

C. Think About It.

1. Do you think an octopus can be described as "intelligent"? Why or why not?

2. Which piece of information about animal intelligence in this unit was the most surprising to you? Why?

To learn more about intelligence and the mind, visit elt.heinle.com/explorer

UNIT 11

Art and Life

WARM UP

Discuss these questions with a partner.

1. Do you have a favorite color? Why do you like that color?
2. Do you think that colors affect people's emotions? How?
3. Who are some of your favorite artists? Why do you like them?

▲ A doll maker paints details onto a *Hina* doll's face in Kyoto, Japan.

147

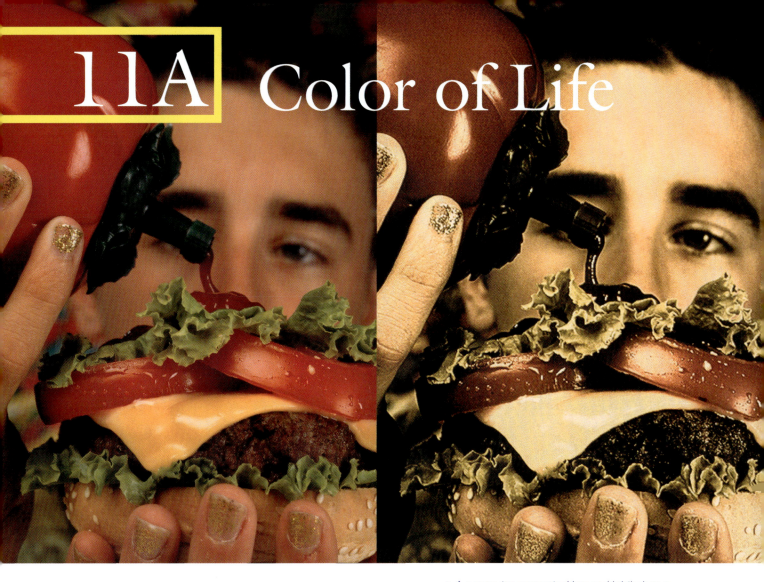

11A Color of Life

▲ A computer-generated image (right) shows what a color-blind person sees.

☐ Before You Read

A. Discussion. Look at the pictures and caption above. Then answer the questions below.

1. How do you think color influences our lives?
2. If you suffered from color-blindness, how would your life be different?

B. Scan. Look quickly at the reading on pages 149–150. Which colors are discussed in the passage? Write them in the chart. What feelings, beliefs, etc. do you associate with each color? Write them in the second column. As you read the passage, add information you learn in the third column.

Color	Things I associate with this color	Things I learned about this color

The Power of COLOR

Thinkers, artists, and scientists have long debated the nature of color:
what are its origins, and how does it affect us?

▲ The sumac leaves of New England, U.S.A, display an amazing range of color.

Early humans watched their fires blacken the ceilings of the caves where they lived. They saw blue and red in the sky and brown and green on the ground. In time, people began to understand that color not only made the world more beautiful, it was also able to convey emotion and symbolize power. Using colors they extracted from insects, plants, and minerals, primitive humans copied animals, painting their bodies to signal aggression toward an enemy or to attract a mate.

Over the centuries, the sources of colors such as blue, purple, and red were carefully guarded and were often worth as much as gold. In the 19th century, a young chemistry student became the first to manufacture a synthetic[1] dye,[2] and suddenly the world became a much more colorful place. By the 20th century, as scientists discovered the psychological effects of colors, everyone from advertisers to educators found ways to make use of color to influence our feelings and behavior.

RED

Red, the color of human blood, has traditionally symbolized intensity, fire, love, and anger. In Eastern cultures, it also represents luck, wealth, and success.

In humans, the color red can send different messages. Some people redden, for example, when they are angry or embarrassed, sending a clear signal to others about how they are feeling. British anthropologists Russell Hill and Robert Barton of the University of Durham found that when opponents in a game are equally matched, the team dressed in red is more likely to win. Why? According to Barton, "red seems to be the color, across species, that signals dominance"—giving those dressed in red an advantage in sporting events. In many animal species (including humans), contact with this bold color causes the heart rate to accelerate. However, one of red's lighter shades, pink, can have the opposite effect on people. Men in prisons are reported to be more passive when the walls are painted a specific shade of pink.

Humans have also used the color red in everything from politics to advertising. Many food products in the U.S., for example, are packaged in red containers. Why? The color makes the product look as if it is advancing toward a shopper.

[1] **Synthetic** products are made from chemicals, not natural materials.

[2] A **dye** is a substance that is mixed into a liquid and used to change the color of something, such as cloth or hair.

YELLOW

55 Yellow, the color we most often associate with sunshine, is found throughout nature and the man-made world as a color that commands attention; indeed, it is one of the easiest colors
60 to see. This highly visible shade is found on everything from school buses to traffic signs and pens used to highlight important information in a text. The color is also used to caution people; soccer players, for example, are shown yellow as a
65 reminder to behave. It can be used as a stimulant[3] as well: in a number of studies, yellow has been found to help children focus on their work and do better in school.

BLUE

70 Blue, the color of sky and sea, has long been associated in many cultures with water, holy or religious objects, and protection against evil. Over the years, darker shades of the color have also come to represent calm, stability, and power. Dark
75 blue, for example, is the color of the business suit or police uniform; it tells others, "I am in control" or "You can trust me." In other cultures, blue has been associated with sadness. It's common in English, for example, when feeling sad or
80 depressed, to talk about "feeling blue," while in Iran, blue is the color of mourning, worn when a person dies.

Like pink, blue has a neutral, calming effect on people. Rooms painted blue help people to relax
85 or sleep. (Sleeping pills are often colored blue to suggest exactly this idea.) The color also seems to inhibit hunger. Blue food is rarely seen in nature, and when it is, such food is usually no longer healthy to consume (with the exception of certain
90 fruits like blueberries). Thus, eating off blue plates may reduce one's hunger. So if you're planning to lose weight, try adding a blue light to your refrigerator—it will make the food inside look less appetizing. It's just one more example of the
95 power that color can hold over us.

[3] A **stimulant** is something that increases your heart rate and causes you to be more active.

▲ Popular with European painters for three centuries, "mummy" was a rich brown color made by grinding the remains of Egyptian mummies.

▲ Legend attributes the color purple to a dye extracted from a kind of shellfish. In the past, 30 g (one ounce) of purple dye for royal clothes required tens of thousands of the creatures. Today, dyeing with shellfish is still done in Oaxaca, Mexico.

☐ Reading Comprehension

A. Multiple Choice. Choose the best answer for each question.

Gist **1.** What is this reading mainly about?
    a. how color influences our lives
    b. the sources of color
    c. how views of color have changed
    d. how color can have a calming effect

Detail **2.** The first non-natural colors were produced _____.
    a. in the 19th century
    b. in the 20th century
    c. only recently
    d. centuries ago

Detail **3.** According to the passage, which color causes the heart rate to increase?
    a. black   c. blue
    b. yellow   d. pink

Detail **4.** Which color has been used to help children study better?
    a. red   c. blue
    b. yellow   d. pink

Reference **5.** In line 86, *this idea* refers to _____.
    a. inhibiting hunger   c. relaxation
    b. blue food   d. painting rooms

Critical Thinking

What evidence does the author provide for the "power that color can hold over us"? Do you agree with the author that color has a powerful effect on people?

B. Completion. According to the passage, which color (red, blue, or yellow):

a. is most easily seen?   _____
b. is associated with mourning in Iran?   _____
c. can cause you to be less hungry?   _____
d. represents success in some cultures?   _____
e. has a calming effect?   _____
f. creates trust?   _____

◻ Vocabulary Practice

A. Completion. Complete the information with the correct form of words from the box. One word is extra.

| bold | caution | extract | neutral | highlight | inhibition |

One of the **1.** _____ of the year in India is *Holi*, also known as "The Festival of Colors." The annual event, which takes place on the day after the full moon in late February or early March, represents the end of winter, and has great significance for Hindus. It is celebrated by lighting bonfires and throwing colored powder and water on friends and family.

Days before the start of the festival, the markets are filled with **2.** _____ colors of all shades, from bright red to the deepest blue. Many families create their own colors at home, often using dyes **3.** _____ from flowers such as *tesu* and *palash*. On the day of the festival, children and adults alike put aside their **4.** _____ and enjoy throwing paint at each other while celebrating the start of spring.

The Holi festival is a popular event with both locals and visitors. However, a note of **5.** _____: Don't wear your best clothes. It's likely they'll be covered with paint by the time you return home!

▲ Powder mixed with water rains on women at a Holi festival in Uttar Pradesh, India.

B. Definitions. Complete the sentences with the correct form of words from the box. One word is extra.

| aggressive | bold | depressed | neutral | package | passive |

1. If you are _____ about something, you feel neither strongly for or against it.
2. If you are _____, you are sad and feel that you cannot enjoy anything.
3. A(n) _____ is a small bag, box, or envelope in which a quantity of something is sold.
4. A(n) _____ person or animal behaves angrily or violently toward others.
5. A(n) _____ person does not take action, but instead lets things happen to them.

Usage

We stress the second syllable of the verb ex**tract**, but the first syllable of the noun, **ex**tract. Other examples are con**trast** (v.) vs. **con**trast (n.); re**cord** (v.) vs. **rec**ord (n.); pro**duce** (v.) vs. **pro**duce (n.); trans**fer** (v.) vs. **trans**fer (n.); im**port**/ex**port** (v.) vs. **im**port/**ex**port (n.).

Master of Color

Dr. Paul Gachet, the subject of this painting, took care of van Gogh during his final months. He is shown staring into space with a sad expression. "Sad but gentle, yet clear and intelligent," wrote van Gogh, "that is how many **portraits** ought to be done."

Like much of van Gogh's work, the painting takes place in a humble **setting**: Gachet is shown indoors, leaning against a simple table.

◀ Portrait of Dr. Gachet

There are two versions of this picture by Vincent van Gogh. Both are widely acknowledged as **masterpieces**. The first version was sold in 1897 for 300 francs. Nearly a century later, it sold for the highest price ever for a painting. The second version (shown here), easily differentiated by its brighter colors, is exhibited in the Orsay Museum in Paris. The location of the first version is currently unknown.

Many of van Gogh's later works followed the basic **principles** of the Impressionist movement, which emphasized movement, light, and unusual visual perspectives. Van Gogh's **techniques** included use of quick, visible brush strokes and bold, bright colors.

☐ Before You Read

A. Completion. Read the information above. Then complete the sentences below using the correct form of the words in **blue**.

1. The _____ of a theory or movement are its basic rules or laws.
2. An artist's _____ are the particular methods that he or she uses.
3. A _____ is a painting, drawing, or photograph of a particular person.
4. The _____ of a painting is the place or type of surroundings in which it takes place.
5. A _____ is an extremely good painting or other work of art.

B. Scan. *Portrait of Dr. Gachet* became the world's most expensive painting in 1990. How much did it sell for? Who bought it? Scan the passage to find out.

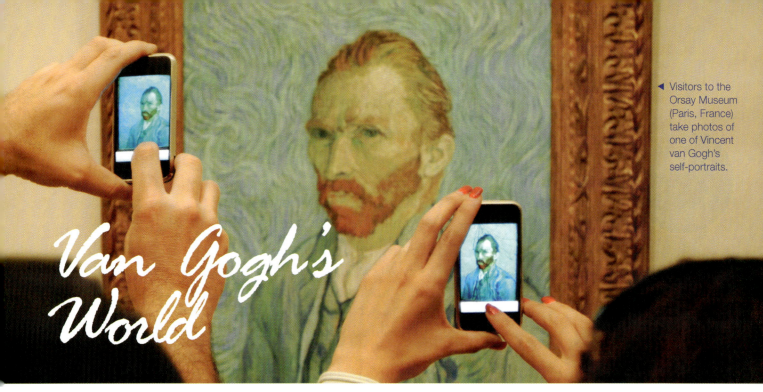

Van Gogh's World

1   Starry nights and sunflowers, self-portraits and café settings—all painted in bold, intense colors. Today, people around the world immediately recognize these as the work of
5   Vincent van Gogh, the Dutch painter. Probably no other artist, at any time in any culture, has achieved such popularity. But who was this man exactly, and why, even today, do his art and life have such an ability to move us?

An artist is born

10 Vincent van Gogh was born on March 30, 1853, in a small village in southern Holland. As a child, he was serious and sensitive. He loved to draw, and his work showed talent, but
15 no one encouraged him to become an artist. Instead, his father thought he should take a "sensible" job—something like a salesclerk or carpenter. As a young adult, he wandered from job to job with little success and very little
20 money, becoming more depressed with each failure.

In March 1880, however, just before his 27th birthday, something changed inside van Gogh. He realized that he was meant to be a painter,
25 and he began to study art, receiving a subsidy from his brother Theo, which helped him to live.

Discovering color

In 1886, van Gogh moved from Holland to Paris, hoping to learn more about color techniques
30 being used by Impressionist artists there. Instead of grays and browns, his work began to emphasize blue and red, and then yellow and orange. Soon he began to see life differently: Go slow. Stop thinking. Look around. You'll see
35 something beautiful if you open yourself. These were the principles that guided his art. With his innovative color combinations, van Gogh wanted to show his viewers how to better appreciate a flower, the night sky, or a person's face.

Descent into madness

40 Few who lived in van Gogh's time appreciated his work, however. Many laughed when they saw his paintings, which hurt the sensitive artist terribly. In February 1888, he moved away
45 from Paris to Arles, a town in southern France. Often he could not eat or sleep, and stayed up into the early morning hours painting.

Days passed, and he spoke to no one. Following an argument with fellow artist Paul
50 Gauguin, van Gogh took a razor and cut off his own earlobe.[1] He never explained why, but by now, many were convinced that van Gogh was crazy, and indeed, his mental health started to decline. He began to have attacks during which

he would hear strange sounds and think
people were trying to hurt him. In the spring
of 1889, he was sent to a mental hospital in
St. Remy, a town near Arles.

What exactly was van Gogh suffering from?
No one knows for sure, but some now think
it may have been a form of manic depression.[2]
Whatever his condition, van Gogh's illness
both inhibited and inspired his creativity.
When his attacks came, he could not paint.
But during his periods of calm, he was able to
complete more than a hundred masterpieces,
including the classic *The Starry Night*.
"Working on my pictures," he wrote,
"is almost a necessity for my recovery."

Final days

Following his release from hospital in May
1890, van Gogh took a room in a town just
north of Paris. For the 70 days that he lived
there, he produced, on average, a painting a
day. Until his death, however, he was unable
to sell a single one; today those paintings
would be worth more than a billion
U.S. dollars.

It was at this time that van Gogh either
borrowed or stole a gun. On the afternoon
of July 27, 1890, he went out to the country
and shot himself in the stomach. Two days
later, Vincent van Gogh died at age 37.

▲ *The Starry Night*, June 1889

What caused him to take his own life—his
lack of financial success, mental illness, his
loneliness? The question, like so many others
in van Gogh's life, remains unanswered.

Van Gogh's legacy

Over a century after his death, van Gogh still
remains extremely popular. His story—of a
man who resisted materialism[3] and greed,
who was alone and unappreciated—gives
people something they need. We find pieces
of ourselves in him. This may also explain the
high prices paid for van Gogh's work. His
Portrait of Dr. Gachet sold in 1990 for more
than $80 million to a Japanese businessman,
breaking the world record for art pieces. Many
of his other works have also sold for millions.

Of course, people are buying great art when
they purchase one of van Gogh's paintings. But
they are also buying a piece of his story, which,
like his work, will live on forever.

[1] Your **earlobe** is the soft part at the bottom of your ear.

[2] **Manic depression** is a medical condition in which someone
sometimes feels excited and confident and at other times very
depressed.

[3] **Materialism** is attaching a lot of importance to money and having a lot
of things.

◄ Showing a view that inspired van Gogh, a window lights
an art room in the mental hospital at St. Remy.

□ Reading Comprehension

A. Multiple Choice. Choose the best answer for each question.

Detail **1.** Which statement is NOT true about van Gogh's youth?
   a. He grew up in Holland.
   b. He was born in a small village.
   c. His parents encouraged his artistic talent.
   d. He tried several jobs but was unsuccessful.

Purpose **2.** What is the purpose of paragraph 3 (starting line 22)?
   a. to advise when van Gogh was born
   b. to describe how van Gogh became a painter
   c. to show that van Gogh was a troubled man
   d. to show how van Gogh survived on his own

Main idea **3.** What is the main idea in paragraph 4 (starting line 28)?
   a. Van Gogh was unhappy working with painters in Holland.
   b. Van Gogh's move to Paris changed his attitude toward art.
   c. Van Gogh was less successful than other Impressionist painters.
   d. Van Gogh's paintings of flowers were very popular in Paris.

Vocabulary **4.** In line 72, the word *took* is closest in meaning to _____.
   a. left   c. stole from
   b. moved into   d. sold

Detail **5.** What is NOT suggested as a possible motive for van Gogh's suicide?
   a. lack of financial success   c. a failed relationship
   b. mental illness   d. loneliness

> ### Critical Thinking
>
> The author says that we can find pieces of ourselves in van Gogh. Do you agree? In what way can you relate to van Gogh?

B. Sequencing. Number the events in van Gogh's life in the order in which they occured (**1–5**).

___ shows artistic talent in his hometown Zundert **(a)**, but receives little encouragement

___ produces a painting a day for just over two months in Auvers **(b)**, near Paris

___ studies the techniques of Impressionist painters in Paris **(c)** and changes his use of colors

___ spends hours painting in the fields of Arles **(d)**; argues with fellow painter Paul Gauguin

___ recovers from depression in a hospital in St. Remy **(e)**; paints *The Starry Night*

Vocabulary Practice

A. Completion. Complete the information with the correct form of words from the box. One word is extra.

appreciation	classic	subsidize	innovative	resist	wander

Many Impressionist painters greatly admired the woodblock[1] prints of Japanese artists such as Hokusai and Hiroshige. The techniques of these woodblock artists, such as the use of strong black lines and uniform shades of color, were new, exciting, and **1.** _____. However, Western artists who **2.** _____ the movement toward Impressionism felt these methods were "vulgar."[2] Instead, they advocated a return to a more **3.** _____ view of art and the use of more traditional techniques.

Van Gogh especially **4.** _____ the work of Japanese woodblock artists. During the time he spent **5.** _____ in the fields near Arles, he felt a close relationship with Japanese art and culture, and even shaved his head to "look like a Japanese monk." From Arles, he wrote to his sister: "Here I need no Japanese woodblock prints, because I am here in Japan."

[1] **Woodblock** printing involves carving an image into a piece of wood, which is then inked and stamped onto a page.
[2] If you describe something as **vulgar**, you think it is in bad taste, or of poor artistic quality.

▲ In 1887, van Gogh's admiration for Japanese art forms led him to paint copies of two famous woodblock designs, including Hiroshige's *Bridge in the Rain*.

B. Words in Context. Complete each sentence with the best answer.

1. If you describe someone as greedy, you mean they want to have _____ of something.
   a. more   b. less

2. When you recover from an illness or injury, you become _____.
   a. well again   b. more sick.

3. If a decision is sensible, it usually means it is based on _____.
   a. emotion   b. reason

4. If you are sensitive to other people's needs or feelings, you _____.
   a. show understanding of them   b. are not aware of them

5. If a government, authority, or person subsidizes something, they _____ of it.
   a. pay part of the cost   b. take ownership

Word Link

The word root **sen(s)** means feeling or being aware, e.g., **sens**ation, **sens**itive, **sens**eless, **sens**ible, **sens**ory, re**sent**, con**sent**.

Graffiti on a wall in Barcelona, Spain.

Urban Art

A. Preview. Read the paragraph below and use the correct form of words in **blue** to complete the sentences.

Urban art—sometimes referred to as "street art"—is a style of art that relates to cities and city life. One **distinctive** form of urban art is **graffiti** art. Art **gallery** owner Chris Murray believes that graffiti art of an important step in the evolution of pop art, an art style that **emerged** in the mid-20th century. Pop art borrows heavily from popular mass culture, such as comic books, advertising, and everyday items, and has brought a new **dimension** to modern art.

Washington, D.C.

1. _____ means belonging to or relating to a city or town.

2. Something that is _____ has a special quality that is easily recognizable.

3. A(n) _____ is a place where people go to look at works of art.

4. When an organization or movement _____, it comes into existence.

5. A(n) _____ of something is a particular aspect of it.

6. _____ is words or pictures that are written or drawn in public places.

B. Summarize. Watch the video, *Urban Art*. Then complete the summary below using the correct form of words from the box. One word is extra.

appreciate	bold	caution	classical	highlight
extract	innovation	resist	wander	package

Urban art is all about **1.** _____—creating something new that has not been seen or heard before. Two new and exciting urban artists in the U.S. are Nick Posada and Jafar Barron.

If you **2.** _____ down a Washington D.C. train tunnel known as the "Wall of Fame," you'll discover the strong, **3.** _____ colors of urban graffiti artists such as Nick Posada. Although the Wall is open to anyone who wants to paint, Posada **4.** _____ that people should follow certain rules if they want to be real graffiti artists.

Posada's art has become one of the **5.** _____ of the Govinda Gallery, where people can **6.** _____ graffiti art in a more traditional setting. Graffiti artists used to be vilified,[1] claims gallery owner Chris Murray, but "now they're being enjoyed, and that's a good thing."

For musician Jafar Barron, urban art means creating a new kind of sound. He mixes **7.** _____ from the rap and hip-hop music of his own generation with the more traditional, **8.** _____ forms of jazz that he learned from his parents. In this way he creates a new kind of musical **9.** _____ that combines the best of both worlds.

[1] If you are **vilified** by someone, they say or write unpleasant things about you.

C. Think About It.

1. Do you think that street graffiti can be called art?

2. What do you think makes someone artistic? Are people born with artistic talent, or can they learn it?

To learn more about art and color, visit elt.heinle.com/explorer

UNIT 12

Medical Challenges

WARM UP

Discuss these questions with a partner.

1. What are some major health concerns for people in your country?

2. What do you think will be some important medical advances in the next 10 years? 100 years?

3. What are some diseases that have been in the news recently? What do you know about them?

▲ Doctors work at a medical laboratory in Shanghai, China.

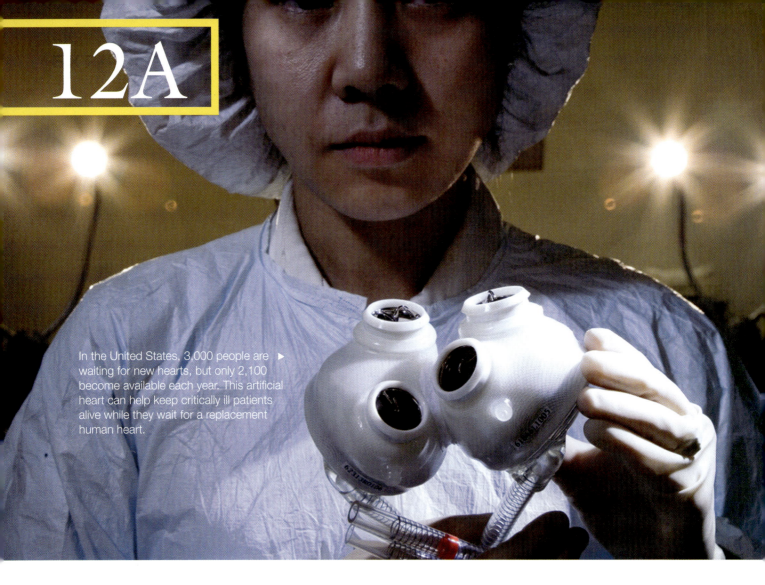

In the United States, 3,000 people are ▶ waiting for new hearts, but only 2,100 become available each year. This artificial heart can help keep critically ill patients alive while they wait for a replacement human heart.

Modern Medicine

▢ Before You Read

A. Discussion. Look at the photo and caption above and discuss the questions below.

1. What are the most serious health problems facing the world today?
2. What major advances in medicine have there been in the past two decades?

B. Skim for the Main Idea. On the next page, look at the title, photos, and captions. What do you think this reading is mainly about? Circle **a**, **b**, or **c**. Then read the passage to check your answer.

a. A new technology involving extremely small particles
b. A new technology taken from animals
c. A new technology that can prevent the spread of killer viruses

Injected into a healthy mouse, nanoparticles of cadmium ▶ selenide glow under ultraviolet light. Such quantum dots can enter cancers and help surgeons remove sick cells without harming healthy ones.

A Cure for Cancer?

1   In the 1966 science-fiction film *The Fantastic Voyage*, a team of scientists and doctors are shrunk to microscopic[1] size and injected[2] into the body of an injured man to save his life. The
5   tiny crew travels through the body's dangerous environment to locate and repair the damaged part of the man's body. Eventually, the group manages to complete their task and the man awakens, fully cured.

10 Such an idea, while fun, sounds extraordinary to many. But what if it were possible to cure a disease like cancer, using tiny particles[3] injected into a person—particles that would not only find the cancer, but also destroy it without
15 harming anything else in the body? Although it may seem like science fiction, tools like this are now being developed and may, in fact, become common in the near future—thanks to research currently being done in the field of
20 nanotechnology.

The main thing to know about nanotechnology is that it's small—really small. The prefix "nano" refers to a nanometer, which is one-billionth of a meter. How small
25 is that exactly? A comma on a page of a book or magazine, for instance, may be more than half a million nanometers wide. Understanding the "science of small" may eventually allow doctors to diagnose and cure illnesses like
30 heart disease and cancer early, before they can do extensive damage to the body.

Researcher Ted Sargent, a leader in the field of nanotechnology, describes how using quantum dots[4]—particles that are a few nanometers in
35 size—will help diagnose disease. The particles, Sargent explains, shine brightly when exposed to UV light. These particles can be inserted into the body and programmed to bond only to a certain type of cell—a particular cancer
40 cell, for example. Doctors can then use a camera and look for the colored particles, which will help them determine where cancer cells are growing in a person's body.

◀ Millions of hairs on a gecko's toes are split into hundreds of tips, each 200 nanometers wide. The faint attraction between each of these tips and a surface, multiplied millions of times, allows a gecko to hold on upside-down to glass.

A nanometer is ▶ one-billionth of a meter. That's like comparing the size of a marble to the size of Earth.

[1] If something is **microscopic**, it is so small you cannot see it with your eyes alone.
[2] If you **inject** something into your body, you put it into your body using a needle.
[3] A **particle** is a very small piece of something.
[4] A **dot** is a very small round mark, like a period (.)

Using this technology, it will be possible
45 to detect cancer at a stage when there are
perhaps only a thousand bad cells. Compare
this to what happens today: doctors can
diagnose cancer only after the dangerous
cells have multiplied into the millions
50 and developed into a tumor. One of the
advantages of detecting and treating cancer at
an early stage is that the cells are less likely to
become resistant to drug treatment. In later
stages, cancer cells often change and adapt to
55 certain drugs so rapidly that many medicines
become ineffective.

Once a certain type of cancer is detected,
nanotechnology will also radically improve
the way it is treated. Right now, most cancer
60 treatments kill not only the cancerous cells
but the healthy ones as well, causing a
number of side effects in people, such as hair
loss, nausea, and intense pain. Nanoparticles,
on the other hand, will allow doctors to attack
65 cancerous tumors without disturbing healthy
cells. The goal will be to deliver cancer-
killing drugs, carried via the nanoparticles,
to the bad cells only. A second method will
be to destroy cancer cells (identified by
70 nanoparticles) using laser rays. Ultimately,
technologies like this will allow doctors to
deliver cancer treatment earlier, faster, and
more thoroughly, with fewer side effects.

Unfortunately, even though nanoparticles
75 have great medical potential, there are serious
concerns that these same materials could have
negative environmental and health effects.
In recent studies, fish exposed to water
containing large amounts of nanoparticles
80 suffered brain damage. And people are at
risk as well. After exposing lab-grown human
cells to water containing large amounts of
nanoparticles, researchers found that half the
human cells died.

85 Because nanotechnology is so potentially
useful, many scientists don't think research
into its many uses should be stopped; learning
more about nanotechnology should remain

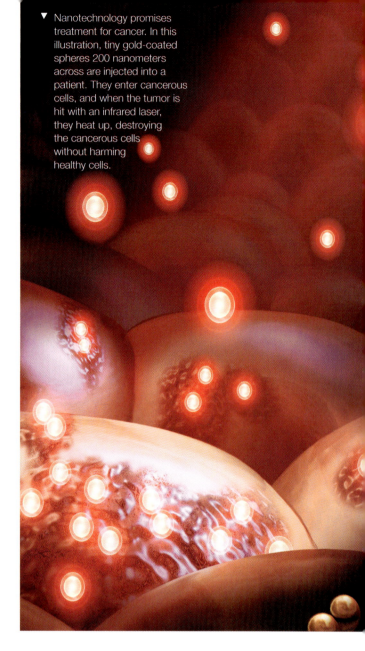

▼ Nanotechnology promises treatment for cancer. In this illustration, tiny gold-coated spheres 200 nanometers across are injected into a patient. They enter cancerous cells, and when the tumor is hit with an infrared laser, they heat up, destroying the cancerous cells without harming healthy cells.

a priority. But scientists do believe that
90 governments should allocate more money for
safety-related studies—to make sure that large
concentrations of nanoparticles do not get
into our food and water supplies and cause
serious problems.

95 Meanwhile, research into the uses of
nanotechnology in health and many other fields
continues. "What's amazing is how quickly this
is evolving," says chemist Vicki Colvin. "Even
ten years ago, a lot of these applications would
100 have seemed pretty unrealistic." Perhaps that
old movie, *The Fantastic Voyage*, isn't so hard to
believe after all.

☐ Reading Comprehension

A. Multiple Choice. Choose the best answer for each question.

Gist

1. What is this reading mainly about?
a. a fantastic voyage
b. how nanotechnology can be used in medical science
c. the dangers of nanotechnology
d. detecting cancer

Vocabulary

2. In line 42, the word *determine* could be replaced by _____.
a. discover   c. miss
b. report   d. hide

Detail

3. Exposing human cells to large amounts of nanoparticles _____.
a. has no effect   c. is how cancer can be treated
b. should remain a priority   d. can result in 50% cell death

Main Idea

4. What is the main idea of the second last paragraph (from line 85)?
a. Nanotechnology has not proved useful and scientists want research halted.
b. Scientists want to see research into nanotechnology continue, but carefully.
c. Nanotechnology is so useful that scientists refuse to stop researching.
d. Many scientists think that nanotechnology is too dangerous to be permitted.

Critical Thinking

Do you think research into nanotechnology should continue? Why, or why not?

Paraphrase

5. On line 98, Vicki Colvin says "Even ten years ago, a lot of these applications would have seemed pretty unrealistic." What does she mean?
a. Nanotechnology has evolved a lot in the last decade.
b. Ten years ago, nanotechnology applications weren't very realistic.
c. Some of these applications are ten years old.
d. In ten years, there have been few realistic applications for nanotechnology.

B. True or False. Which of these statements are true (**T**) and which are false (**F**)?

1. A nanometer is the size of a comma.   **T F**

2. Doctors use X-rays to see colored quantum dots.   **T F**

3. Nanotechnology may make diagnosis of cancer possible earlier.   **T F**

4. Resistance to drugs is a problem in the treatment of cancer today. **T F**

5. With nanotechnology, doctors can avoid destroying healthy cells. **T F**

6. Nanotechnology is completely safe for humans.   **T F**

Vocabulary Practice

A. Completion. Complete the information with the correct form of words from the box. One word is extra.

allocate	bond	insert	laser	thorough
meanwhile	multiply	priority	radical	

Cancer is one of the biggest killers in the world today, and finding ways to prevent and cure it is a medical **1.** _____. Every year, governments and private companies **2.** _____ huge amounts of money to cancer treatment. Here are two recent developments:

The new science of nanotechnology is receiving a lot of attention, both because it is revolutionary, and also because there have been great claims for its potential. For example, some scientists claim that it will be possible for doctors to **3.** _____ nanoparticles into a patient's body to find and attack cancer cells before these unhealthy cells **4.** _____, group together, and become a tumor.[1]

5. _____, a **6.** _____ new way to detect cancer uses dogs. It works on the fact that many animals' sense of smell is much better than that of a human. Dogs, because of their unique **7.** _____ with that of a human, are the obvious choice of animal for this. The method hasn't been **8.** _____ tested yet, but early studies have found that dogs can identify a person who has cancer by sniffing either sores on the skin, or the person's breath.

[1] A **tumor** is a mass of diseased or abnormal cells in a human or animal body.

B. Definitions. Complete the definitions using the words in the box. One word is extra.

meanwhile	priority	multiply	laser	extensive	allocate

1. the most important thing _____
2. give to someone for use for a particular purpose _____
3. covering a wide range or area _____
4. a narrow beam of concentrated light made by a special machine _____
5. while a particular thing is happening _____

Word Link

The prefix **multi–** means *many*, e.g., **multi**colored, **multi**ply, **multi**media, **multi**national.

Skin cancer can be a particular problem for light-skinned people ▶ living in environments with a lot of sunlight. 84-year-old Australian beach lifesaver Don Bennewith has had over 600 skin cancers removed.

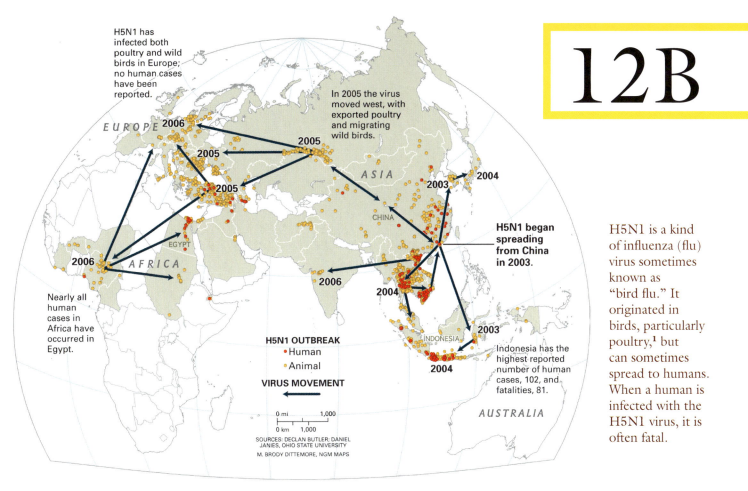

H5N1 has infected both poultry and wild birds in Europe; no human cases have been reported.

In 2005 the virus moved west, with exported poultry and migrating wild birds.

EUROPE **2006**

2005

2005

2005

2005

ASIA

2003

2004

CHINA

H5N1 began spreading from China in 2003.

EGYPT

AFRICA

2006

2006

2004

2003

Nearly all human cases in Africa have occurred in Egypt.

INDONESIA

2004

Indonesia has the highest reported number of human cases, 102, and fatalities, 81.

AUSTRALIA

H5N1 OUTBREAK
- Human
- Animal

VIRUS MOVEMENT

0 mi   1,000
0 km   1,000

SOURCES: DECLAN BUTLER; DANIEL JANIES, OHIO STATE UNIVERSITY
M. BRODY DITTEMORE, NGM MAPS

H5N1 is a kind of influenza (flu) virus sometimes known as "bird flu." It originated in birds, particularly poultry,[1] but can sometimes spread to humans. When a human is infected with the H5N1 virus, it is often fatal.

Virus Hunters

☐ Before You Read

A. Discussion. Look at the map showing the spread of the H5N1 virus. Then answer the questions.

1. Where did the first cases of H5N1 occur?
2. In which continent were there the most human cases of H5N1?
3. Where are there cases of H5N1 in birds, but not in humans?

B. Predict. The passage on pages 166–167 is about zoonotic diseases. What do you think *zoonotic* means? Check (✔) your guess. Then read the passage to check your ideas.

❏ Diseases that spread very rapidly
❏ Diseases that spread from animals to humans
❏ Diseases that cannot be treated
❏ Diseases that affect the lungs

[1] **Poultry** includes birds like chickens and ducks that are kept for their eggs and meat.

DEADLY CONTACT

1 In September 1994, a violent disease erupted among a group of racehorses in a small town in Australia. The first victim was a
5 female horse that was last seen eating grass beneath a fruit tree. One of her caretakers noticed that the horse didn't appear to be well, and brought the
10 animal back to her stable[1] for observation. Within hours, the horse's health declined rapidly. Three people worked to save the animal—the horse's trainer, an assistant, and a veterinarian.[2]
15 Nevertheless, the horse died two days later, leaving the cause of her death uncertain. Had she been bitten by a snake, or eaten something poisonous?

Within two weeks, most of the other horses in
20 the stable became ill as well. All had high fevers, difficulty breathing, facial swelling, and blood coming from their noses and mouths. Despite efforts by the veterinarian, 12 more animals died. Meanwhile, the trainer and his assistant
25 also became ill, and within days, the trainer was dead too. Laboratory analysis finally discovered the root of the problem: the horses and men had been infected by a previously unknown virus, which doctors eventually labeled *Hendra*.
30 This virus had originated in bats that lived in the tree where the first horse had been eating grass. The virus passed from the bats to the horse, which then transmitted the virus to other horses and to people—with disastrous results.

35 Infectious disease is all around us. Disease-causing agents, such as viruses, usually have specific targets. Some viruses only affect

A young rhesus macaque monkey is tested to see whether he carries human diseases, or diseases that could be passed to humans.

humans. Other viruses live in or affect only animals. Problems start when animal viruses are
40 able to infect people as well, a process known as zoonosis. When an animal virus passes to a human, the results can be deadly. Often, our immune systems are not accustomed to these viruses, and are unable to stop them before
45 they harm us.

In the last three decades, more than 30 zoonotic diseases—the kind that live only in animals but somehow pass to people—have emerged around the globe. HIV is an example;
50 it evolved from a virus originally carried by African monkeys, and later chimps. Today, conservative estimates suggest that HIV has infected more than 40 million people, though this number may be higher. SARS, a type of
55 flu which jumped from chickens to humans, is another type of zoonotic disease.

Hendra survivor Ray Unwin still suffers from the aftereffects of the disease. "I can't get the tiredness out of my body," he says.

[1] A **stable** is a building where horses are kept.
[2] A **veterinarian** is an animal doctor.

But how do these viruses—like Hendra, SARS, and HIV—pass from animals to humans? Contact is crucial. Human destruction of animal habitats,[3] for example, is forcing wild animals to move closer to the places people live—putting humans at risk for exposure to animal viruses. The closer humans are to animals, the greater the risk of being bitten, scratched, or exposed to animal waste, which can enable a virus to pass from an animal to a human. Raising animals (for example, on a farm) or keeping certain kinds of wild animals (like monkeys) as pets increases the risk of exposure. Eating animals that are diseased can also result in a virus being transmitted.

The factor that is probably most responsible for the spread of zoonotic diseases worldwide is international travel. In 1999, for example, a deadly disease—one that had never been seen before in the Western Hemisphere—appeared in the United States. There were several incidences that year of both birds and people becoming sick and dying in New York City, and doctors couldn't explain why. Subsequently, they discovered that the deaths had been caused by the same thing: the West Nile virus, found typically in birds and transmitted by mosquitoes that live in parts of northern Africa. Somehow, this virus—

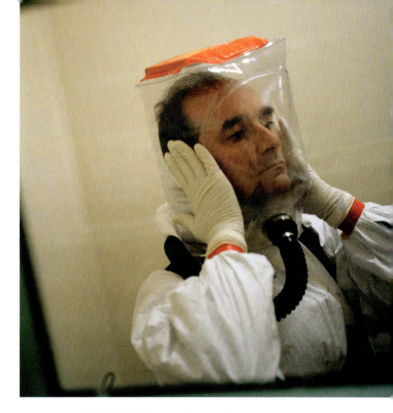

▲ Scientist Eric Leroy studies another very serious disease: Ebola. At his lab in Gabon, his research points to fruit bats as carriers of the disease.

probably carried by an infected mosquito or bird on a plane or ship—arrived in the U.S. Now, birds and mosquitoes native to North America are carriers of this virus as well.

West Nile cannot be transmitted from person to person. But zoonotic diseases, which can be spread by a handshake or sneeze, create medical emergencies: they can potentially circle the world and kill millions of people before science can find a way to control them.

Today, researchers are working to create vaccines for many of these zoonotic diseases in the hope of controlling their impact on humans. Other specialists are trying to make communities more aware of disease prevention and treatment, and to help people understand that we are all—humans, animals, and insects—in this together.

[3] An animal's or plant's **habitat** is the natural environment where it normally lives and grows.

◄ Hendra was eventually traced to fruit bats, like this little red flying fox, living in a nearby tree.

Reading Comprehension

A. Multiple Choice. Choose the best answer for each question.

Gist
1. What is this reading mainly about?
- a. the unexplained deaths of horses
- b. the symptoms of zoonotic diseases
- c. the effect of international travel on the spread of disease
- d. the rise in the spread of viruses from animals to humans

Reference
2. In line 76, *a deadly disease* refers to _____.
- a. Hendra
- b. Ebola
- c. West Nile Virus
- d. HIV

Inference
3. Which of the following is at the greatest risk of contracting a zoonotic disease?
- a. a nurse
- b. a teacher
- c. a chicken farmer
- d. a zookeeper

Detail
4. How is it thought that the West Nile virus found its way into the United States?
- a. An infected passenger traveled from Africa to the U.S.
- b. An infected African doctor came to work in a U.S hospital.
- c. A U.S. citizen picked up the virus while in Africa.
- d. An infected mosquito or bird was transported from Africa to the U.S.

Detail
5. Which virus is not mentioned in the passage as being zoonotic?
- a. SARS
- b. HIV
- c. the common cold
- d. Hendra

B. Completion. Complete the notes below with words from the passage. Use no more than two words for each gap.

Critical Thinking

What do you think people or governments can do to prevent zoonotic diseases spreading to humans?

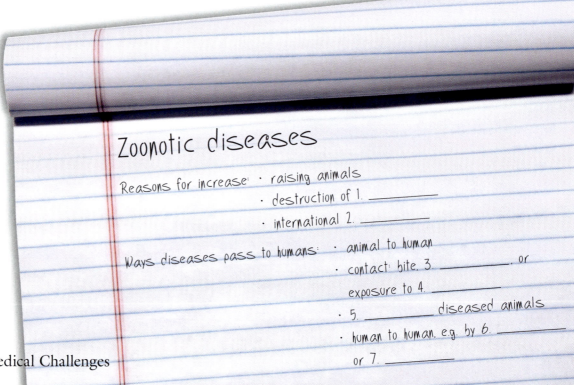

Zoonotic diseases

Reasons for increase:
- raising animals
- destruction of 1. _____
- international 2. _____

Ways diseases pass to humans:
- animal to human contact: bite. 3. _____. or exposure to 4. _____
- 5. _____ diseased animals
- human to human. e.g. by 6. _____ or 7. _____

Vocabulary Practice

A. Completion. Complete the paragraph with the correct form of words from the box. Three words are extra.

accustom	conservative	emergency	fever	incidence
poisonous	root	swell	transmit	victim

Polio is a very serious disease, the **1.** _____ cause of which is a virus called *Poliovirus*. The virus is easily **2.** _____ to other humans through contact, especially in a humid or wet environment. It is particularly common in summer. One of the first symptoms of polio is a high **3.** _____, making it seem like ordinary 'flu. Later, **4.** _____ of polio may suffer from varying degrees of paralysis[1] affecting the arms and legs. In severe cases, the heart and lung muscles are also paralysed, causing death, unless **5.** _____ treatment is received.

In the first half of the 20th century it was one of the most feared of childhood diseases, affecting, at a(n) **6.** _____ estimate, tens of thousands of people a year. There was great pressure to create a vaccine,[2] and in the 1950s and 60s vaccines created by Jonas Salk and Albert Sabin become widely available. This managed to reduce the global **7.** _____ of polio from many hundreds of thousands a year to around a thousand. Polio vaccination programs are so effective that there is a possibility that—at some point in the future—the disease could be completely wiped out.

[1] **Paralysis** is the loss of the ability to move and feel in all or part of your body.

[2] A **vaccine** is a harmless form of a disease given to people to prevent them getting that disease.

▲ A child receives the polio vaccine as part of a vaccination program in Bangladesh.

Word Partnership

Use *emergency* with:
(*adj.*) **major** emergency, **medical** emergency, **minor** emergency;
(*n.*) **state of** emergency, emergency **care**, emergency **surgery**, emergency **vehicle**

B. Words in Context. Complete each sentence with the best answer.

1. If something is poisonous it is _____ to eat.
   a. safe
   b. dangerous

2. When something swells it becomes _____ in size.
   a. larger
   b. smaller

3. You are more likely to be accustomed to something you have had _____.
   a. for a long time
   b. for a short time

4. A conservative estimate of a number is probably _____ than the real number.
   a. higher
   b. lower

5. If you discuss something's incidence, you are concerned with _____.
   a. how old it is
   b. how often it happens

Paraguay Shaman

A. Preview. Read the definition of a *shaman* below. Are plants widely used for medicine in your culture? Do you know any examples?

> **sha • man** /ˈʃeɪmən/
> (*n.*) A **shaman** is a person who is believed by members of his/her tribe to have powers to heal sick people, or to remove evil spirits from them. Many shamans have extensive knowledge of traditional plant medicines.

▲ 65-year-old Victoriano is a tribal shaman in Cuyabeno, Ecuador.

B. Summarize. Watch the video, *Paraguay Shaman*. Then complete the summary below using the correct form of words from the box. One word is extra.

bond	emergency	extensive	fever	poisonous
root	meanwhile	multiply	priority	victim

The rainforests of Paraguay have a huge variety of plant species. Some are **1.** _____ as they contain chemicals that are dangerous for humans. Others, however, contain chemicals that are potential cures for illnesses. Some chemicals may even help malaria **2.** _____, or people with common **3.** _____ and colds.

Paraguay

Paraguay's renowned healers, called "shamans," have a deep knowledge of the parts of the plants of the forest, such as their leaves, flowers, and **4.** _____. Many shamans claim to have a special spiritual connection, or **5.** _____, with the forest. Researchers believe it should be a top **6.** _____ to record the shaman's **7.** _____ knowledge. Paraguay has one of the highest deforestation[1] rates in the world, so the knowledge must be recorded before the forest disappears.

Recording and analyzing Paraguayan plants for possible medical cures is urgent business. Some may even call it a(n) **8.** _____. Medicinal plants that were once healthy and **9.** _____ are now disappearing—and so too is the possibility of finding new medical cures.

[1] **Deforestation** is cutting down or destroying all the trees in an area.

C. Think About It.

1. If you were ill, would you be willing to try traditional plant medicines?

2. Do you think that plant-based cures or nanotechnology has the best chance of solving the world's medical problems? Why?

To learn more about medical challenges, visit elt.heinle.com/explorer

A. Crossword. Use the definitions below to complete the missing words.

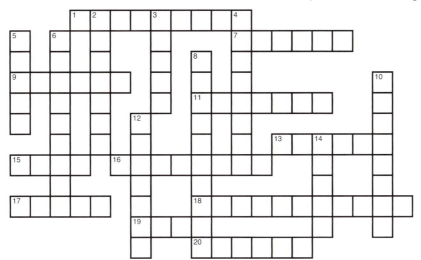

Across

1. to indicate and give emphasis to
7. to stand firm against or oppose
9. a person or thing that is hurt or killed by something or someone
11. not taking an active part
13. to _____ a skill, is to learn to do something very well
15. to join together (with something)
16. to give to a particular person, or for a particular purpose
17. excessive desire for something, such as food or money
18. to recognize or admit
19. the cause of something (usually bad)
20. something (natural or abstract) that exists and has its own identity

Down

2. to restrain or prevent
3. a device that produces a very narrow intense beam of light, which is used for cutting
4. to pass something, such as a message or disease, from one place or person to another
5. illness characterized by an abnormally high body temperature
6. frequency with which something (usually bad) occurs
8. to value (something/someone) highly; to be grateful for (something)
10. complete and careful
12. health, comfort, happiness (usually of a group of people)
14. to grow bigger

B. Notes Completion. Scan the information on pages 172–173 to complete the notes.

Field Notes

Site: Banks of the Seine

Location: Paris, France

Information:
- Highlights include the _____, which houses art from late 19th to early 20th centuries, and the Conciergerie, which was once a palace and then a _____
- Visitors shouldn't miss two famous churches: Notre Dame Cathedral and the smaller _____
- Oldest surviving bridge in Paris is the "New Bridge," which was built in _____.
- A popular place to eat _____ is the 50-year-old store called Berthillon
- The Eiffel Tower and New York's _____ were both designed by architect _____ Eiffel

Banks of the Seine

Sites: **Banks of the Seine**

Location: **Paris, France**

Category: **Cultural**

Status: **World Heritage Site since 1991**

Paris, France

For centuries, the heart of Paris has been the area surrounding its river, the Seine. The **banks** of the Seine contain so many places of historical importance that the entire central part of the city, totaling 365 **hectares** (900 acres), was made a World Heritage Site in 1991. Although it is possible to see the river's highlights in a single day, most tourists allocate at least a few days to wander along its banks, to fully appreciate the area's many attractions.

One of the city's highlights is the chance to explore its extensive collection of art treasures. The Louvre, which began as a public museum in 1793, contains some of the world's most famous works of art, such as Leonardo da Vinci's classic *Mona Lisa*. The Orsay Museum houses sculptures and paintings from 1848 to 1914, including masterpieces by Vincent van Gogh. Visitors in search of more modern, abstract art should head to the Pompidou Center, famous not just for its innovative exhibits but also for its radical architecture.

Sainte-Chapelle

Although its big sister Notre Dame is more famous, visitors should not dismiss the more humble 13th-century church known as Sainte-Chapelle. Once accustomed to the dark inside the church, visitors can appreciate a fascinating series of 16 brightly colored painted windows, which together reveal up to 1,000 detailed scenes.

Conciergerie

Originally built as a luxurious royal palace, this 700-year-old building was later transformed into a prison, which was used to hold more than 2,700 prisoners during France's Reign of Terror (1793–94). The victims included France's Queen Marie Antoinette, who was later taken from the prison to be **executed**.

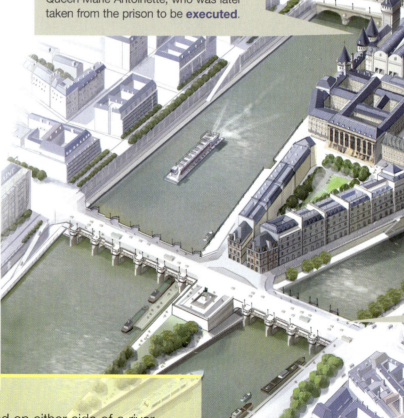

Glossary

banks: raised areas of land on either side of a river
cathedral: a large and important church
execute: to kill someone as punishment
hectare: an area of 10,000 square meters (2.471 acres)

Berthillon

On warm weekends, long lines of hungry sightseers wait outside this 50-year-old ice cream store. The secret to the store's success lies in the ingredients—fresh milk, chocolate from West Africa, and vanilla from Madagascar.

Notre Dame Cathedral

Constructed between 1163 and 1345, Notre Dame is wivvdely acknowledged as a magnificent accomplishment of European architecture. Today's visitors come to admire Notre Dame's astonishing painted windows, statues, bell towers, and the strange-looking gargoyles carved on the **cathedral** roof.

The Eiffel Tower

Today, it would be difficult to visualize the Paris skyline without its most distinctive landmark. But few people appreciated Gustave Eiffel's radical architecture when it was created in 1889, and 20 years later it was almost taken down. Fortunately, the tower survived and continues to delight visitors from around the world, particularly on special occasions when it is lit up in a spectacular laser show. Eiffel's other world-famous creation, the Statue of Liberty, was given to the U.S.A. and stands in New York City.

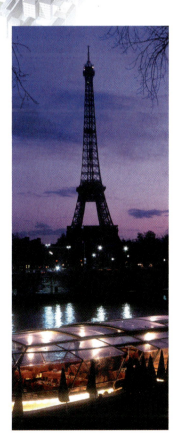

Pont Neuf

Despite its name (meaning "New Bridge"), Pont Neuf is actually the oldest bridge in Paris. It has been extensively restored and reinforced several times during its long history, most recently in 2007, the year of its 400th anniversary.

▲ The area comprising the islands of Ile de la City (foreground) and Ile Saint-Louis has been the historical center of Paris since settlers first arrived here more than 2,000 years ago.

Cultural Heritage

A Global View

In 1972, the United Nations Educational, Scientific, and Cultural Organization (UNESCO) established a definitive list of high priority heritage sites. Together, the 900 plus sites on the World Heritage list—unique landscapes, ecosystems, buildings, monuments, and cities—represent the natural and cultural heritage of the world.

The purpose of the World Heritage list is to encourage countries to identify, maintain, and preserve cultural and natural sites that are important to the heritage of humanity. UNESCO programs assist countries in the preservation of sites by supplying technical and professional training, and by allocating funds and providing emergency assistance to immediately threatened sites.

Approximately 75 percent of the places on the World Heritage list are cultural sites—masterpieces of human creative genius and surviving remains of unique cultures and civilizations. These precious cultural sites not only highlight outstanding examples of architecture and art, they enable us to trace the footsteps of humanity across the Earth and across time.

Mesa Verde National Park
Colorado, U.S.A.

More than 4,400 sites built by the Anasazi people, dating from the 6th to the 12th centuries, have been found in the steep cliffs of Montezuma County, Colorado. Although some Anasazi cliff houses were small and **primitive**, others were much bigger—the largest had more than 100 rooms.

Brasilia
Brazil

Brazil's capital city was visualized and designed in the 1950s by urban planner Lucio Costa and architect Oscar Niemeyer. Every element—from the residential and **administrative** districts (shaped like a bird in flight) to public buildings such as the city cathedral (pictured below)—is **sensitively** designed to be in harmony with the city's overall plan.

Word Link

We can add –ive to some words (mostly verbs) to create adjectives meaning "to have the quality of (something)," e.g., impress—*impressive*; create—*creative*; innovate—*innovative*.

Critical Thinking

Are there cultural sites in your country that you think should be preserved? How would you decide which sites receive the most funds?

Works of Antoni Gaudí
Barcelona, Spain

During his lifetime, the architect Antoni Gaudí (1852–1926) was criticized by **conservative** architects for being too radical. Today, his buildings, such as Sagrada Familia cathedral (pictured above), are a highlight for any visitor to Barcelona.

Historic Center of Florence
Tuscany, Italy

Florence became Italy's predominant economic and cultural center in the 15th and 16th centuries. Visitors to the city can appreciate masterworks such as Michelangelo's *David* (pictured left) and the Uffizi museum's **extensive** collection of classic paintings.

The Old City of Sana'a
Yemen

Located in a mountain valley at an altitude of 2,200 meters, the old city of Sana'a has been inhabited for more than 2,500 years. Close by the city is the impressive Imam palace, located on a high rock in Wadi Dhar (pictured below).

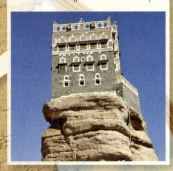

Rock-cut Churches of Lalibela
Amhara Region, Ethiopia

Each of these extraordinary cross-shaped churches was created from a single **massive** block of stone, in the ground or in the side of a hill. The 30-meter high church of St. George (pictured below), which dates from the 12th-century rule of King Lalibela, ranks as one of the greatest architectural accomplishments in Africa.

Borobudur Temple
Java, Indonesia

In 1814, explorers on the island of Java made an astonishing discovery: an isolated Buddhist temple, dating from the 8th and 9th centuries and hidden for centuries in the jungle. The vast temple area, comprising huge stone platforms and **distinctive** carvings and statues, has since been restored to its former magnificence. The reason why it was abandoned remains a mystery.

Sydney Opera House
Sydney, Australia

Designed by **innovative** Danish architect Jørn Utzon, the Sydney Opera House is an acknowledged masterpiece of 20th-century architecture, and has become one of the world's most famous landmarks.

A. Completion. Use words in **bold** from pages 174–175 to complete the passage.

The magnificent city of Angkor, a World Heritage Site in Cambodia, was the religious, cultural, and _____ center of the Khmer Empire from the 9th to the 15th centuries. Its most famous site is the 213-meter (699-foot) high temple Angkor Wat, which was constructed using _____ stone blocks. Today, its _____ shape can be seen everywhere in Cambodia from drink cans to paper money.

Archeologists recently studied the area using highly _____ radar that can detect small details in the landscape. They concluded that "even on a _____ estimate, greater Angkor . . . was the world's most _____ pre-industrial urban complex." The Khmer also had technology that was far from _____; their _____ system of irrigation, for example, was very advanced for its time.

B. Word Link. Several phrasal verbs are of the form **verb + "up"** (for example, tears or emotions can *well up*). Complete the passage using the correct form of the verbs in the box.

give	grow	pick	set	speed	swell	take	turn	well

Baby born two days after mother died

A British champion ice skater who died from a brain hemorrhage gave birth to a baby girl two days later. Jayne Soliman, 41, was 25 weeks pregnant[1] when she suddenly suffered severe bleeding inside her head, which caused part of her brain to _____ up. She was quickly taken to hospital but was pronounced dead at 8:00 p.m. Although the mother was dead, the doctors did not _____ up on the baby. They used steroids[2] to help _____ up the development of the child's lungs, and within 48 hours, on January 9, 2009, the baby was born by Cesarean section,[3] weighing just 0.95 kg (2 lb 1.5 oz).

Soliman's husband, Mahmoud, was at first not allowed to _____ up the baby because it was so weak. Lucine Phillips, who witnessed the birth, said that Mahmoud was filled with emotion: "It was just _____ up inside him. He took one look at his daughter and . . . said, 'That's my Jayney.'"

Jayne Soliman _____ up in the U.K. and later spent time in Dubai, where she taught skating and met her future husband. The couple eventually _____ up home in southern England. Soliman _____ up free skating professionally, and in 1989 became British champion and the seventh ranked free skater in the world. More than 300 people _____ up to Soliman's funeral, which was held at the Jamia mosque in Reading, England.

[1] If a woman is **pregnant**, she has a baby developing inside her.

[2] A **steroid** is a type of chemical substance found in your body.

[3] A **Cesarean section** is surgery performed to deliver a baby.

Target Vocabulary

Target Vocabulary

High Altitude Peoples

Narrator:

Even with the best equipment, mountain climbing can be hard work. In fact, at high altitudes, simply walking is more tiring than doing the same activity at sea level. That's because air automatically becomes thinner the higher you climb.

This means that a person takes in less oxygen with each breath. It's this lack of oxygen in the body that causes mountain sickness, or hypoxia. Now, researchers are studying three high-altitude peoples that may give us a better understanding of human evolution. Dr. Mark Aldenderfer of the University of Southern California has been studying how native Tibetans have adapted to their environment.

Dr. Mark Aldenderfer, Anthropologist:

"Tibetans deal with hypoxia apparently by breathing faster, in other words, obtaining more oxygen into their lungs and moving it through their systems much more rapidly."

Narrator:

On the other side of the world, native people of the South American Andes developed a different strategy for living in high mountain air.

Dr. Mark Aldenderfer:

"Andeans, on the other hand, how they seem to adjust to hypoxia is to have more hemoglobin in their blood. So, in other words, their blood, in one sense, you could say is thicker."

Narrator:

People in the highlands of Ethiopia have also adapted to high altitudes—but scientists still don't know exactly how. Ancient peoples were originally attracted to mountain heights by the prospect of good hunting, despite the lack of oxygen. At first, their survival could be attributed to human culture.

Dr. Mark Aldenderfer:

"You need controlled use of fire. You need to be able to make a fire, and you need to be able to use that fire to keep you warm, and if you move, you have to be able to take the fire with you."

Narrator:

Humans also needed clothes for survival—not just animal skins, but clothes that were warm enough to protect the wearer from the intense cold.

According to Dr. Aldenderfer, the first tools needed to make complex clothing, such as needles, appeared just as people were moving into the high altitudes of Tibet.

In addition to cultural adaptation, evidence suggests that biological adaptation was also important in enabling humans to live in such high altitudes.

Data from DNA studies may provide us with proof that people are genetically adapted to these high-altitude environments.

2 Skin Mask

Mike, Special Effects Artist:
"Hi Cassandra, I'm Mike and this is Rick."

Narrator:
In a London special effects studio, a brave model waits to have her face preserved as a lifelike mask . . .

Mike:
"This is a silicone material."

Narrator:
Silicone is an often rubber-like material that includes silicon and other chemical elements.

Mike:
"I'm hoping this is going to do it."

Narrator:
First, a cap is placed over Cassandra's hair.

Next, a thin layer of Vaseline is brushed over her eyebrows and lashes to prevent them from sticking to the mask.

Then a crucial step in the process—the gooey stuff. Artists paint her face in quick-drying silicone, starting with the eyes, nose, and mouth. She has to sit motionless as they devote about an hour to brushing the icy cold silicone onto her face.

It takes about three or four minutes for the silicone to dry. Then the model's face is wrapped in bandages . . . rather like a living mummy.

Mike:
"Nice and solid."

Narrator:
The hardened material comes off, followed by the newly created mold, which conforms to the shape of the model's face.

Cassandra, Model:
"Who said modeling was easy?"

Narrator:
At a workshop, the artists create a series of positive and negative masks. A master mold is then prepared.

The artists mix a soft silicone with a combination of chemicals to alter the mask's color, creating a natural, uniform shade that's similar to human skin. The mixture is then injected into the master mold. When it's dry, a face is created. A touch of makeup helps bring the skin to life. Eyebrows and lashes are carefully added. It can take up to three hours to do one eyebrow.

The completed mask has all the fundamental aspects of real human skin.

It has more than just the look. It has the feel— a record of one person's face, preserved in a moment in time.

Leopard Under Threat

Narrator:

Leopards spend much of their time in trees. They eat there, they sleep there. In fact, leopards spend more time in trees than any other big cat.

This leopard is in a tree in the Mala Mala Game Reserve in Kruger National Park, South Africa.

The reason leopards spend so much time in trees is because other cats—like lions—kill leopards, and because hyenas and wild dogs love to steal their precious kills.

This gives leopards a great incentive to master the art of tree-climbing, never failing to know exactly which branch will support their weight.

Well, almost never failing . . .

Sometimes a leopard must carry himself and his dinner up a tree.

The leopard has incredibly strong neck muscles. These enable it to drag its prey up into trees, where it won't be troubled by predators. The prey might be double—even triple—the leopard's own weight.

You might think that finding and killing an impala would be the hard part, but, in fact, the really difficult thing is knowing which branch will support all that weight.

And then, after all that trouble, a lucky hyena grabs the kill and runs away.

Seeking to reverse its fortune, the hungry leopard goes out and kills another impala, and, again, tries to drag it up the tree.

Another hyena arrives and decides it would like the leopard's precious prize.

Who'll win this conflict? Well, consider this: relative to their weight, hyenas have the strongest jaws in the Mala Mala Game Reserve.

Nothing is going to make this hyena let go.

Well, except maybe this . . . a lioness.

The hyena quickly runs off, and the leopard doesn't hesitate to leap upwards with its kill.

But the lioness decides that she has eyes for the prize and also heads up the tree.

Survival in this landscape often requires great skill. But this time, the leopard has estimated the strength of the tree branches perfectly.

Even though the lioness is a short distance from a juicy meal, she knows that she's too heavy to climb any higher.

At last, the drama is over and the leopard is rewarded with a well-earned meal—in peace.

4 Tsunami: Killer Wave

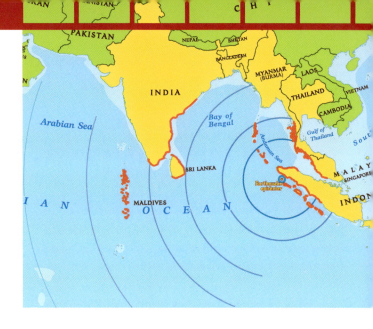

Narrator:

The warnings are few. The signs are sudden.

The ground shakes. The tide goes into reverse. A great roaring sound fills the air.

And then . . .

It strikes. Wave after wave of crashing, crushing water. And when it is over, nothing is left.

A tsunami.

The word in Japanese means "harbor wave."

Japan has been hit by many tsunamis in its history, as a result of its location. It lies across the edges of four tectonic plates, where most earthquakes—the principal cause of tsunamis—are born.

When two tectonic plates push together, the resulting earthquake sends enormous amounts of energy up through the ocean . . . displacing huge amounts of water.

A series of waves expands in all directions. In deep water, these waves travel fast—up to 500 miles an hour—but reach a height of only a few feet. A passing ship may not even detect them.

But as the waves enter shallow waters, friction with the ocean floor lowers their speed and raises their height.

As they move onto land, the waves can rise to a height of a ten-story building.

A tsunami wave doesn't break like an ordinary wave. Instead, it advances like a wall of water, crashing over everything in its way, sometimes reaching more than a kilometer inland.

More damage is caused when the wave moves back out to sea, dragging everything in its path underwater and out to sea.

Most tsunamis have several waves, arriving between ten and 60 minutes after the first strike—just when survivors think the danger has passed.

The deadliest tsunami ever recorded occurred in December of 2004. An earthquake off the coast of Indonesia caused a tsunami that rushed across the Indian Ocean and reached as far as the coast of Africa.

Whole sections of cities were destroyed. More than 200,000 people died. Most had no way of being warned.

Five thousand miles away in Hawaii, scientists at the Pacific Tsunami Warning Center monitor the earth's movements 24 hours a day, hoping to prevent a similar disaster from happening in the Pacific region.

If they detect a quake big enough to cause a tsunami, the scientists track where the wave will head and warn the people in its path.

Their advice is simple: abandon coastal areas and move to higher ground. Wait for news that the danger has passed. And be ready to deal with the destruction that a tsunami inevitably leaves behind.

Pacific Paradise

Narrator:

Humans have a long history of migrating across great oceans, eager for new destinations. Ultimately, we have been searching for, among other things, paradise.

In the Tuamotus—a small, isolated group of islands located in the vast Pacific, just over 320 kilometers northeast of Tahiti—paradise means . . .

coconuts . . .

digging for clams . . .

spear fishing . . .

and camping on the beach, with mild ocean winds and the sounds of the sea singing you to sleep.

But paradise today is not without its tensions. The biggest worry here is global warming.

The more than 75 little islands, called atolls, that make up the Tuamotus are thin coral reefs. Some are only just visible above the water; the highest are just ten feet above sea level.

The average temperature of the oceans is climbing. As the seas rise, scientists estimate that many of these living, breathing reefs, and the diverse sea life they protect, may disappear in the next 50 to 100 years.

Frank Murphy is a trained marine biologist from the University of California, Berkeley.

Frank Murphy, Marine Biologist:

"Fishing is a primary source of both food and income in the Tuamotus."

Narrator:

Gerard catches big mahi-mahis from his boat and sells them on the island of Fakarava.

Gathering and drying the white meat of coconut, known as copra, is the region's biggest business. A 45-kilogram sack sells for 38 dollars. A hard-working family will produce 100 sacks a month.

In the past 20 years, a new economy has grown quickly in the Tuamotus—black pearls.

Pamela and Veldo are 22 and have their own pearl-growing business at a place called Tureia, on a tiny island of sand surrounded by water.

They have boxes filled with thousands of oysters tied just below the surface. Veldo takes daily care of the boxes of oysters, making sure they are closed tightly to protect them from natural predators. Pamela works eight-hour days, preparing up to 400 oysters a day. Each oyster will take a year and a half to produce a pearl.

Visitors come pursuing the dream of paradise, and leave with many questions.

Is it peaceful here? Certainly.

Is it paradise? Perhaps as close as you can get.

A tropical dream come true.

Yet it is clear these tiny but magnificent islands in a giant sea of blue are at some risk.

These visitors are happy to have seen a bit of paradise, since it may soon change forever.

6 Ancient Little People

Narrator:

Lee Berger has spent his professional life searching for evidence of our human past.

He is a paleoanthropologist who studies and searches for the graves and fossil remains of ancient humans.

He's done most of his work in Africa, but it was during a vacation on the Pacific island of Palau, on a walk through one of its many caves, that he made an astonishing find.

Lee Berger, Paleoanthropologist:

"You see that? This is just packed full of bone. I mean you can actually see there's still some actually exposed here. But what's cool is that there was a whole skull here."

Narrator:

Berger thinks these bones may be the remains of some of the earliest humans ever to populate these islands.

Previous estimates trace the earliest humans found here by Berger to about 2,900 ago.

But all the bones previously found by Berger were above something called a "flowstone."

A flowstone is a common phenomenon in caves, where water flowing over the ground deposits minerals that harden into stone.

All of Berger's previous digging was above a flowstone that dated back about 2,900 years.

Today, Berger has returned and is going to break through the flowstone. He hopes that he will find bones from an even earlier age underneath the flowstone.

Lee Berger:

"It is also making me personally consider my understanding of what is normal human variation."

Narrator:

Berger published a paper suggesting the bones he found are astonishing because they show how varied early humans were in their size and shape.

This new understanding of the potential for human variation makes some people doubt whether the hobbit is a special species.

The controversies will likely continue. But in the meantime, Berger will return.

Lee Berger:

"What has struck me on this second scientific visit is how phenomenally little research has been done on these islands."

Narrator:

Berger hopes to change that in the coming years, by continuing his search for more definitive answers to our human past.

Solar Power

Narrator:

The most powerful source of energy on the planet is actually out in space. It's our sun. More energy falls as sunlight on the U.S. in a single day than the U.S. uses in a year. But it's been difficult to turn that sunlight into electricity.

Many people already utilize some solar energy. But the world's need for power is great . . . and for solar power to be a real substitute for other energy sources, it has to be both affordable and dependable.

A major advocate for solar energy can be found in California. Sacramento, the state capital, is one of the nation's leaders in solar power. Many new homes in Sacramento are equipped with solar cells. And solar panels shade parking lots and city buildings. But most importantly, Sacramento has shown that by buying a lot of solar power at one time, it's possible to significantly reduce the price per unit—so people can actually save money using solar power . . . or make money.

California, along with many other states, has started "net metering." Net metering lets citizens profit from their extra solar power by selling it back to the utility company for exactly the price they would normally pay for it. If they use less power than they produce, the utility company sends them a check for the difference.

In California's Mojave Desert, there is a solar-generating plant that makes all other solar plants seem small by comparison. The Kramer Solar Junction power facility covers over 400 hectares of land. It creates more energy from solar power than every other solar panel in America combined—a total of 150 megawatts.

David Rib, Vice President, Kramer Solar Junction:

"Which at that full capacity is enough power for the residential needs of about half a million people."

Narrator:

Unlike photovoltaic systems, which capture the energy in sunlight directly, these mirrors reflect the sunlight onto a tube filled with a special oil. The hot, 700-degree oil then goes into a boiler that powers an electric turbine. Each section also has a natural gas generator so the plant can guarantee a supply of power even during periods of bad weather.

Furthermore, it can do all this while creating very little carbon dioxide or pollution. So long as the sun rises, solar power will continue to offer hope for a dependable—and cleaner—solution to the world's energy needs.

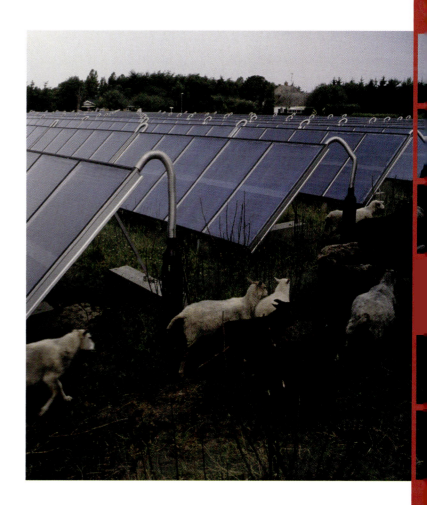

8 | Mecca

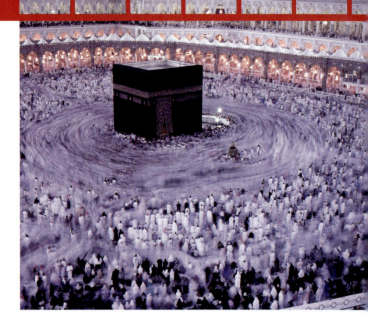

Narrator:

The holy city of Mecca is located in the western mountains of Saudi Arabia, in an area of approximately 250 square kilometers. Since long before Islam, it has been considered a sacred place where no one could hunt, cut trees, or fight. At the heart of the city is a great mosque called Al-Masjid Al-Haram, and at its center is the Kaaba. Muslims don't worship the Kaaba. They worship what it represents: the one God.

Hajj takes place in and around Mecca. The Hajj comprises a series of rituals that take place between the 8th and 13th days of the last month of the Islamic calendar. Circling the Kaaba is the first thing pilgrims do when they get to Mecca, and also the last.

For Muslims who have prayed in this direction every day for years, seeing the Kaaba for the first time is almost overwhelming. Now to the Valley of Mina where the Prophet Muhammad stopped and rested on his Hajj nearly 14 centuries ago. This is a town whose population grows to two million people in one night.

At sunrise, the camped pilgrims prepare excitedly for the greatest day of the Hajj. Two million people depart for the Plain of Arafat. Some 50,000 vehicles accumulate, filling the roads. Arafat is eight miles east of Mina. It's the place Muslims believe Adam and Eve found each other after they were forced to leave the paradise of Eden. The ritual at Arafat is seen by many as a practice for the Day of Judgment. A strange quiet descends in the afternoon, as people turn inward. It's called the Standing at Arafat.

Only when the sun has set can pilgrims leave Arafat. Nearly two million people stand ready to move as soon as the sun begins to set. The pilgrims move back toward the white tents of Mina, where tomorrow they will join in a symbolic struggle with the devil.

Here, Muslims believe, God commanded Abraham to sacrifice his son, but the devil challenged him not to.

According to one tale, Abraham attacked the devil with stones three separate times, chasing him away. Three stone pillars mark the spots where Abraham stood his ground.

At a place called Muzdalifah, on the way to the pillars, pilgrims pick up small stones to stone Satan themselves. The ritual is called the Jamarat.

With all other rituals complete, pilgrims return to Mecca for a grand final visit. They have all earned a special title—Hajji for the men, Hajja for the women. Many pilgrims arrive in Mecca alone, but they find themselves accompanied by a million strangers. Finally, after their brief visit, they depart for home riding a spiritual wave of rebirth.

Coast Guard School

Aaron Ferguson, Instructor:

"You're not in control all the time out here. We never come out to beat Mother Nature, but if you can go home calling it a draw, then that's a good day."

Narrator:

In a place where nature can be at its worst, the United States Coast Guard tests its toughest people.

Boat Driver:

"Kind of scary, tense, adrenaline rush all mixed up into one. It's like a rollercoaster ride sometimes."

Narrator:

Rescue boat drivers learn how to deal with the most violent of seas. In the Coast Guard's national motor lifeboat school, students are at the mercy of waves that can kill.

So many ships sink in the rough waters where the Columbia River empties into the ocean. This area is known as the graveyard of the Pacific. Coast Guard boat drivers come from around the country to learn skills that will sustain them as they perform their tough life-saving missions.

Aaron Ferguson:

"The motor lifeboat school gives the students and the upcoming boat drivers a base, a base to build on. The skills that we teach them here apply everywhere to boat driving."

Narrator:

Aaron Ferguson has been an instructor here for over two years.

Aaron Ferguson:

"It's an exciting job every time we come out. I've never come out and had the same thing twice. It's always different no matter what day you're here."

Narrator:

The only thing that stays the same is that danger is always present in the rough surf.

Aaron Ferguson:

"The last two weeks it all pays to be right today. It's right now. If something happens and we get knocked down and we go in the water, you go in the water, pop up smoke, remember to breathe. If we come back up, and I'm not here, Ty will take over and depart the surf zone. Okay, let's do it."

Narrator:

For student and instructor alike, pulse rates accelerate heart rates rise as soon as the sea becomes more dangerous

Aaron Ferguson:

"There's a huge range of emotions. You're scared, you're nervous, it's anticipation, there's conditions that you just can't believe that the boats will make it through."

Narrator:

The two-week class ends with the students mobilized for the man overboard drill.

Student Ralph Johnston must prove he can move the lifeboat through heavy surf while keeping it steady. He must position the boat so that his crew can recover the person in danger.

Aaron Ferguson:

"He needs to learn to control his fear of the elements. He needs to understand the strength of the ocean, and we give them an exposure to that and some experience with it."

Ralph Johnston, Student:

"It helps us to learn our limitations or to push our limitations to get us more comfortable in the weather. If we're more comfortable, then our crew's going to be more comfortable, and we'll be more effective."

Aaron Ferguson:

"Onboard, okay, good job, good job."

Narrator:

For the instructors, there is satisfaction in knowing that the skills students learn in the graveyard of the Pacific might one day prevent a terrible tragedy.

Aaron Ferguson:

"On those nights when they're out on their own, it's rough, it's scary, it's nasty. If they fall back to the base, the very basics, they'll go home, they'll get home that night, they'll take their crew safely home with them and the people they're out there to help. I get the knowledge of knowing that on those nights they do go home."

10 Shark vs. Octopus

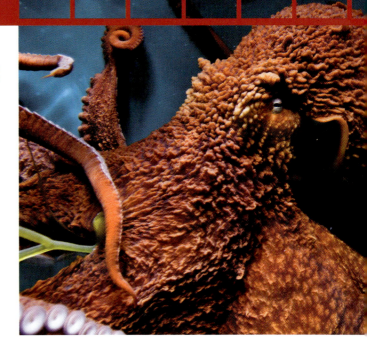

Narrator:

Here's a giant Pacific octopus in an equally giant aquarium tank. The giant Pacific octopus is from a group of entities known as octopods, meaning "eight legs or arms."

Now, there are also sharks in this tank as well.

This is a spiny dogfish shark, known to be a fierce predator. Usually, dogfish sharks eat fish, but they have also been known to attack and eat an occasional octopus.

Could this octopus be in danger of being eaten?

Well, don't dismiss it yet.

The giant Pacific octopus is an extraordinary creature. It can camouflage itself from predators, by transforming its skin color to match its surroundings. And if that doesn't work, it can release a dark ink at an attacker, and escape by forcing water out of its body.

The spiny dogfish shark got its name from two sharp spines on its fins, which contain a mild poison. Dogfish sharks are known to travel in large schools, or packs, like dogs.

When bodies of sharks began appearing at the bottom of the tank, the aquarium staff became worried about the sharks' welfare.

The giant octopus usually dines on fish and small sea creatures like shrimps and crabs, so no one expected the humble octopus to be responsible for the dead sharks.

But they soon discovered what was happening . . .

Each of the octopus' flexible arms contains two rows of suckers, used for catching prey. In its mouth is a beak which it uses to kill prey and tear it into pieces.

Including, it seems, fearless sharks . . .

The aquarium staff had learned something new about the giant Pacific octopus. They hadn't expected it to be a master shark-killer.

Well, it's clear we can pronounce the octopus the winner in this fight.

There definitely was a dangerous animal in this aquarium tank. But the danger had eight legs—and powerful suckers!

Urban Art

Narrator:

Urban art is all about innovation . . .

From using buckets on a busy street . . .

To filling an art gallery with local graffiti . . .

To mixing jazz with spoken word—inviting us to listen with new ears . . .

To look with new eyes.

Wander down this train tunnel in Washington D.C., and you'll discover the bold colors of urban graffiti artists. It is Washington's Wall of Fame, and Nick Posada's work is here.

But unfortunately the art he's created has been covered by other people's graffiti.

Nick Posada, Graffiti Artist:

"This is what happens when nobody respects any type of work that someone spent their paint and their time on. This is what the Wall of Fame in D.C. has come to."

Narrator:

Although the Wall of Fame is open to everyone, Posada cautions there are rules to be followed in the world of graffiti—rules that not everyone appreciates. He says that real graffiti artists understand how to use color and how to make their work distinctive.

Nick Posada:

"So you would use colors that contrast one another. Ah, my piece is still there. I did this in, like, '99."

Narrator:

Nick's work is also highlighted here at the Govinda Gallery in Georgetown.

Chris Murray, Govinda Gallery:

"Graffiti art has certainly brought to public art a whole new dimension."

Narrator:

According to Chris Murray, graffiti art is special because it's fast, uninhibited, and always inventive. Murray is convinced that graffiti is just one more step in the evolution of pop art. The works have sold well—to young people and to collectors of pop art. In the gallery, people can appreciate the art in a traditional setting—and they like it. It's good for the artists, too.

Chris Murray:

"It was a real reversal for them because they're used to being vilified and now they're being enjoyed, and that's a good thing."

Narrator:

People are beginning to appreciate the talents of Jafar Barron, too. The 28-year-old trumpeter grew up in this neighborhood north of Philadelphia. Both his parents are jazz musicians. But Jafar chose to mix more traditional, classical forms of jazz with the rap and hip-hop music of his own generation. His first CD is an innovative mix of both worlds.

Jafar Barron, Jazz Musician:

"I like to think that the whole of creation is all about music, to me, you know what I'm saying? I believe that the Most High is a musician. I guess it came from my exposure to hip-hop, and the poetry that comes from that, and from some friends of mine."

Narrator:

Jafar now plays in clubs in the city where he grew up. He also now has a deal with a major recording company.

The stories of how these two artists developed—one musical, one visual—are not surprising to art history professor Don Kimes.

Don Kimes, American University:

"It's about sort of taking what it is that you come from, what you emerge from, what's authentic for you and pushing it to the edge of its envelope, to the edge of its boundaries, its limits, and taking one more step."

Narrator:

Kimes says artists need to build on their own cultural background—as anything else would be false. It is said that art is fundamentally about exploration and discovery. Urban artists—whether musicians or painters—can take us to places we've never been before . . . Even if it's as close as a nearby city street.

12 | Paraguay Shaman

Narrator:

Somewhere in this forest, maybe in this plant or that herb, there might be a cure for an illness like diabetes, malaria, or even common fevers and colds. But as the plants disappear, so too do the potential cures. The rainforests of Paraguay have long been a source of medicinal cures. Traditional folk healers often lead the way to the plants that provide the medicines.

Paraguay's renowned healers, called "shamans," have a deep knowledge of local medicinal plants—the equivalent of the knowledge contained in an entire medical library. But Paraguay has one of the highest deforestation rates in the world. That's why researchers believe it's a priority to record the shaman's extensive knowledge—before the forest disappears.

The journey begins in Paraguay's isolated Mbaracayú Forest Nature Reserve and the nearby native community of Tekoha Ryapu, where shaman Gervasio lives.

To reach Gervasio, a group of researchers set out on a long journey through the reserve.

Meanwhile, at the village, Gervasio is using chants and prayers, perhaps to establish a spiritual connection, or bond, with the forest. When he feels ready, Gervasio and his wife lead the group on the search.

They are looking for a root called Suruvi, also known as Jatropha isabelli, which is used to treat and cure various illnesses. Scientists are very interested in this family of plants for cancer research. Gervasio brings the root back to the village, where his wife inserts it in a pot of water to prepare tea.

Scientists have published a book to help record and transmit Gervasio's forest knowledge. The book helps people to easily identify and study local plants. Recording and analyzing Paraguayan plants for possible medical cures is urgent business; some may even call it an emergency. Medicinal plants that were once healthy and multiplying are now disappearing—and so too is the possibility of finding new medical cures.

Photo Credits

3 Karen Kasmauski/National Geographic Image Collection, 4, 5 (clockwise from l) Sarah Leen/National Geographic Image Collection, B. Anthony Stewart/National Geographic Image Collection, W. Robert Moore/National Geographic Image Collection, The Bridgeman Art Library, Cary Wolinsky/National Geographic Image Collection, Medford Taylor/National Geographic Image Collection, Thomas Marent/Minden Pictures/National Geographic Image Collection, 6, 7 (t from l) Steve McCurry/National Geographic Image Collection, Bob Sacha/National Geographic Image Collection, Bob Sacha/National Geographic Image Collection, Lynn Johnson/National Geographic Image Collection, David Doubilet/National Geographic Image Collection, Sarah Leen/National Geographic Image Collection, Chris Johns/National Geographic Image Collection, 6 (c, l) Tim Laman/National Geographic Image Collection, 7 (r, c) John Dawson/National Geographic Image Collection, 6, 7 (b from l) Fan Jun/Xinhua/Landov, Steve and Donna O'Meara/National Geographic Image Collection, Katherine Feng/Minden Pictures/National Geographic Image Collection, Kenneth Geiger/National Geographic Image Collection, Ethan Myerson/iStockphoto, 8 (t) Todd Gipstein/National Geographic Image Collection, 9 Alaska Stock Images/National Geographic Image Collection, 11 Albert Moldvay/National Geographic Image Collection, 14 Chris Howey/Shutterstock, 15 (t) Dylan Martinez/Reuters/Landov, (b) Fan Jun/Xinhua/Landov, 16 (t) Joe McNally/National Geographic Image Collection, (b) Joe McNally/National Geographic Image Collection, 17 Joe McNally/National Geographic Image Collection, 19 Chen Xiaowei/Xinhua/Landov, 20, 179 Fritz Hoffmann/National Geographic Image Collection, 21 Jodi Cobb/National Geographic Image Collection, 22 (l) Paul Chesley/National Geographic Image Collection, (c) Robert Clark/National Geographic Image Collection, (r) Jodi Cobb/National Geographic Image Collection, 23 Jodi Cobb and Stephen R. Marquardt/National Geographic Image Collection, 24 (t, l) Jodi Cobb/National Geographic Image Collection, (b, r) Jodi Cobb/National Geographic Image Collection, 26 Photoshot/Landov, 28 Jodi Cobb/National Geographic Image Collection, 29 (t) Sarah Leen/National Geographic Image Collection, (b) Thomas J. Abercrombie/National Geographic Image Collection, 31 Winfield Parks/National Geographic Image Collection, 32, 180 Sarah Leen/National Geographic Image Collection, 33 Norbert Wu/Minden Pictures/National Geographic Image Collection, 34 (A) Taylor S. Kennedy/National Geographic Image Collection, (B) Katherine Feng/Minden Pictures/National Geographic Image Collection, (C) Katherine Feng/Minden Pictures/National Geographic Image Collection, (D) Katherine Feng/Minden Pictures/National Geographic Image Collection, 35 Michael Nichols/National Geographic Image Collection, 36 Fritz Hoffmann/National Geographic Image Collection, 38 Katherine Feng/Minden Pictures/National Geographic Image Collection, 39 (1) Beverly Joubert/National Geographic Image Collection, (2) Steve Winter/National Geographic Image Collection, (3) Beverly Joubert/National Geographic Image Collection, (4) Roy Toft/National Geographic Image Collection, (5) Tim Fitzharris/Minden Pictures, 40 Steve Winter/National Geographic Image Collection, 41 (t) Steve Winter/National Geographic Image Collection, (b) Steve Winter/National Geographic Image Collection, 43 Andrejs Jegorovs/Shutterstock, 44, 181 Kim Wolhuter/National Geographic Image Collection, 45, 47 Mark Cosslett/National Geographic Image Collection, 46, 47 (bg) Thomas Marent/Minden Pictures/National Geographic Image Collection, 47 (t, l) Thomas Marent/Minden Pictures/National Geographic Image Collection, (b) 20th Century Fox/The Kobal Collection, 48, 49 (t from l) John Dawson/National Geographic Image Collection, Vincent J. Musi/National Geographic Image Collection, Flip Nicklin/National Geographic Image Collection, Vincent J. Musi/National Geographic Image Collection, Tim Laman/National Geographic Image Collection, Katherine Feng/Minden Pictures/National Geographic Image Collection, Steve Winter/

National Geographic Image Collection, Chris Newbert/Minden Pictures/National Geographic Image Collection, (clockwise from macaw) Marc Moritsch/National Geographic Image Collection, Patricio Robles Gil/Minden Pictures/National Geographic Image Collection, 50 (t from l) John Dawson/National Geographic Image Collection, Katherine Feng/Minden Pictures/National Geographic Image Collection, Tim Laman/National Geographic Image Collection, Vincent J. Musi/National Geographic Image Collection, (r) Chris Johns/National Geographic Image Collection, 51 Carsten Peter/National Geographic Image Collection, 52 (l) John Stanmeyer/National Geographic Image Collection, (r) Mike Doukas/USGS, 53 Karen Kasmauski/National Geographic Image Collection, 54 (t) Sarah Leen/National Geographic Image Collection, (b) Sarah Leen/National Geographic Image Collection, 56 Steve and Donna O'Meara/National Geographic Image Collection, 59 (t) Reza/National Geographic Image Collection, (b) James P. Blair/National Geographic Image Collection, 61 Karen Kasmauski/National Geographic Image Collection, 63 Jodi Cobb/National Geographic Image Collection, 64 (1) Franck Camhi/Shutterstock, (2) Daniel Wiedemann/iStockphoto, (3) Ricardo De Mattos/National Geographic Image Collection, (4) Celso Pupo/Shutterstock, 65 (t) Michael Melford/National Geographic Image Collection, (b) Panoramic Stock Images/National Geographic Image Collection, 66 (t) Daniel Wiedemann/Shutterstock, (b) Franck Camhi/Shutterstock, 69 (A) Jonas Bendiksen/National Geographic Image Collection, (B) Nakheel PJSC, (C) George F. Mobley/National Geographic Image Collection, (D) Jeff Banke/Shutterstock, 70 (t) Richard Nowitz/National Geographic Image Collection, (b) Ralph Lee Hopkins/National Geographic Image Collection, 71 Ralph Lee Hopkins/National Geographic Image Collection, 73 Yanfei Sun/Shutterstock, 74, 183 Panoramic Stock Images/National Geographic Image Collection, 75 Kenneth Geiger/National Geographic Image Collection, 76 (1) Robin Chapman/iStockphoto, (2) Kenneth Geiger/National Geographic Image Collection, (3) Ethan Myerson/iStockphoto, 77 Kenneth Geiger/National Geographic Image Collection, 80 (t) Gordon Wiltsie/National Geographic Image Collection, (b) Hashim Pudiyapura/Shutterstock, 81 Rebecca Hale/National Geographic Image Collection, 82 Ira Block/National Geographic Image Collection, 83 (b) Kenneth Garrett/National Geographic Image Collection, 85 (b) Joy Tessman/National Geographic Image Collection, 86, 184 Kenneth Garrett/National Geographic Image Collection, 87, 88 Medford Taylor/National Geographic Image Collection, 88, 89 (bg) Skip Brown/National Geographic Image Collection, 89 (t) Michael Melford/National Geographic Image Collection, (b) Melville B. Grosvenor/National Geographic Stock, 90, 91 (t from l) Panoramic Stock Images/National Geographic Image Collection, Steve and Donna O'Meara/National Geographic Image Collection, Tim Fitzharris/Minden Pictures/National Geographic Image Collection, Pablo Corral Vega/National Geographic Image Collection, James P. Blair/National Geographic Image Collection, Karen Kasmauski/National Geographic Image Collection, 92 (t from l) Steve and Donna O'Meara/National Geographic Image Collection, Panoramic Stock Images/National Geographic Image Collection, (c) Pablo Corral Vega/National Geographic Image Collection, 93 Sarah Leen/National Geographic Image Collection, 94–96 (all) Bob Sacha/National Geographic Image Collection, 98 B. Anthony Stewart/National Geographic Image Collection, 99 Sarah Leen/National Geographic Image Collection, 100 Sarah Leen/National Geographic Image Collection, 101 (t) Sarah Leen/National Geographic Image Collection, (b) Lynn Johnson/National Geographic Image Collection, 103 Midkhat Izmaylov/Shutterstock, 104, 185 Sarah Leen/National Geographic Image Collection, 105 Emory Kristof/National Geographic Image Collection, 108 Michael Yamashita/National Geographic Image Collection, 110 Aladin Abdel Naby/Reuters/Landov, 112 EcoPrint/Shutterstock, 113 (t) James L. Stanfield/National Geographic Image Collection, (b) Cotton Coulson/National Geographic Image

Collection, **115** Jeff Moore/Maxppp/Landov, **116, 186** Reza/National Geographic Image Collection, **117** Skip Brown/National Geographic Image Collection, **118** Larry Minden/Minden Pictures/National Geographic Image Collection, **119–120 (all)** James Vlahos, **122** Courtesy Alison Wright, **123** Steve McCurry/National Geographic Image Collection, **124 (t)** Steve McCurry/National Geographic Image Collection, **(b)** Mark Thiessen/National Geographic Image Collection, **125 (all)** Steve McCurry/National Geographic Image Collection, **127** Mark Thiessen/National Geographic Image Collection, **128** Kent Kobersteen/National Geographic Image Collection, **129, 131** Justin Guariglia/National Geographic Image Collection, **132, 133 (t worker at nuclear plant)** Lynn Johnson/National Geographic Image Collection, **(others)** Sarah Leen/National Geographic Image Collection, **134 (t, c)** Bob Sacha/National Geographic Image Collection, **(t, r)** Lynn Johnson/National Geographic Image Collection, **135** Rebecca Hale/National Geographic Image Collection, **137 (t)** Cary Wolinsky/National Geographic Image Collection, **137 (b)** Maggie Steber/National Geographic Image Collection, **138** Cary Wolinsky/National Geographic Image Collection, **141–143 (all)** Vincent J. Musi/National Geographic Image Collection, **145** Frans Lanting/National Geographic Image Collection, **146, 188** Vincent J. Musi/National Geographic Image Collection, **147–152 (all)** Cary Wolinsky/National Geographic Image Collection, **153** The Bridgeman Art Library, **154** Raul Touzon/National Geographic Image Collection, **155 (t)** The Bridgeman Art Library, **(b)** Lynn Johnson/National Geographic Image Collection, **157** The Bridgeman Art Library, **158** Scott S. Warren/National Geographic Image Collection, **159** Justin Guariglia/National Geographic Image Collection, **160** Robert Clark/National Geographic Image Collection, **161 (t)** Mark Thiessen/National Geographic Image Collection, **(b, l)** Mark Thiessen/National Geographic Image Collection, **(b, r)** Thomas Mounsey/Shutterstock, **164** Sarah Leen/National Geographic Image Collection, **166 (all)** Lynn Johnson/National Geographic Image Collection, **169** Karen Kasmauski/National Geographic Image Collection, **170, 190** Michael Nichols/National Geographic Image Collection, **171, 173** Richard Nowitz/National Geographic Image Collection, **172** James L. Stanfield/National Geographic Image Collection, **173 (b)** W. Robert Moore/National Geographic Image Collection, **174, 175 (t from l)** James L. Stanfield/National Geographic Image Collection, O. Louis Mazzatenta/National Geographic Image Collection, David Doubilet/National Geographic Image Collection, Shutterstock, O. Louis Mazzatenta/National Geographic Image Collection, Richard Nowitz/National Geographic Image Collection, Justin Guariglia/National Geographic Image Collection, Brian J. Skerry/National Geographic Image Collection, **(clockwise from Mesa Verde)** Theresa Martinez/Shutterstock, Vladimir Sazonov/Shutterstock, Ronald Sumners/Shutterstock, Vladimir Melnik/Shutterstock, Pokrovskaya Elena/Shutterstock, Neale Cousland/Shutterstock, Martin Gray/National Geographic Image Collection, Franck Camhi/Shutterstock

Illustration Credits

4, 5 (bg), 10, 31, 36, 43, 44, 48–49 (all), 52, 56, 57, 58, 62, 64, 68, 72 (all), 73, 74, 76 (globe), 80, 84, 85, 86, 90–91 (all), 98, 103, 104, 106, 111, 115, 116, 118, 122, 123, 127, 128, 132–133 (all), 145, 152, 156, 158, 165, 170, 174–175 (bg), 182 National Geographic Maps, **11, 12** Beaudaniels.com/National Geographic Image Collection, **27** Keith Kasnot/National Geographic Image Collection, **46, 88, 130, 172** iStockphoto, **76 (large map)** bluliq/Shutterstock, **78 (all)** Kazuhiko Sano/National Geographic Image Collection, **83 (t)** Lars Grant-West/National Geographic Image Collection, **107** Hongnian Zhang/National Geographic Image Collection, **108** Greg Harlin/National Geographic Maps, **130–131 (bg)** Bruce Morser/National Geographic Image Collection, **131 (r)** Javier Zarracina, **136** Courtesy of Dr. Arthur W. Toga, Laboratory of Neuro Imaging at UCLA, **140** Jonny Goldstein/Flickr, **162** Ken Eward/National Geographic Image Collection, **172–173 (bg),** Javier Zarracina

Text Credits

11 Adapted from "The Beautiful Game: Why Soccer Rules the World," by Sean Wilsey and Brenna Maloney (accompanying supplement): National Geographic Magazine, June 2006, **16** Adapted from "Pushing the Limit," by Rick Gore: National Geographic Magazine, September 2000, **23** Adapted from "The Enigma of Beauty," by Cathy Newman: National Geographic Magazine, January 2000, **28** Adapted from "Unmasking Skin," by Joel L. Swerdlow: National Geographic Magazine, November 2002, **35** Adapted from "Panda, Inc.," by Lynne Warren: National Geographic Magazine, July 2006, **40** Adapted from "Out of the Shadows," by Douglas H. Chadwick: National Geographic Magazine, June 2008, **53** Adapted from "Fuji: Japan's Sacred Summit," by Tracy Dahlby: National Geographic Magazine, August 2002, and "Popocatépetl: Mexico's Smoking Mountain," by A. R. Williams: National Geographic Magazine, January 1999, **58** Adapted from "The Next Big One," by Joel Achenbach: National Geographic Magazine, April 2006, **65** Adapted from "The Five Thousand Mile Beach," by Stanley Stewart: National Geographic Traveler, March, 2008, **70** Adapted from "Adventure Guide: Iceland," by Steve Casimiro: National Geographic Adventure Online, and "Iceland: Europe's Land of Fire, Ice, and Tourists," by Stefan Lovgren: National Geographic News, **77** Adapted from "If the Stones Could Speak," by Caroline Alexander: National Geographic Magazine, June, 2008, **82** Adapted from "The People Time Forgot," by Mike Morwood, Thomas Sutikna, and Richard Roberts: National Geographic Magazine, April 2005, **95** Adapted from "Caffeine," by T. R. Reid: National Geographic Magazine, January 2005, **100** Adapted from "Tapped Out," by Paul Roberts: National Geographic Magazine, June 2008, and "Future Power: Where Will the World Get Its Next Energy Fix?," by Michael Parfit: National Geographic Magazine, August 2005, **107** Adapted from "China's Great Armada," by Frank Viviano: National Geographic Magazine, July 2005, **112** Adapted from "In the Wake of Sindbad," by Tim Severin: National Geographic Magazine, July 1982, **119** Adapted from "Alive: Then and Now," by James Vlahos: National Geographic Adventure, April 2006, **124** Adapted from "A Life Revealed," by Cathy Newman: National Geographic Magazine, April 2002, **137** Adapted from "Beyond the Brain," by James Shreeve: National Geographic Magazine, March 2005, and "Remember This," by Joshua Foer: National Geographic Magazine, November 2007, **142** Adapted from "Minds of Their Own," by Virginia Morell: National Geographic Magazine, March 2008, and "Almost Human," by Mary Roach: National Geographic Magazine, April 2008, **149** Adapted from "The Quest for Color," by Cary Wolinsky: National Geographic Magazine, July 1999, **154** Adapted from "Lullaby in Color," by Joel L. Swerdlow: National Geographic Magazine, October 1997, **161** Adapted from "Nanotechnology's Big Future," by Jennifer Kahn: National Geographic Magazine, June 2006, **166** Adapted from "Deadly Contact," by David Quammen: National Geographic Magazine, October 2007